ROCK THE NATION:
MONTROSE, GAMMA AND RONNIE REDEFINED

MARTIN POPOFF

WYMER
PUBLISHING
Bedford, England

First published in Canada, 2016
Wymer Publishing
Bedford, England www.wymerpublishing.co.uk
Tel: 01234 326691
Wymer Publishing is a trading name of Wymer (UK) Ltd

Copyright © 2018 Martin Popoff/ Wymer Publishing.
This edition published 2019.

ISBN 978-1-912782-09-3

The Author hereby asserts his rights to be identified
as the author of this work in accordance with sections
77 to 78 of the Copyright, Designs & Patents Act 1988.

All rights reserved. No part of this publication may be
reproduced or transmitted in any form or by any means,
electronic or mechanical, including photocopying, or any
information storage and retrieval system, without written
permission from the publisher.

This publication is sold subject to the condition that it shall not,
by way of trade or otherwise, be lent, re-sold, hired out or
otherwise circulated without the publisher's prior consent in any
form of binding or cover other than that in which it is published
and without a similar condition including this condition
being imposed on the subsequent purchaser.

Every effort has been made to trace the copyright holders of the
photographs in this book but some were unreachable. We would
be grateful if the photographers concerned would contact us.

Printed and bound by
CMP, Dorset, England

A catalogue record for this book is available from the British Library.

Typesetting, layout and design by Eduardo Rodriguez.
Front cover photograph © Jim Summaria
Back cover photographs © Jim Summaria & Paul Vincze

TABLE OF CONTENTS

Introduction		5
Chapter 1:	Early Years: "Being loud and distorted really added to that"	9
Chapter 2:	Montrose – ***Montrose***: "Fuzzy, clean, dirty, edgy"	23
Chapter 3:	Montrose – ***Paper Money:*** "I'm going through a process."	59
Chapter 4:	Montrose – ***Warner Bros. Presents:*** "Where's Ted? Where's Ted?"	85
Chapter 5:	Montrose – ***Jump on It:*** "Bobby, what's the name of this band?"	115
Chapter 6:	Gamma – ***1:*** "And he's hungry, Ronnie. He's hungry!"	153
Chapter 7:	Gamma – ***2:*** "Powering it through"	175
Chapter 8:	Gamma – ***3:*** "Jack said, 'I don't hear a lot of guitar.'"	201
Chapter 9:	Montrose – ***Mean:*** "I was just continuing on the path, my brother."	213
Chapter 10:	Gamma – ***4:*** "What Davey likes to call it is 'Gamma grown up.'"	231
Chapter 11:	Dying of Nothing – "That Saturday Ronnie changed his mind and it was over."	249
Chapter 12:	Epilogue – Ronnie's Legacy: "Continually moving forward and wanting to be remembered for that"	263
Discography		285
Credits		289
About the Author		294
Martin Popoff – A Complete Bibliography		295

INTRODUCTION

Wow. A day or two away from finishing this harrowing trip, and that was tough, depressing, at times an entirely distasteful exercise and possibly a disservice. I knew it was going to be haunting writing this book, even though I was trying to cling desperately to my usual modus operandi, which is talk about, write about, deconstruct the albums, chapter by chapter. In this case, it was going to be satisfying but not entirely, first due to the modest mess of the catalogue. There are four Montrose albums and then an anomaly called *Mean*, in 1987. With Gamma, there are three albums in quick succession, all for the same label before a quick break-up of the band, and then an even more disconnected anomaly almost 20 years later. Indeed, the mess of it was a factor in having me not dig further into the murk and make this two separate books.

So yeah, that's a little messy, particularly when you stick the oddness of Ronnie's below-the-radar meanderings in-between, but hey, I was up for it, being a huge fan. Like anybody else, I hugely respected and rocked hard to the first Montrose album, and then quite liked the next three as well. But more so, I'm a massive fan of Gamma 1 and Gamma 2, to the point where I probably admire those two records, even before and above the superlative, stone-cold classic from 1973 called Montrose – *Montrose*, the record so good they hadda name it twice.

But then two things started happening. Unsurprisingly, Ronnie's shocking suicide hung over this whole, laborious, complicated journey like a black cloak. I was prepared for that, but then not really prepared for how many people had opinions on what happened, throughout the subsequent interviews I did for the book. And so sadly, I guess what I'm saying, I ended up spending more time than I wanted to on this tragic end to Ronnie's life and career, overshadowing by proxy emphasis on the albums, song by song.

But then a second thing happened: much more negativity from my interviewees than I bargained for, that I expected, that I welcomed, that I wanted to include. Some of it seemed deliberate and aggressive, but a whole pile of it just seemed occasional and offhand, from well-meaning people really trying not to be negative. And in this case, it was somewhat heartening, that what you were hearing was the story of a complicated man, as many a' speaker put it.

Believe me, there were plenty of things I left out, because they were too damaging to Ronnie's reputation, or they would hurt his extended family, or cause arguments. Plus there was a bunch of "This is off the record" or the more casual "Between you and me," which I respected in all cases.

But as I kept grinding on, getting depressed by the whole process and periodically wishing to abandon the book, I eventually got to the point where the critical mass of the compliments versus the put-downs began to swing back to the point where you couldn't help but admire the totality of the man that was Ronnie Montrose. As I was arriving at an enlightenment toward that profile of the man, again, I began to feel assured that at the end of all the pluses and negatives, this book was going to serve as not only an accurate portrayal of the man, but also a positive albeit complicated one.

To help drive this thesis, one of which I grew to believe in through education and through consistency and confirmation of viewpoints, I decided to discuss his suicide in the second to last chapter, with a long passage of testimonial as to his legacy serving as the final chapter. This was just one more subtle way to leave the reader with an impression that stresses Ronnie's finest attributes, imagining that as the reader closed the book on this book Ronnie himself slammed shut, the last thing they read is the last thing they would remember.

An additional thing I wrestled with was the idea of seeing if Ronnie's last wife, Leighsa Montrose would talk to me for the book. I decided, after weighing all the pros and cons, that I wouldn't bother her, mostly out of respect for not making her have to discuss a painful chapter in her life, but also because I didn't want to add even more material to the darkest part of this book. In other words, it was a check on sticking to the method and the mandate I've used for all my books, which is a celebration of the records. Despite this, her image weighed on my mind the entire time I was devoting to this cause that I feel was ultimately noble.

So again, happy thoughts, among the many other expressed throughout, to me personally, Ronnie Montrose is a bit like a Ronnie James Dio, in that in the course of his productive life, he had managed what in my opinion are some of the finest full-length albums of all time across two completely different bands, in Ronnie's case, *leading* these two acts. For me, again, this would be *Montrose* and Gamma 2, although as I say, I worship Gamma 1 as well.

In summation, what can I say? This has been a strange, and as I've alluded to, debilitating and demoralizing bunch of months, for which I blame Ronnie the same way that people who love someone who commits suicide, blame their dearly dead. I mean, given Ronnie's curiosity and enthusiasm for so many facets of life, this was not supposed to happen.

On the positive, I got to make the acquaintance with a bunch of new and interesting characters, including most of the guys spread across these great records, and some other smart and engaging people who knew Ronnie and played with Ronnie in other situations. As we all get older, this becomes more valuable, these tentative connections, the weaving and extending of these friendships, however cursory they may be. I guess what I'm saying is, I've listen to Jim Alcivar's, Bob James', Bill Church's, and certainly all kinds of Denny Carmassi's music for years, but now I've gotten to put voice with name, so to speak. And so my listening to their music becomes all that much richer. That's a personal selfish thing—I just relish, for myself, the opportunity to make the engagement with their artworks that much richer.

But of course, as I've said many times, the additional satisfaction of writing these books is that hopefully after you read this thing, you're going to go scurrying back to your Montrose and Gamma catalogues and reengage with all of this wonderful music again. In fact, as bonus for me, chasing the same thrill that any DJ has, I imagine that maybe I'm the one to send you into the man cave for a serious listen of Gamma 1 and Gamma 2 for the first time ever. Because hey, I fully recognize that a large swath of the readership for this book might not of given a damn that there's a big chunk devoted to Gamma, that it's basically a Montrose book with a weird extra bit. Well, I hope I've stated my case richly enough that Gamma, Ronnie's second life of a band, is as much testimony to Ronnie's greatness as is the much more recognized Montrose. I mean, you are going to hear a bunch of people offer some fresh ideas on why Ronnie was so cool, but my contribution to the conversation is pretty much, "Take a look at Gamma." And in the spirit of this book being about records, a large bunch of the credit goes to the massive vocal charm of Davey Pattison, along with the lyrics he wrote and his cool presence as front man, but yeah, mostly that deep, rich, bluesy voice of his.

Having said that, those who might've wished that I would spend equal amount of time and energy on Ronnie's instrumental albums... you're out of luck. I really couldn't give a damn about instrumental guitar albums by Ronnie or anybody else, and so those are dispensed with fairly quickly as we march on towards the inevitable, violent end.

And so really, we're back at the beginning, and so here I wanted to reiterate that I had an original goal, i.e., talk about the entire Montrose and Gamma catalogues, but that what I ended up with was in uneasy amount of re-living Ronnie's death, marbled with a lot of analysis of why Ronnie was the often difficult person he was.

And on the subject of his untimely death, as restated in the title of the second to last chapter from an anecdote related to me by Tal Morris, did Ronnie indeed "die of nothing?" Well, there's a resonance to that phrase "dying of nothing" wrapped up in Tal's amusing story reproduced near the end of this book, as related to him by Ronnie, about his time on tour with Lynyrd Skynyrd. So I decided to lift it and use it in that chapter title for this reason. As you will find out, Ronnie died of all sorts of things, but any one of them on its own, is arguably senseless or meaningless or nothing.

Additional to that, again, given Ronnie's status as an intellect and an explainer, a participant in life and an avid commenter on life, and as a guy that had a rich life, the nothing in that phrase also refers to the idea that nothing should've been so onerous as to cause him to annihilate this life force within himself.

The idea of dying of nothing is also reflected in another large and recurring theme all throughout this book, the idea that Ronnie was constantly in the process of throwing away his career, sabotaging himself, turning something—or the promise of something—into nothing. Again, it is hoped that all the articulate discussion of the positives and the negatives around this aspect of Ronnie's character will lead the reader to be educated as to the very commendable quality of a guy who follows his muse.

I mean, even in Tal's funny tour tale, the lesson of the story from Ronnie's end of it was that life was so precious that food had to serve the life force Spartan and business-like and not be celebrated hedonistically. The Skynyrd guy had other ideas. It's neither here nor there that half of Skynyrd ends up dying in a plane crash. In fact, if you think about it, that dark moment in rock history actually proves the guy right. And then again, Ronnie goes and chooses the void, or "nothing," over checking out whether his early instincts towards an ascetic (not to mention aesthetic!) life were to be proven correct and productive, over the philosophy that the best way to go was to live large and burn out like a southern rockin' whiskey rock 'n' roller.

Anyway, enough dwelling, because there is certainly a bunch of dwelling to come in the following pages. Suffice to say, that by the end of this trip down a dark hole, I hope that there's been enough celebration of Ronnie while alive—not to mention celebration of all the other interesting and sometimes odd characters in this tale—to take you to a place where you are ultimately focusing on the nine albums for which I intended to focus on in the first place.

There's the goal, and that's always the goal, to champion a bunch of great music, and convert a few extra people to my way of thinking along the way. With that in mind, and again, with the sincere hope that you will get to know Ronnie better and ultimately end up liking the guy, well, read on...

Martin Popoff
martinp@inforamp.net

CHAPTER 1: Early Years: "Being loud and distorted really added to that"

People have called the likes of Cactus and Mountain "America's Led Zeppelin." Cute, approximate, and I can somewhat see the point, but no—America's Led Zeppelin was Montrose. Or I suppose, unfortunately, Montrose was America's *Led Zeppelin*, and it's pretty much universally agreed upon that we never got *II*, *III* and *Physical Graffiti*. And the origins of this remarkable band, like Led Zeppelin's in fact, are unremarkable. Magic can happen in many ways, and this time it was like that time: four guys shuffling around found each other and made history.

The members of the original Montrose band—Denny Carmassi, Bill Church, Sammy Hagar and Ronnie Montrose—were essentially unknowns and lacking in much experience, save for Ronnie, this band's Jimmy Page, who had found some mild success as adjunct to the likes of Van Morrison and Edgar Winter.

Bill Church was somewhat tested as well, I suppose, also emerging from the shadows in Van Morrison's band. Church, 26 by the point Montrose got going in early 1973, had played with Ronnie in that situation, as well as a band from back in '69 called Sawbuck.

"When I first met Ronnie," says Church, "he lived in Boulder, Colorado, and he was from a band that I'd met in Boulder called Daddy Long Legs. And I told him, 'You guys, if you're ever in the Bay Area, look me up.' Well, Ronnie comes out there, having been back and forth from Boulder, and he decided to move to San Francisco. And my friend, my ex-drummer from Weed Straw, was now in the band Sawbuck. And Sawbuck needed a lead guitar player, so we got Ronnie. And Kootchie Trochim moved to Canada to be in The Wackers, with a friend of mine, Bobby Segarini. So I went into Sawbuck and that's how I met Ronnie. But I go way back; I played my first professional gig in 1959. I was in Europe in a band called The Blue Stars, and I lived in a place called Kaiserslautern, Germany."

Bill and Ronnie were also in an acoustic band together called The Corn Brothers. "Yes, and he actually didn't want to be in the acoustic band, so that was fairly short-lived," explains Church. "He didn't want to do acoustic music. And the guy who wrote all the songs in Sawbuck, Mojo Collins, he and Ronnie, their egos clashed."

Denny Carmassi, 27, by this point, came from a family full of drummers, having started playing clubs in and around the Bay Area while still in high school. His main claim to fame, other than a swell percussion education, was with a black female artist called Sweet Linda Divine (Linda Tillery), who recorded an album in New York with Al Kooper and Columbia. Issued in 1970, *Sweet Linda Divine* is now quite the collector's item.

Notes Bill of Carmassi's pre-Montrose ramp-up, "Denny is the king of the heavy foot and snare. He's an original Bay Area guy. Sammy and Ronnie are not Bay Area guys. But Denny is. He's East Bay grease like me, from Oakland, and I first met him when he thought he was black and was with Linda Tillery—big, fat, black blues singer, Sweet Linda Divine. And that's when Denny wore a dashiki and one of those weird floppy hats like black people wore (laughs). Before we ever played together, he and I would go to Raiders games and Oakland As games. And of course, his little brother was the very first drummer in the Sammy Hagar band. He did a tour with us, but did not record."

Sammy Hagar, also 27, had been bouncing around the music industry without much success for six years before his fateful collaboration with Ronnie. Family life was brutal for young Sammy, with a violent alcoholic father, but if anything good came out of it, Sammy was a hardened born leader, a characteristic that was going to come into play with respect to the impression he would make with "America's Led Zeppelin," not to mention his long run as boss of his own joint and as front man for a little something called Van Halen.

And for his part, Ronnie Douglas Montrose, also 26 in '73, was born in San Francisco on November 29, 1947, but spent much of his youth in Denver, Colorado, playing in bands like The Grim Reapers and the aforementioned Daddy Long Legs before lighting out for fame and fortune as an axe-wielder, winding up once more in the Bay Area. San Francisco was destined to remain his home forever, Ronnie succumbing to the same charms that result in nearly every musician that was raised there staying there rather than uprooting to LA. As indication of how magic could happen there, at one point he played host, at his rented garage apartment behind a house known as Thin Blue, to Band of Gypsies drummer Buddy Miles, who brought along his buddy Jimi Hendrix. Ronnie was living there with his wife Jill and baby son Jesse, practising in the main house with his band at the time, Sawbuck.

"I don't recall getting a first guitar," begins Ronnie, offering a bit of background to his ascendance to rock royalty. "I shared guitars before I actually got one of my own and played a guy's Silvertone and played another guy's Danelectro 12-string and it was at about age 17 that I actually started playing. I don't recall the specific guitar that was mine. I was too broke to buy a guitar so I borrowed guitars from friends. I'll tell you what! If you don't think it's rough playing lead on a 12-string... bloody fingers, man! I would say seeing the original Yardbirds with Jeff Beck and Jimmy Page at the old Fillmore was a pretty powerful influence on me. Seeing

Cream at Winterland was very powerful for me. Hendrix obviously was without peer, those early bands, that kind of stuff. I much more liked the Yardbirds with Beck and Page than I did the live Zeppelin things."

"When I first started playing, I wanted to be the best guitar player in the world," Ronnie told Steve Rosen, back in 1976. "But then I came to realize, it was a big world. That was a pretty wide goal, and there is no 'best' guitar player. I just wanted to be as expressive as I could with what I did, and reaches many people as possible. I wanted to be a sincere guitarist. Now, the goal I've set for myself—of course, I'm always trying to be a better finger picker and acoustic player—is to be as sincere with the notes as possible, so that what I'm playing is what I really mean. It sounds kind of corny, but that's the way I feel."

"Playing with Van Morrison," is what Ronnie cites as his first big break. "Being offered the chance to play in Van's band and do the *Tupelo* album was a pretty serious break. Then came the offer to play with Edgar Winter. Another break, to say the least! So yeah, I played with Van Morrison and came out of this Van Morrison thing, moved to California, I think I was 19, and went from Denver, Colorado... I'd heard there was this thing going on in San Francisco, the hippie movement, so I went out and tried my hand at becoming a hippie, which I did a really good job at doing. But I was just playing guitar and jamming around with everyone and going out and playing on little projects with people, just nothing of note."

"My acoustic band, the Corn Brothers, was opening for Van Morrison, in the Bay Area," recalls Bill. "And they really liked the idea that I was a mandolin/guitar/bari-uke player, as well as a bass player, right? And so he started having me come out to his studio and hanging out. And one day he asked me if I knew a guitar player. I said, 'I know the best guitar player in the Bay Area,' Ronnie. And at that time, I didn't realize it was the wrong kind of guy for Van (laughs)."

Not as a guitar player as such, but in terms of Ronnie's personality, the pattern forming early that Ronnie would have to lead, run things, be the centre of attention, or it wasn't going to work.

"Yes, absolutely. You know, at a gig, Van would go out front and start singing, and Ronnie would go right out to the front of the stage and stand right in the same line, like he was in a band, you know? And you don't do that. You can imagine if one of Frank Sinatra's guys did that, or James Brown even, you know? I don't think so. And of course, in Van Morrison's band, the famous quote when I asked him what was happening with Ronnie, he turned around and looked at me and said, 'Church, when the bus stops, somebody's gotta get off.' And that was it. Van is his own show. And Ronnie, of course, he would always go to the front of the stage and try to be the rock star. And of course, that's the reason that the original Montrose would split. Because of his need to control every friggin' thing."

And how did Ronnie find out in the first place? Well, Van had broke it to him using an old Irish expression of bad news, telling him, "Ronnie, it looks like rain." Ronnie had to wait until Van's manager explained it to him that he had just been let go.

Continues Ronnie, now plotting his next move, "Long story short I got a call from doing one project with a guy who knew a guy, and a guy who worked at CBS Records in New York and heard the project that I was working on and he called me and said that Edgar Winter was looking for a guitar player. That Edgar didn't want to do the *White Trash*, southern funk band, but wanted to do a rock band."

On the strength of Ronnie's playing on a friend's demo, Edgar made the offer, but Ronnie insisted on a two-way plane ticket, just in case he couldn't make the coastal leap psychologically speaking; after all, Ronnie considered himself a "California hippie."

"And there it was, they hired me to go and play guitar with them. So I went out, and I'd already been with Van Morrison playing *Tupelo Honey* and on those things. But when I went with Edgar, I was sort of thrown into the—no pun intended—the rock arena. I met him and a week later we were playing in coliseums. Playing big… well not big—well we were, actually, later—but we were playing in big college houses, field houses and everything. And it was amazing for me because I didn't really have chops at the time. Some say I do but they were very young chops. I had limited vocabulary, but what I did was, I guess, very effective for what was needed. And so that lasted, and then we just decided it wasn't the right situation for me because I was just really starting to feel my wings and wanting to get out there and do things."

To recap, Ronnie's stint with Van Morrison lasted a year-and-a-half (amusingly, part of the reason Van tapped Ronnie is because Van, a big Western and Americana fan, considered the Colorado native a "cowboy"). Montrose also did a nationwide tour with Boz Scaggs, who had just left the Steve Miller Band. The Edgar Winter gig was at the behest of mover and shaker Steve Paul, who flew him out for a tryout and then, as Ronnie chuckles, he never left, trying out on a Tuesday and playing a headline show on Friday. Ronnie did other less recognized session work as well, including the official *Roller Derby* theme song. "I was kicking around all over the country doing sessions for anyone who would ask me. I even played with Herbie Hancock once. I was doing a lot of sessions for David Rubinson of Fillmore Productions, and word came down that Hancock wanted a 'chickawawa' guitar player. So I went and did a wah-wah track. With Van, I played quieter, arranged parts. Van taught me an incredible amount about dynamics and things that didn't show on the first album, but have been included on the ones that followed."

"With Van, it was basically acoustic or subtle electric work," Ronnie told Rosen. "I used a Fender Princeton set on about four. With Edgar, it was a totally different concept—giant amps, right out in the middle of the stage, and guitar solos to death. There really wasn't much difference between Edgar's and my own thing."

Recording *They Only Come Out at Night* in September of '72 and leaving The Edgar Winter Group in the Spring of '73, Ronnie attributes to "growing pains. There just wasn't quite enough room for the talent and the desire that everyone had. There was Edgar, Dan Hartman, me... Rick Derringer was in producing the group for a while. There were so many influences that I needed a creative vehicle to be something that could drive myself as opposed to being in someone's band and working for someone."

Providing an indication of how there was more to the story than Ronnie's delicate version would attest, Bill recalls how Ronnie busted open the gold record he had gotten for *They Only Come Out at Night*, and on the little picture of the album cover designed into these things, X-Acto-knifed out the picture of Edgar. "Yeah, that's what happened. Ronnie and I, of course, were best friends for years and years, and usually every morning, I went over to his house and had coffee, and he called me up one morning, 'Are you coming over tomorrow? Because I just got in the mail my gold record.' Cool. So I went over the next morning, and there it is on the wall, and the only thing missing, in the little square picture, he had cut out Edgar (laughs). I don't remember exactly what I said, because I knew how much he hated Edgar anyway." As for why Ronnie would do this, Bill says, "Same with Van—two giant egos clashing."

They Only Come Out at Night would reach #3 on the charts, receiving its gold certification on April 30, 1973, in other words, pretty much right away. But as Church alludes to, "Free Ride" and "Frankenstein" would live on as perennials, the result being platinum as well as double platinum certification taking place November 21, 1986. And so at this point, including the assorted bits and bobs, Ronnie had under his belt a couple of albums in *Tupelo Honey* and most relevantly *They Only Come Out At Night*. Ronnie had one writing credit on the album, for "Rock 'n' Roll Boogie Woogie Blues." But as Ronnie says, he was "feeling his wings;" in other words, his own persona as natural born leader was struggling to the fore, arriving at a new place from the diametrically opposed position of mere sideman to two dominating figures.

At this juncture, as Ronnie explained to Steve Rosen, he was an avowed Gibson Les Paul man. "I had never been out of the Denver area to be able to look around and find good guitars. And I really didn't have any desire to own another one, because what I had was fine for me. I got out on the road with Edgar, met J. Geils, and developed a little friendship with J., who said, 'Look man, get rid of that thing. I can get you a sunburst.' So I bought my first real Les Paul Sunburst from J. This was in the good old days when sunbursts went for $700 or $800."

"So I came back and left his group," continues Montrose, "and came back to California looking to put a rock group together. So as it turns out, Sammy was with his band back in the day—he had a little cover band in a nightclub called The Justice Brothers—and they had seen me at Winterland playing with Edgar actually a month beforehand. And back in those days—I remember this vividly because I put out the word to Rik Elswit, who was with Dr. Hook & the Medicine Show. I lived in Sausalito, California, and everybody who lived in Marin, everybody gave everybody else their number. There was no big managers and road managers and a curtain or wall of fire you had to walk through to get to anybody. You handed out your phone number."

"So I told Rick I was putting a band together and blah blah blah. He had seen Sammy, he knew Sammy from some place, and Sammy had just seen me and called me up on the phone and said, 'I'm your man'—that straight-ahead. He said, 'I just saw you play with Edgar. I love your playing and I'm the guy for you.' Extremely confident. So I went down and saw him and his band play cover songs at this nightclub called the Wharf Rat in San Francisco, and he had the whole look thing going; he had the hair... it was like a young Robert Plant. And he had that voice, and the voice is still there. It's always there, because Sammy has got that unique voice and he's still good to this day."

Bill Church recalls the hook-up with Sammy a little differently, with other background characters involved. Beginning with the connection to Carmassi, Bill explains that, "What happened was, when we were deciding who was going to be drums and who was going to be singing, it was my job to go up to Northern California to check out Denny playing in his band Thunderstick, and talking to him and seeing if he wants to do a band and all that. Same time, what happened was Tawny, friend of Ronnie and mine, who at that time was a female disc jockey on the big San Francisco station, along with her friend Tom Donahue, the greatest DJ ever, right? Anyway, Tawny was turning us onto people. And she called and said, 'You want to check the singer out at the Wharf Rat tavern.' So Ronnie went down by himself a couple of times without introducing himself, more or less incognito, you know? Because even though he was in Edgar's band, he could get away with not being recognized down there. And so I became friends with Denny before we had a band. And that's pretty much it."

Continues Bill, "So one night we got Denny, and then one night me and Ronnie went down to the Wharf Rat and hear Sammy up there with his band doing James Brown covers. And Ronnie, you know, he's coming out of the Edgar Winter Band, he's got a $2000 fur coat on. Back then, the lead guys in bands wore fur coats. I don't know if you remember that era. Mick Jones and all those guys, full-length fur coats that cost thousands. And Ronnie's got his on, and Sammy is playing in the Wharf Rat tavern. Anyway, sat down and said, 'Do you want to be in this band?' And, of course, Sammy, his eyes blew wide open, because obviously, he realizes this is his chance. Sammy wanted to be a star. His big influence and big hero—and why he named his son Aaron—was Elvis Aaron Presley. He saw Elvis on TV when he was a kid, and he wanted to be Elvis ever since. And Denny and I had been friends ever since that first meeting. Of course, he's on a couple of Sammy Hagar band albums. He never toured in the Sammy Hagar band. But he did play on two of the albums."

Harper's Bizarre drummer and soon-to-be star producer Ted Templeman even claims a role in the introduction, having said he had told Ronnie about this R&B singer down at the Fillmore, thinking the two would work well together. Some of the incongruence with Sammy's particular telling of the story are muddied by the fact that Sammy knew Denny, having been asked by Carmassi about recording a demo of Thunderstick's original material, which he actually didn't do, not having been convinced about the viability of the act.

Continues Ronnie, once a connection is established, "Sammy and I got together and he brought some cassettes out, some little songs that he'd been writing and I'd been writing, and he had done a session with Denny Carmassi at that time, and I went out to see Denny, and obviously Denny was the right drummer, and I hired Denny on the spot. I said, 'You wanna be in a band?' 'Yep.' We shook hands and that was it. And I had played with Bill Church. We tried a bunch of bass players out but I played with Bill Church and he was an old buddy of mine and he was actually the right bass player for us, so we went with him and we started this thing."

But it didn't exactly go that smoothly, qualifies Bill. "Then Ronnie and I had a big giant fight, right? And it wasn't settled now whether I was going to be the bass player! So he has the audacity to try out other bass players. You know, amongst them, Pete Sears (ed. Rod Stewart, later Jefferson Starship), Ross Vallory (ed. later Journey), Andy Fraser from Free, who I don't think actually made it out. And he keeps doing this, and then about three weeks later, sooner or later, he says, 'Well, are you coming down to S.I.R. or not?' And I said, 'I thought you weren't talking to me anymore.' I said, 'All right, I'll be there.' So that was that. That's a weird story, huh? But believe me, I didn't... that's the third band I'd been in with him, so believe me, we'd had words before that (laughs)."

And for the record, further complicating the story behind Bill Church being available for all these head games in the first place was the fact that Bill had earlier been informed by Van Morrison that he had swapped his entire band for Jesse Colin Young's, and that, by the way, you are now Jesse Colin Young's bass player.

"Well, that actually only happened in theory," laughs Bill. "What happened is, Van and Jesse were friends, of course, and neighbours. They decided they wanted to trade bands—that was the theory. The end result was that the remaining few of Jesse's band, they all took off on their own. All of us from that particular version of Van's band went their separate ways and that was that. And the only exchange that actually happened was that Van's new bass player was Jesse's old bass player, David Hayes. There's no way I was going to go play with Jesse Colin Young. He was a combination of acid, folky and hippie, but no, Jesse thought of himself as a Van-type of dude, but they were two different leagues. I wasn't going back from the big leagues to triple A."

"I would have to say my dad," answers Denny Carmassi, in conversation with John Wardlaw on the roots of his life in drumming. "He played the drums, his brother played the drums, my brother plays the drums. So I come from a family of drummers. Some of my earliest memories as a child are of my dad rehearsing his band in our kitchen. He had a small group—five, six guys—and they played big band arrangements of standards. These guys all worked regular jobs during the week and played on the weekends. He used to let me sit in when I was a kid. I guess I saw him play more than anyone at an early age. He also hipped me to some pretty cool drummers. We always watched Buddy Rich when he was on TV. He took me to see an absolute bitch of a show drummer named Jimmy Vincent who played with Louie Prima. I think when I saw that I thought, 'That's what I would like to do.' He also had a Ray Charles live at the Newport Jazz Festival album (ed. Ray Charles - At Newport) that I used to listen to and practice with. I think the drummer's name was Richard Goldberg."

"I was also influenced a lot by what I heard on the radio," continues Carmassi. "This was mid-'50s, so I heard drummers like Earl Palmer. Little Richard, Fats Domino, Eddie Cochran... anything with a wicked groove on it was probably Earl. D.J. Fontana (ed. Elvis) just layin' it down. Then in the late '50s/early '60s it was Al Jackson Jr., who played with Booker T. and did all the Stax Volt stuff. I think I actually learned to play the drums from listening to and playing along with Booker T. & the M.G.s' 'Green Onions.' I'm a firm believer in what goes in your ears comes out your hands. Then I guess the whole British Invasion thing. But, we had the baddest drummer of that era right here in our own back yard, and that was Dino Danelli of The Rascals. He blew all those English cats away. Then the Tamla Motown records with Bennie Benjamin. James Brown with Clyde Stubblefield and Jabo Starks. Then I would have to say Cream with Ginger Baker, Jimi Hendrix with Mitch Mitchell and Led Zeppelin with John Bonham."

"I have to mention Tony Williams," adds Denny. "Not that I could even remotely begin to grasp his style and facility behind the drum set. He was deep. But he was such an inspiration with the fire and command he had of the instrument. I went to see him every chance I got. I saw him play in a little club in Oakland about a month before he died. My brother and I sat two feet away from him for two sets. He was the master. So, I guess my dad got me started, but I was influenced by many drummers. And like any self-respecting musician, I stole from the best."

As for instigating his career in drumming, Denny says that at the beginning, it was "just really local Bay Area stuff. I started right out of high school playing topless clubs in San Francisco. Top 40. Learning my craft. I was in a band called Sweet Linda Divine that went to New York, recorded one album on Columbia, produced by Al Kooper. It broke up soon after that. Then it was just one local band after another. Trying to get signed, trying to get a break. The usual stuff."

"This thing" that Sammy, Ronnie, Denny and Bill would soon cook up, namely the lighting rod of a mind-wrecker called *Montrose*...well, it was the inevitable by-product of a shift from psychedelic culture to something louder. We have to remember, Montrose emerged from San Francisco, birthplace of psychedelic music, but also birthplace of Blue Cheer, who some call the world's first heavy metal band, pretty much due to the trio's 1968 debut album *Vincebus Eruptum*.

"I grew up in this working class California town called Fontana that had nothing to do with LA, even though it was just down the road apiece," reflected Sammy Hagar, in conversation with Lenny Stoute from Music

Express, "My dad was a Golden Gloves champion, so by the time I could stand up, there were guys trying to knock me down. How tough was it? It was so tough, I was 16 before I realized I could unfold a fist. It was so tough there was an express line at the church confessional for eight sins or less. Television saved my soul for rock 'n' roll. I used to watch the groups on *American Bandstand* and it looked like they were having a good time and getting lots of girls. It didn't look like they worked too hard, and I said, 'That's for me.' But I never had any doubt that I would be making a living from rock 'n' roll."

Sammy takes us through the history of the music scene as it existed in his home town, setting the stage for the conditions in which a harder rock could thrive and in fact become a replacing new flavour against the hippie music of the '60s.

"In the '60s I was in the middle of all that," begins Hagar, addressing the subject of the Vietnam War, speaking with Sam Dunn. "It was just the times. Everyone was just feeling that. People were in an age group where a large amount of people were being drafted at the same time, and a large amount of people were starting to listen to rock 'n' roll, a harder-edged music, and a lot of people were starting to smoke dope and take drugs and all that. Man, you get high and get through it with a Les Paul and a Marshall stack. You get high and plug into that mother and it gets good to you. And there's an audience there accepting it. I just think it's more fun to play music really loud and powerful. Before that, the Elvis generation and all that, the only thing coming through the PA was the guy singing, and they had these little speakers and everybody had to play soft and it was all down. As equipment and technology started getting better, people started saying wow, I can play this loud and hey, we're playing in a stadium for 70,000 people for God's sakes; I'll play as loud as I want. And pretty soon it just got to you. The amount of volume that puts out, it changes the way you play. And when you're playing guitar through a small amp with a clean sound, you play a certain way. You crank that sucker up and you start playing a whole different kind of way, and it brings out more of an aggressive attitude in you, and I think the noise actually affects people and it makes other people respond and it just catches on like a snowball effect, you know? It just starts getting good to you. It really does. Loud music is powerful."

For his part, Ronnie downplays the effects of politics on what was driving him personally to make rock 'n' roll. "As far as I'm concerned, there wasn't too much politics going on. Except for the—and this is an absolute ludicrous thing to say—we had the war going on. But after the war and after everybody came home and in the '70s, it was sort of like a little lull, you know? Life was good, people were making money, Detroit was making shitty cars and things were just sort of going on. Yeah, there was a gas crisis, but as far as I could see, there wasn't any reason to do anything extremely political because it was just business as usual. Watergate, to all of my friends and everyone else, was more of like an amusement park, a cartoon more than anything else."

"I was kind of really into the surf music," laughs Sammy, offering more on his own roots and motivations. "I really was for a couple years there. It seems like it was a couple summers in a row, and then The Seeds and those things kind of came right on the heels of that, didn't they? I'm trying to put my time frame on there. I'm old, man. It's like trying to say was that before or after? I think Iron Butterfly, The Seeds and those kinds of bands started coming right along the same time as Cream and all that. Plus I was listening to the blues. I was listening to John Mayall and the Blues Breakers. I was listening to B.B. King because when I got turned onto Clapton and Jeff Beck and those guys, and Hendrix, all they were talking about were the blues guys. So I went back immediately and I started digging into the blues. The rest of the country, I don't really know what they were doing because at that stage I was smoking dope all day with my little turntable and my guitar and I'm learning Eric Clapton solos and Jeff Beck solos and even Hendrix. I wasn't as big a Hendrix guy as I was Clapton. I liked the way Clapton always played. The blues seemed to be more authentic. I don't know, I went to Monterey Pop Festival, for instance. Three days I was there, and I saw Otis Redding, Eric Burdon and the Animals, the new Animals, The Association, and that's all I remember. I didn't see Hendrix, I didn't see Janis Joplin. I was there. I was a different kind of guy."

"I wasn't a big Iron Butterfly fan either," continues Hagar, "because I saw them once, and if you weren't high and didn't catch that whole buzz you didn't go with them, you know? I think the drug scene really had a lot to do with everything going in that direction, the more I think about it. It's like okay, here you are, you're seeing things starting to work in concerts. Bands that wanted to be experimental, that weren't pop bands, they weren't just writing pop hits. They were going out and laying down a vibe like The Dead and bands like Iron Butterfly. They wanted to go out and create an experience, so everybody got high and they just kind of started playing, and I think they found out that being loud and distorted really added to that. And then as that started growing, pretty soon the dark side started becoming less commercial and wasn't getting them anywhere, so then some band comes along and just takes a piece of that and tightens it up a little bit and makes more of a hit. I mean Iron Butterfly had a huge hit. The biggest album of the year was *Ball*. I remember that, because my favourite band was Cream, and they weren't as big as Iron Butterfly and that sickened me. I'm going how could this be? I was such a Cream fanatic."

Makes sense, for Cream was a power trio, as was essentially The Who and Led Zeppelin and Montrose. But the template for a pure three-piece power trio was right in Montrose's backyard, and that would be none other than Blue Cheer.

"I think Blue Cheer is still the loudest band ever," laughs Hagar. "Like I say back then they didn't have huge PAs. Technology was still starting to come in, so you had to be really loud coming off the stage to be heard in the back of an arena if you were playing a 10,000, 3000, 4000 seat place. You ain't gonna do it through this little amp because you're probably not going to be in the PA system. The PA system was for the drums and the vocalist. And the guitar and bass, like in Blue Cheer, I don't even think they were in the PA. I mean they were in everything because they were playing so loud, but they had three Marshall stacks or four Marshall stacks apiece. I saw Blue Cheer a lot of times, and they just took acid and played loud. It was like that was their trip, and if you took acid and liked loud music, you went to see Blue Cheer. And if you didn't like the music... because they weren't great. I mean they were in their own way, but they could have some pretty bad nights."

As for the rest of the San Francisco bands, Sammy says they were "loud but clean. It wasn't distorted. Blue Cheer was the only distorted band, although there may have been others. But bands like Quicksilver, the guy was playing through PA horns and stuff, you know? Cipollina had the most projected friggin' guitar sound. It was thick but not big and fat; it was just like… it would make you go deaf. And Jerry Garcia had walls of Altec Lansing and JBL speakers, the cleanest speakers you could get. So those guys were really into the big clean wall of sound, but loud. So for some reason, the San Francisco sound was real clean. That's the one thing I didn't dig about it, because I like a distorted sound."

As evidenced by Montrose... "Yeah, and Montrose was a San Francisco band. People don't realize that. We came in in San Francisco, the Bay Area, all of us. So yeah, we were a bit more like Blue Cheer than anyone else. But the hard part about being part of all these different scenes, I never stepped out and analyzed it, so I'm trying to now. That's where I'm having the problem. I can only tell you what I felt, you know what I mean? The San Francisco scene was real exciting times. There was a lot going on. It wasn't just drugs. It was music everywhere and art everywhere. Somebody was doing something wacky everywhere. It was like living in Disneyland."

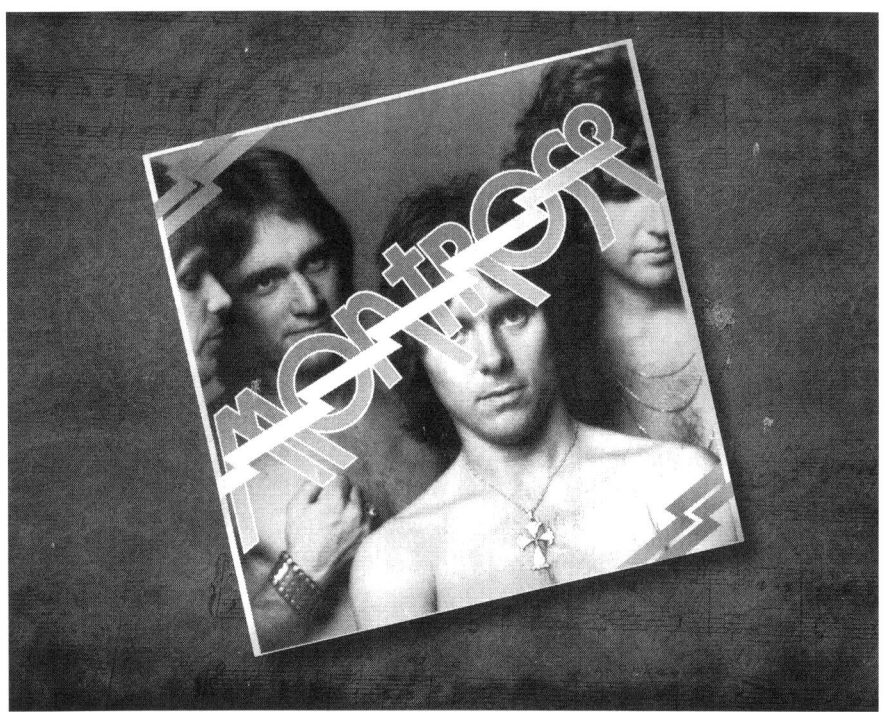

CHAPTER 2: Montrose – *Montrose:* "Fuzzy, clean, dirty, edgy"

After three years of grand British heavy metal and nothing from America, save for the likes of the aforementioned Cactus and Mountain, no one saw the *Montrose* record coming. Who were these guys anyway? Sure, we had heard of Ronnie Montrose, bit player in a somewhat successful band of dated funky hard rockers led by the striking Edgar Winter. But the rest of them? And like a shot from the land of the rock gods, who was this belter, this Sam Hagar? He was a presence, that's who, a rock lion who would quickly outstrip the impression of his boss for which the band was named (and therein lies the seed of discontent).

Fact is—and of course this is all neat, encapsulated, cemented in history by people like myself repeating it everywhere—*Montrose* is considered one of the greatest debut records of all time, certainly way, way up there in the tighter realm of hard rock. What else gets the nod? Well, of course it's that other Ted Templeman-produced debut for Warner from five years later, *Van Halen*. Strange how things work out. But one could also call *Montrose* the first American heavy metal album and even something like "Space Station #5" the first American heavy metal song. The album was that groundbreaking, and this from a baby band, not someone's third or fourth album.

Baby band yes, but as has been established, not a bunch of young firecrackers: these guys were all into their late 20s. But picture them in their birthday suits on the pink and pastel front cover, and then again amidst the misty soft blues of the back cover, and subliminally the record buyer is led to believe these guys were mere babes in the woods—I mean, given the pink on one side and soft blue on the back, the *Montrose* jacket is practically a cardboard nursery.

Notes Denny Carmassi on the cover, "Those were Norman Seeff's photographs. At the time, I guess he was a hot photographer but we didn't even know who he was. We just kind of went and did it. Generally, they would just bring in ideas. Or Ronnie would bring in a bunch of ideas, and we would look at it and say, yeah, we like this, we don't like that. That's the way I remember the album covers being picked. He would have some ideas, he would show them to us and we would discuss it. But what is in that album is the most important thing, you know? That piece of vinyl is really important. But the first one was cool; those photographs were great and sort of captured what we were."

"I like it a lot," says Bill. "The original shots that were rejected, because they were considered pornography by Joe Smith and Warner Bros., were even better. Norman, who is by the way one of the all-time great photographers, we went into a swimming pool and he shot us breaking water as we were coming up together, all naked, and it was a really cool shot. And Warner Bros. says, nah, too much pornography. And the only thing they would finally go for, was, if you're going to go naked, you can do it from the waist up, end of story. And so I liked the cover. Now, in Europe, Warner Bros. Europe, they were not allowed anything naked back then. And so the album cover in Europe, on the continent, is the one with the cartoon caricature girl with the four boobs. They wouldn't allow any nakedness at all, so we had to change it."

What Bill is referring to is the issue of the album re-titled as *Rock the Nation*, where, in fact, the girl doesn't really have four breasts, but rather both her sleeves are mischievously illustrated to look like two additional breast. Plus, there's clearly nipple showing through her burst-ready shirt, and really, it's hard to say which album cover actually came out as more "pornographic;" in fact, one could envision this German image getting over-ruled by any given major label stateside. What's more, it wasn't always a given that the band would take on Ronnie's last name, the guys having struggled over a moniker for a while, with White Dwarf having been in the running for a spell.

"We were trying to figure out what this band was going to be called," remembers Church. "And so after we went through names and laughing and crying about all of them, we got down to Sammy's choice, which was White Dwarf. You know what a white dwarf is, don't you? It's not a Hollywood midget, it's a type of star. Anyway, so we had to take a band vote. It came down to two choices: White Dwarf and Montrose. And so it went to a vote, and Sammy and Denny voted for White Dwarf. Ronnie, of course voted for his own ego. I made the choice to go with Montrose simply because I thought it would help be a springboard. Because Ronnie at that time had just quit the band that had the top album in the world, with Edgar. I still hear those songs on commercials to this day. Anyway, I thought about it; I didn't want it to be called after anybody's name. We were all against that except Ronnie. We didn't want it to be called anybody. I wanted a band. But I just thought, well, I don't really like White Dwarf that much, and I thought it's a springboard, because Edgar's album is still in the Top 10, and here we are coming out with his guitar player in a new band and stuff, so I'll just go along with being called Montrose. And so that was the tying vote. I was the tying vote. In that case, when it's a tie vote, guess who decided? (laughs)."

MONTROSE

It is said that Sammy, when he got hired on with the band, went and got his astrological chart drawn up. Sammy also tells—quite convincingly—the story of having been abducted by aliens. Ergo, the White Dwarf idea is right up his alley.

"You have to know that out of all the four guys in that band, Sammy is the one that is into the occult," explains Bill, although one gathers, not intending to equate Hagar with the likes of Jimmy Page here! "That's why he's always trying to name things after stars and stuff. White Dwarf wasn't the last time. When he started the Sammy Hagar band, the original name of that band was Sammy Hagar & Dust Cloud. You know what a dust cloud is? When a supernova explodes, all that is left is a cloud of dust. And you know why we didn't end up being called that? We actually did a couple gigs, I've got a couple posters of gigs... we hired a guy, an artist, to do our album cover, right? And so one of the first things he came up with was this stagecoach riding across the prairie with this big cloud of dust behind it. And I turned to Sammy and I go, 'Hey, if we call it Dust Cloud, everybody in America is going to think it has something to do with cowboys and shit out in the dirt. Nobody knows what a dust cloud is.' But of course there's 'Space Station #5,' and on some of the early Hagar tunes, we were trying to be a science band."

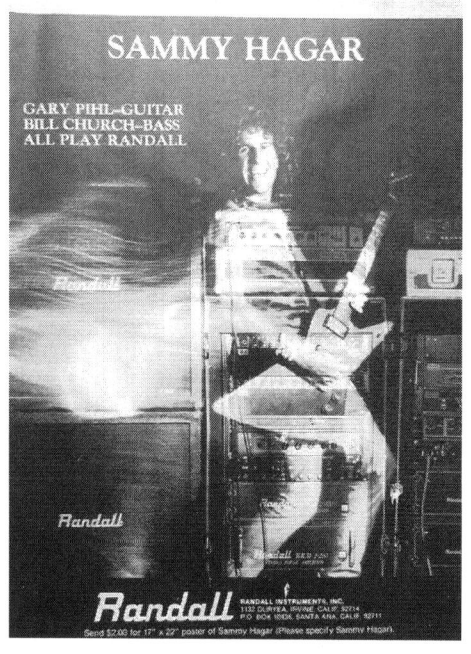

"Silver Lights," "Crack in the World"... "Yeah, a bunch of the early Sammy Hagar stuff was basically directed at that. And then we shifted gears and decided to go back to women and cars."

Besides renaming the album for Europe and changing the cover, Warner also played a heavy hand in this new band's business arrangements as well, reveals Church, who first establishes the framework in which Montrose was to operate. "Being a San Francisco-based band, we were right in the middle of the whole psychedelic type trip. And their music didn't have a lot of discipline to it at that time. A lot of jamming going on and all that kind of stuff. And so we absolutely did realize we were making something different. We were not going to have rambling solos and stuff. We were going to save that for live. And we wanted to be a little bit more mainstream."

"It was to be a short-lived band, but we were coming into it with heavy credentials. Our producer, Ted Templeman, even then, was one of the top producers in the world. And all of us were personal friends, because I was already with Warner Bros.. Joe Smith, of course, was the president then, and I was personal friends with him, because I was already with Warner Brothers. I was in the Van Morrison band. And Joe himself, gave us a list of five managers, and said, 'You have to go out and get one of these guys, no matter what it takes.' These five guys, as I recall, amongst many of them, the one that we wanted was Alice Cooper's manager, Shep Gordon. And Alice wouldn't let Shep sign us. And that's why we ended up with a New

York manager—Dee Anthony, was our manager. That's why we ended up out there. But anyway, Joe Smith had given us this list of five names, and said, you have to have one of these as your manager. He and Ted set us up for success, and success eluded it. Most people call it a classic album, and indeed it is, but it didn't sell shit during the period. And it almost cost Ted his position, because the band was so short-lived."

But before getting set up with management, Bill Graham was on the spot, setting the band up to rehearse at S.I.R. Studios (Studio Instrument Rentals) in San Francisco, with the understanding that the label that eventually signs the band would be paying the bill. A nascent version of Journey was down the hall, and that band's manager, Herbie Herbert made a play for Montrose to no avail.

As Church explains, "Bill wanted the action (laughs). He was willing to do anything. Even through the Sammy Hagar band, he was always trying to buy 5% of everything. But Bill Graham was not a manager. He was an amateur manager at that time. He managed the Airplane and all them, the local guys up there, but he was a booking agent. He was not really what a record company at that time would've considered… Well they wanted somebody to be a full-time manager. Bill Graham, was already way too spread-out. And he was a booking agent, basically, anyway. These are people that think they could be managers."

Why the band would have wanted Shep, Bill says, "Alice was really hot, and chances are that we would break in with his shows. Because he was about the biggest of the American rock bands in that particular year. And so with Shep we would automatically have a vehicle into American hard rock. But Dee, for example, Dee had everything, because at that time, that was the Mafia—him and Frank Barsalona. Frank Barsalona promoted every show east of the Mississippi, right? Every one! And of course we got a springboard there too, because of the in with Dee Anthony's other bands. Here we are playing with Humble Pie, who was huge at that time. And ELP was another one of his. He had loads of them."

"I didn't know I was that good that fast, or I never thought about it," reflects Ronnie, asked to look back on what the band had unleashed, October 17, 1973. "The only references I had were I loved Jeff Beck, loved Eric Clapton, loved Hendrix, loved Deep Purple. Those were my sort of… what I grew up on. There was nothing else as a reference. Basically I was just so involved at that time in exploring my instrument with my limited experience. I was just trying to discover what it was I was doing. As Mitchell Froom told me at one time, when I'd said well, we weren't really that skilled, he said, 'Yeah, but you were playing up to 100% of your ability.' Which is true. I mean we were maxed-out. I mean, I've heard great records that are just a simple three chords and that's it, but if that's all you know, and you're playing it balls to the wall..."

Although Ronnie also cedes that, "I wouldn't say that it was much of a surprise because we were already playing that kind of heavy rock with the Edgar Winter Group, basically an extension of that; if not exactly an extension of that group, an extension of the way my playing was evolving. For me there wasn't any intention to make a specific kind of music. It just happened to be where I was at at the time , a.k.a. the words to 'Rock the Nation,' 'I've got it in me, ain't gonna quit until it all comes out.'"

And to reiterate, there wasn't anything going on at this intensity level at the time. "No, honestly, you'd have to look at the... I forgot who the managers were; I think they were Earth, Wind & Fire's managers. But you'd have to look at the music that was around in the '70s, and there just wasn't anything there. There wasn't any American things there. I mean the only things that came out even close to us, obviously there was the three: there was Montrose, Kiss and Aerosmith. And this little old band from Texas called ZZ Top. Bill Graham told me one time, 'Ronnie there's this band in Texas, they book their own shows, they're just phenomenal, they're called ZZ Top. They made it on their own without anybody helping them. They moved up.'"

So true, there was ZZ Top three records in, and there was also one wobbly Aerosmith album, no Kiss yet, there was Foghat getting their sea legs, there were second and third stringers like Bang, Sir Lord Baltimore and Captain Beyond, but there was nothing close to the molten proto-metal levels of a record like *Montrose*. Heck, Ted Nugent's only two Amboy Dukes albums that were even remotely analogous were 1973 and 1974 records.

But it all had to start with the songs, and the baking and making of those is a clinic in explosive, youthful, apocryphal rock 'n' roll chemistry bordering upon alchemy.

"No difficulties with lyrics," says Hagar, recalling those shiny times brightly. "In those days, that was my first record and I could sing about anything. I mean, I could write about anything because I hadn't written any songs before. Now, I've written about a motorcycle, I've written about I can't drive 55, I've written about my tequila, you know (laughs)? I've written about my divorce and my new love, I've written about my children. So pretty soon you're sitting they're going, God, what am I going to write about? In Montrose, I was fresh as a daisy, man. There was nothing I had written about. So that was simple, and lyrics were a lot simpler back then as well. I don't think I could get away with writing some of that now."

"I learned so much from Ronnie Montrose, it's ridiculous," continues Sam. "He taught me without even trying. I mean, if he would have had his way, he wouldn't have taught me anything, but... he had a really big ego and it really held him back in his career. He's a really talented guy; he was one of the innovators of that kind of music and I learned so much from him about playing guitar. I learned as much from Ronnie Montrose on guitar as I ever learned from Eddie Van Halen. And Eddie, you know, not taking anything away from Eddie, Ronnie in his day was a hot guitar player and I learned so much from him. Writing, arranging a song and all that. But as soon as I started blossoming... I was a kid who didn't have any experience on the road. I'd never been on the road and I'd never been in a recording studio. I'd been in a recording studio, but not for real, making a record."

Adds Ronnie, "One of the great things about Sam's writing was he had this booklet of lyrics, not necessarily all cohesive, but he would just write lyrics down. So when I put those songs together... I mean he had written some of the songs as well, but when I started looking at his lyrics I realized that it was one of those things that you could actually mix and match and cut and paste. So I put a couple of things together with him like that, just said this would work good with the bridge here, and it just came out that way. So we just started jamming, rehearsing, and we really liked what we were doing. We didn't know what we were doing, but musically we liked it. And we actually had managers come up—I've told this story before—a couple of well-known managers came and saw us play 'Rock Candy,' 'Rock the Nation,' 'Bad Motor Scooter,' all of those songs, 'Space Station #5' and say—and this was in 1973—'Guys, it's good music but if this was just five years ago we could go ahead and do something with you. But right now this is kind of dated. This is not good music for the time.' And we looked at each other and went fuck you. No. We're doing this no matter what. And so then we just started playing around."

The end result of all this however—the *Montrose* album as it would exist as launched in October of 1973—is considerably more forceful and fiery than the original songwriting and arrangements would let on. There's a live-in-studio session recorded at the Record Plant in Sausalito, California, for local classic rock station KSAN on April 21, 1973, that displays the Montrose songs very differently than what we would hear once producer Ted Templeman got hold of the guys. Soon to be monolithic metal sledges like "Rock Candy" and "Make It Last" sound comparatively twee, lacking in distortion, lacking in bombast, but also regularly stuffed with extra licks (one supposes, later deemed gratuitous), compared to the renditions on the record. "Bad Motor Scooter" and "I Don't Want It" are practically poppy, boogie rocking modestly like Edgar Winter or James Gang or ZZ from the first two records. "Good Rockin' Tonight," "Rock the Nation" and "One Thing on My Mind," on the other hand, sound close to fully cooked.

Of note, included on the session are two non-LP compositions, "Roll Me Nice" and "You're Out of Time," the former being dull buffalo burger rock like BTO or Kiss, the latter being a bit of a progressive Hendrix rave, commendable, but one conjectures an ill fit to what would emerge as a damn near perfect record. Bill recalls that these two songs were never properly recorded for consideration with respect to making it onto the album. "That was one of the earliest live things, when we were testing things. You know who that DJ is, don't you? That was Tom Donahue. He's about the most famous San Francisco DJ ever." Tom "Big Daddy" Donahue would die barely two years later, of a heart attack at the age of 46.

Not ceding too much credit to Ted and his engineer Donn Landee, Denny clarifies, "Well, yeah, I mean, they recorded it, but we had to play it. You know, they captured what we were. But man, when I first heard that KSAN thing... are you hip to the way 'Rock Candy' is? It's way, way different than it came out on the record. Man, I was playing it way different. I don't even remember it. When I first heard it, I went, oh my gosh. It was more like a funky beat, yeah, more like Little Feat—you're right."

And so a survey of these sessions could and should lead one to believe that Templeman had a big part in making *Montrose* sizzle and fry and send off heat the way it would.

"We did a demo, actually with Ted Templeman," begins Ronnie, articulating the connection. "who I worked with in Van Morrison. We flew down to LA, did this demo. I remember I liked Ted. And also Don Ellis, I believe, from Epic Records, who had just signed Jeff Beck to his solo record with Epic, he had flown out to my house, was sitting in my living room in Sausalito and said we'd like you to come with us on Epic because we'll pay a lot of attention to you. And Ted flew me down there and we had dinner together, and Ted said we'd like to have you on Warner Bros. So the bottom line is I liked Ted. They were both good, but I liked Ted and I'd known him and he was a California boy and it just worked out like that. And as far as the sound goes, we told Ted we liked Zeppelin, and he went and researched Zeppelin records and said, 'Well here's what we need to do, guys.'"

Except *Montrose* isn't produced like Led Zeppelin—it's several times better. Ronnie himself would later produce one of the band's albums very much in a Zeppelin mode, but that's a story for later.

Scratching his head for the link, Ronnie figures, "We did most of the music at Amigo Studios, which was the Warner Bros. studios there in Burbank, California, and 'Rock Candy' happened to be so heavy. It was a situation with 'Rock Candy' where I was jamming some riff and I always would put my cassette player on when we were rehearsing. You couldn't hear anything because it was distorted because we were playing louder than concert level in probably a 12' x 12' room. The only thing in the PA was the voice and then everything else was loud. And then Denny... I'm sure he was playing something along the lines of 'When the Levee Breaks' because we all loved Zeppelin, and it was something like that kind of a slow power groove. And then I put that riff together; I just played that riff for 'Rock Candy' and then it was a couple days later and we're going what was that thing we were doing? It was cool. And Sam already had the 'Rock Candy' lyrics with no song, just the lyrics. And I went back, referenced my cassette player, and the rest was history. We decided, yeah, this is a pretty good song right here. So Ted, when we told him that we wanted something as heavy and powerful as that, he booked Sunset Sound on Sunset Blvd. in LA because Zeppelin had worked there, and done... I don't know which tracks. So we went in and did 'Rock Candy' there. The rest of the album we did at Amigo Studios, and you can tell the difference in the actual big giant drum room sound and everything else. But doing the record, it wasn't like we were using big amps. We were playing little... I had a little 310 Fender amp. I mean it was like a little 40 watt amplifier, but it was just up to the max and mic'd well and it sounded huge. And everybody to this day says, 'What kind of Marshalls did you use? Did you use stacks in the studio?' No."

Adds Sammy on the topic, somewhat contradicting the above, "It was Donn Landee. The engineer was Donn Landee, who is Ted Templeman's engineer all through the... after us, after Montrose, Van Halen—it was Ted Templeman and Donn Landee. They were doing Doobie Brothers, they just did everything and anything together. But Donn really knew how to get that big heavy guitar sound that Ronnie was looking for. Ronnie came in with the Marshall stacks and everything else, and a Les Paul through the Marshall stack—what more do you need than that to be heavy in the studio? And Ted was just open-minded to layering, I think. Ted's a great producer because he allows an artist to get the best of themselves out. He doesn't come in and tell you what to do; he brings the best out of you. And to me that's a great producer. That's why he can produce Van Morrison, Doobie

Brothers, Montrose, Van Halen—who else can do something like that? Captain Beefheart. He can do them all because all he's really doing is he's in there getting the best of the artist. And I think Ronnie felt he was stifled in Edgar Winter and Van Morrison, making him play through a little amp and probably just one guitar part. This ain't your band, pal. So he's going, 'This is my band; I'm going to put on 300 guitar overdubs.' And Ted let him go, and Donn Landee just got each one of them sounding good, spreading them out. I mean there's a wall of sound, that *Montrose* album. When it kicks off with 'Rock the Nation' or 'Good Rockin' Tonight,' I think is the first song on that album, I mean that guitar, man, it just sounds like wow. It's fuzzy, clean, dirty, edgy—it's just got it all."

"Donn Landee was a super great technician," agrees Bill. "In those days, you had two guys; you had a producer and you had the technician, the guy who would turn the tape. And Landee was really good with that, plus mic placement and running the board and stuff. That's all part of the technician's duty anyway. The producer is just going to tell the technician, 'Look, I don't like the sound of this—do something,' and then the technician, in this case Donn, would move stuff around. And subsequently, Landee was on his way up too. Because Ted went on to become vice president of Warner Brothers, and Landee went on to be a producer and not a technician anymore. Which was a step up."

"I think it was a really good synergistic situation between myself and Ted," affirms Montrose. "I happened to have a really good band together and Ted was really into it. Ted and I happened to know each other from the Van Morrison project, because he had produced *Tupelo Honey* that I played on. Certainly Ted was majorly involved, plus Donn Landee I dare say, the engineer, both of them. They were going about it as a situation as producer and engineer making a great contemporary record."

As Ronnie alludes to, not only did Ted produce, but he was instrumental in Warner Bros. snatching the deal away from Epic, who, besides what Ronnie says about Jeff Beck, was Edgar Winter's label, one that was also in the process of working out solo deals for Rick Derringer and Dan Hartman.

Ted, now a Warners staffer on the behest of Lenny Waronker, had kept Ronnie in mind, furthermore liking what he had done on *Tupelo Honey* follow-up *St. Dominic's Preview*, limited to acoustic work on an 11:00 track called "Listen to the Lion." But again, interestingly, there's the presence of Jeff Beck in the story, a fiercely independent and commercially fearless axeman who loves sounds and gear and instrumental music, and also a man prone to put his singer in his place when he has to grit his teeth and work with one. In the mindsets of both Ronnie and Jeff, front men inevitably get LSD—lead singer's disease.

In any event, *Montrose* was a big first for this consortium of music tinkerers—indeed all of them—in the world of big, fat rock. And what was the end result of all this luck and yearning and seasoned talent at the ready? *Montrose* is an album, in fact, that sounds a good five years ahead of its time. Van Halen, Riot, Moxy, the Aerosmith and Ted Nugent of 1977... these are more apt comparatives than Mountain, Captain Beyond, the first couple Foghats and the Aerosmith of the dodgy 1973 debut.

"Ted was producing Little Feat, and I think he had done the first Doobie Brothers record, but nothing as heavy as this," recalls Montrose. "I do remember that when we went in to meet with Warner Bros., they were asking what our favourite record was and we were saying stuff from Led Zeppelin and Deep Purple. Their thrust was to get as big a sound as they could."

"Ted was a genius," says Bill. "He had the golden ear and he was a genius in all aspects. He is the pioneer of American heavy metal. Believe me. I mean he took Van Halen, same lineup, same American thing, same type of music... he took them in and did what he had to do. I could tell you stories that Ted told us about them, and how long it took them to do the singing and stuff (laughs). Ted Tempo-man, as I've always called him. And of course I worked with him before Montrose, because he did Van. And he also did one of my favourite bands of all time, and one of my great friends, rest in piece, Lowell George and his band Little Feat. Great band and a great production job by Ted. And he's just a genius, he has that gift of an ear, and he taught it to his engineer, Donn Landee, right? After Eddie and Ted had that big fight, Donn went on to be the producer now. And he learned all those gifts from Ted. A true genius; the most gifted producer that I've ever worked with. And that is why Ted is part of the band. Because the sound of that album is still unmatched in heavy metal. You can put it up—as long as you do it on vinyl, because they've remastered everything—but if you take the original vinyl, and you put on the first Led Zeppelin album, the Montrose just blows them away. They, of course, have separation in their instruments, but they're heavy and loud—ours was saturation and loud."

Adds Sammy, "Well *Montrose*, first of all, it was the first time I was ever in a recording studio and I'm in there with Ted Templeman, first class Grammy award-winning producer at the time, probably, and Ronnie had done it with Boz Scaggs and he had played with Edgar Winter Group; he had just come out of that. So he was kind of a veteran. Bill Church, same thing, played with all the same people. And so I was like really the new guy on the block and just in awe of the whole thing. So for me, it was really like I didn't even know what we were doing. I was just giving it my heart and soul. I'd written these songs, and Ronnie was playing in a very heavy metal style. I didn't come from a heavy metal background at that stage. I was a blues/R&B guy. I was singing Otis Redding, Wilson Pickett and Tower of Power in a cover band. The best rock we'd do would be like the Stones or The Who, and the Stones were a blues band, too, you know? So I kind of came from that."

"And I started singing against the way Ronnie was playing guitar—I think that's what created the Montrose sound. I had this bluesy voice and was using all blues chops and playing blues riffs, writing songs like 'Make It Last' and 'Rock Candy' and those kind of songs. Those are blues riffs, you know. And Ronnie didn't come from the blues. He came from almost more country, and then he just wanted to play really loud through a Marshall. Denny Carmassi the drummer, he had a heavy foot, he was a John Bonham freak. None of the rest of us were really into Led Zeppelin that much. I dug them but I wasn't a Led Zeppelin freak at that time. So I think what made Montrose unique was it was heavy, and with Ted Templeman's sound, he made us a metal band. Ronnie had 11 guitar overdubs on 'Rock the Nation' for God's sake, and it sounds like just one. So as I say, a wall of sound and there was a unique chemistry between the four of us that kind of made that sound."

And to be sure, Ronnie's guitar tone is white hot and electric, but Sammy is roaring to be heard, to be noticed as the rock god he will fight and scrape to become. The rest of the band, its bruising rhythm section, Bill and Denny, they're as live and boomy as the band's sparring stars. Says Ronnie, "We went in beforehand and rehearsed the material, and the one thing that sticks out in my mind is that the record was completely 100% analog tape because there wasn't such thing as digital tape. Small console, small room... I've always been a sort of a tech head, so I was always accompanying Donn Landee as he was crawling around in the live echo chamber throwing packing blankets around to get the right amount of dampening for the reverberation. That was literally what you had to do in those days. It was a physical hands-on thing. Ted and Donn's view of me by the way was that I was always on the other side of the console leaning over with my head as if it were one of the knobs on the meters—always involved."

"It wasn't a question of working together," explains Montrose, with respect to his procedures with Hagar. "The material was written and it was still a situation at that point where we weren't cutting live vocals. We were cutting live rhythm tracks, and then we overdubbed the vocals and solos, because we were a trio obviously. We overdubbed guitar solos, any other extra little add-ons and Sam's voice. Sam was there for the recording, but literally, we would finish up the track, and I think we finished all of the tracks and then Sam came in and finished his vocals and we added the backgrounds as needed."

Into the steaming guts of the record, nothing satisfies like the opening chords to track one, side one, "Rock the Nation." What ensues is a hot clockin' anthem, buttressed with a bit of boogie, a great bass line from

Church, and a novel architecture that surges onward and upward in heady heavy metal dementia. Amusingly, one gets the drift Sam alludes to about the simplicity of lyrics back in the early '70s—indeed Zeppelin should take more stick for this than they're known to get.

As Ronnie remarked in the liner notes we did together for *The Very Best of Montrose*, "I actually started writing this one when I was still in the Edgar Winter Group and was planning to submit it for the group's then-upcoming album. As it turned out, we parted ways before that time, and I ended up recording it for the first Montrose album. I was unsure about the lyrical content, thinking it might be a little too Broadway musical (as in, 'Shake my hips, throw my head back and shout!'), but it has stood the test of time."

Instantly, with "Rock the Nation," one is struck by how "electric" the record sounds. And "heavy metal." "The music itself just sort of happened, you know?" shrugs Bill. "If you listen to the stuff that we had all done before that, not really a lot of connection. So it just sort of happened. And I think that Sammy was lucky, because he was getting his first taste of doing anything original. And Denny came from a different type of bag. He'd been in blues bands and stuff, and he was trying to be more like a Ginger Baker-type guy; he wanted to pound pretty heavy, you know? And all I did was just write bass lines that went along with what Sammy and Ronnie were throwing at us."

"I will say one thing that helped spur it," continues Bill, shifting to the audio side of the equation. "And this can be proven to this day. One of the things that spurred it is that both Ronnie and I were audiophiles, and we were using state of the edge amplification and speakers that would later on influence big companies—literally. This is the truth. The stuff that I was doing and experimenting with later went on to be the whole line of Randall. And Ronnie was using Macs and things because there was a limit to the availability of high-powered amps made specifically for guitar. Fender in those days were incredibly underpowered, still are today. But we had some amps, and we went and played at the Fillmore West, the one on Market Street, and blew the back walls off with it. It amazed even us, but we knew we were on the cutting edge of things. So that helped get the sound happening."

"And I'll tell you what else that most people don't know about the *Montrose* album. You know what kind of speakers Ronnie used for the guitar? He's using what's called an Altec Lansing Capistrano, which is a low-boy piece of furniture made by James B. Lansing that is a living room stereo speaker that came out of Ted Templeman's living room. He hauled it out, down to

Amigo Studios, put it out in the middle of the room and powered it, not with a stereo that would normally power it at home, but he powered it with McIntoshes, and a Mac preamp, and that's how that sound is on there. And as you know, to this day, a lot of guitar players consider that one of the exemplary heavy metal sounds."

Describing the Capistrano further, Church says it's "large, about eight-foot long, and oiled teak. I mean, these were expensive cabinetry. It was made like a piece of furniture to go into a rich man's home. And it's powered by... back in those days, you had separate components and a whole separate cabinet. And it has a curved, concave teak front that the sound actually bounces off of. And inside of it is the famous JBL 8SR system. Which is real famous; many recording studios in our day used the 8SRs in their control rooms for studio monitors. But this is built into this little box. This thing was three-way. And of course, in those days, James B. Lansing was like the Rolls-Royce of speakers."

Stressing the difference between industrial and home use, Church adds that, "We're talking about commercial JBL. Because this Capistrano of Ted Templeman's, that did not come out of JBL's musical catalogue. But all the speakers that I used in all my cabinets, I only used JBL speakers that came out of their musical factory—two different things all together. And I used what were called C5 folded horn cabinets with 15 inch JBLs. Because nothing made in those years had the power. The biggest thing you could get was Fenders, which had been around forever. But Fenders always were designed for country players (laughs)."

As if manna from heavy metal heaven, Montrose follow up "Rock the Nation" with "Bad Motor Scooter," again, a new modern metal offering a deft link to the past with a touch of boogie. Central though is Ronnie's slide guitar-sourced motorcycle revving, the perfect foil to Sam's vocal and lyric, which both establish Hagar's character right then and there as rock 'n' roll's fun guy. For slide work, Ronnie preferred a 2" glass slide that was fitted to his ring finger to allow for chord work, along necks that were uncommonly wide to allow him "lots of room to operate."

Recalls Hagar, "The one memory I have is that I had a rear molar that was just all swollen up, you know, coming in. What are those, I guess it's a molar, right? Wisdom tooth, right, there you go! And boy, was I getting wisdom. But it was growing in and it wouldn't break through the gum so the gum was all swollen up on top of the tooth and I couldn't close my mouth, and I was doing vocals. So Ted Templeman, the producer, gets the dentist appointment. I go in and the guy puts me out, asleep, under anaesthetic; I was dead, goodnight, asleep. Pulled both my wisdom teeth out, both sides, so that I wouldn't have to come back, and stitched them up, and when I woke up I was so grogged-out, I didn't even know who I was, where I was. Send me back to the studio, and did the vocal on the original 'Bad Motor Scooter' with a chunk of cotton with blood in it, in the back of my mouth. But in those days, I would rather have sang and been in that studio making that record more than anything. You couldn't keep me out of the studio because it was my first record and I was so excited. And you know, nowadays, I'd take two weeks off (laughs). Straight up with you—I ain't going to lie to you."

"'Bad Motor Scooter' and 'Make It Last' were the first two songs I ever wrote in my life," continues Sam. "I had written those songs—'One Thing on My Mind,' 'Make It Last,' 'Bad Motor Scooter' and 'I Don't Want It'—I wrote those songs before I was in Montrose. And when Ronnie auditioned me. I went to knock on his door, actually and said, 'I heard you're looking for a singer' and he said 'Yeah, you got any songs?' I said yeah. I came in with my guitar in my hand and I played him four songs, those four songs. And he went, 'Wow, you've got songs! You write lyrics too?' And I said yeah, and I had a notebook right in my guitar case and I took it out and he saw the 'Space Station #5' lyrics and he said, 'Do you have any music for this?' And I said, 'No, I've just been writing that lyric.' And he picked up the guitar and started going (sings the riff) and that's the kind of energy we had on the first record. He played me 'Rock the Nation.' We shook hands, I said I know a drummer, Denny Carmassi and he said I know a bass player. Within a month we were in the studio recording the first album, and within a couple months after that we were on the road for three years. So everything happened so fast that we didn't even know what we were doing. I mean, we wrote that first record and recorded it in like two weeks or something like that; it was crazy."

Says Ronnie, "This little ditty was penned by Sam. We recorded it, but it never really jumped out until one day in the studio when I was messing around with an open-D tuning with fuzz box and slide. I started to play what became the ever-popular signature motorcycle-rev-up intro, and I vividly remember Ted Templeman and Donn Landee running for the reel of tape that had this song on it. They were throwing up their arms and yelling into the talk-back system, saying, 'Hold it right there! That's the song intro!' They were right."

Affirms Church, "Sammy to this day uses that in his set, right? The start is ingenious, because Ronnie, being adept at playing slide guitar, said, 'Let's do an open tuning on my guitar, and I'll start it like a friggin' motorcycle.' And Sammy, to this day, takes a lap steel and starts the song with that effect—to this day."

As alluded to, the *Montrose* album was recorded in LA, at Warner Bros. Studios as well as Sunset Sound. But as the credits attest, additional guitars were added on "Make It Last," "I Don't Want It," "Bad Motor Scooter" and "Space Station #5" on home turf at Wally Heider in San Francisco, engineered by Steve Jarvis. The overall production credit in fact goes to "Montrose & Ted Templeman" with Donn Landee credited as engineer.

Moving forward, "Space Station #5" is the first album's epic, blessed with a vicious delicious riff, a nice fantasy lyric and a proggy psychedelic stoner rock break before the band crashes back in, grooving impossibly, even more so when one notices how truly heavy metal the song is. The eerie intro to the track is in fact four voices put through a synthesizer, accompanied by acoustic guitar. Or, as Ronnie explained in more detail in our compilation liner notes, "I think I've received more inquiries about this song than any other—not for structure, tone or the standard stuff, but, 'What the hell is that on the intro?' What it was, was this: after recording a backing acoustic guitar track, I put a microphone into my Big Muff distortion box, which went through a Leslie speaker cabinet, and then through tape delay in the control room. All sounds other than the acoustic guitar were my voice tracks processed through that set-up, including the 'synthesizer' sounds. This was one of the most enjoyable songs I co-wrote with Sam. He had a book of many different lyrics, and I was able to mix and match verses, choruses, bridges, etc., with him to put this one together."

Bill remembers it differently, but then concedes that he might not have seen the entire process. "I think Ted came up with the idea to start 'Space Station.' Ronnie is in the control room, and he's using a bag. You ever heard of a bag? Peter Frampton, his biggest hit record is that thing, he puts it in his mouth and blows." Talkbox? "I guess, but bag is its real name. Anyway, Ronnie has that, not attached to a guitar, but just going straight to the board from his mouth, right? And he starts making the noises, and Ted is turning the joystick on the console in 360° circles, all around (makes a yipping sound)."

Told about Ronnie's description of the process, Bill says, "Nah, I don't remember that, because I wasn't in the control room. It was too small for all of us to be in there. Ted, Donn and Ronnie... at Amigo, there's a control room, there's a small studio that faces part of it and it faces the big studio this way. And then you walk across the small studio and then there's another room with soundproof doors and that has TVs, and it's like a kickback room. So Ronnie would be in there trying to do that over and over again, and none of us want to sit there and listen to that crap for three hours straight. So I didn't really bother. I just knew what they were doing and he's taking the bag and I watched him for a few minutes until I got bored."

Once again, breaks, shifts, segues... they are all placed perfectly, and in service of the happy, accessible, crushingly heavy riff. Approach the demise of the track, and the band gradually speeds up while Ronnie solos exotically, a final screech of effects lifting this classic to the ether.

Sammy's vocal is downright heroic on this classic, a kerranging construct that, again, one could call America's first heavy metal song. "There were two things vocally that made my voice the way it was," reflects Hagar. "Number one, I was just a young kid and I had a high screechy voice.

Because I came from a club situation where we didn't even have monitors. I was always pushing really hard because I couldn't hear myself. So I would sing at a high register at least so I could get overtop of the instruments, and I came from that school. And then trying to sing like an 80-year-old black guy, trying to sound like I was Howlin' Wolf or somebody... I was this 20-year-old kid. I pushed my voice to get it to be raspy, because I didn't want to use a fake voice. A lot of guys would just use a fake voice. They'd go falsetto, you know, but I wanted to be a good singer so I pushed myself really hard."

"We were so loud, the first thing Ted Templeman said is, 'Oh great, you've got a voice that can cut through all that volume.' Because I was singing in that high register. So everyone pushed me into that high register and that's why I sing the way I sing today. I used to always play guitar and sing, and then I joined Montrose and I was just a singer, so I didn't even know what key songs were in. I would have written a song, Ronnie would work it up, and then I don't know what key he was doing it in, and then I would just sing whatever I felt in my heart, and 90% of the time it was at the peak of my range. I used to get on tour and after about 100 shows in a year, I'm going why in the hell am I singing in this register? It really is hard. It's hard on your stomach, your back, your neck, your balls. But I just was always in that supersonic range and everyone liked it so I just kept doing it."

Notes Church, "I like 'Space Station #5' because the album got done, and we all went down together to see the premiere of *2001: A Space Odyssey*. And when the Space Station #5 floats by, you would think that didn't blow our minds?! Yeah, there you go. No, so 'Space Station #5' was just, we needed a number for it, and so we tried out the numbers, which one works best when we were vocalizing it. So, okay, 'Space Station #5.' And the album comes out, and out comes *2001*, the movie, and we all pile down together to see it on the debut. I think we were in New York; I can't remember that far back. But anyway, we all went down there, and boom, and here comes that thing, and right across the side of it... yeah, that was mind-blowing."

"I Don't Want It" closes side two of the original vinyl, and again the band is moving hard rock boulders, even if the riff's a bit funkier than what came before. Highlight of this one is Hagar's wisecracking lyric, as well as Bill Church's weaving and bobbing bass line. There's also a nice modulation of the chorus, before the band settle back into a groove o'er which Ronnie turns in an April Wine-like harmony solo.

Side two opens with a fat, hard, southern rock-ish version of old rock 'n' roll chestnut "Good Rockin' Tonight." Why a cover? If Sammy's comments are any indication, speed was of the essence. "Well, the thing is, we got a record deal in like two weeks. After I met Ronnie, he says, 'We've got a band but we need a drummer; I've got a bass player.' He had Bill Church and I had Denny Carmassi. His band had actually asked me to join their band, and I said, 'Go check this drummer out.' So he checked the drummer out that night, and we got together and within two weeks we had a record deal. So we really didn't have time to write any songs. I had most of those songs. Ronnie had 'Good Rockin' Tonight,' the guitar riff, and he said that's the way he heard it—'Good Rockin' Tonight.' And I just sang it. So that kind of became our version of that song, which is an old song."

Discrepancy on how Denny got corralled into the band aside, Bill notes that, "We wanted to do a white American rock 'n' roll idol remake. And so we had two songs. We had, of course, Bobby Brown's 'Good Rockin' Tonight,' but it wasn't his version, not the black version. Of course, we based ours upon Elvis', right? And then we had 'Twenty Flight Rock,' Eddie Cochran. And I think we laid both of them down, although one made it, and the other, they went back and redid that one again for *Warner Bros. Presents*. But other than maybe doing 'Twenty Flight Rock,' those were our first eight tunes. We didn't have any other tunes."

Metallica's Kirk Hammett, Bay Area neighbour and lifelong Montrose fan, offers an interesting perspective on this first of many covers Montrose would cook up for consumption. "I've got to tell you, man, that *Montrose* album was a huge, huge influence on me. I know Sammy pretty well. I never got to meet Ronnie, but I know a lot about Ronnie. And even to this day I'm still figuring out how to play stuff off that *Montrose* album. Which is unusual, because it's not difficult; those songs were not difficult to play. But I found that there are all these subtle nuances that Ronnie used to do, and playing those songs, I'm just figuring them out now."

"Like the intro to 'Good Rockin' Tonight.' I always thought that was two guitar players or an overdub, but no. Ronnie Montrose played that on one guitar. He played both part simultaneously. And he uses his thumb. It's a really difficult thing to play, if you're just not used to playing that kind of chord grip. And when I figured that out, I couldn't believe it. I was like, that's how he does it. And then that January we played a show here and Sammy came to it, and I pulled him over and said, 'Sammy, I know you're probably sick of me always talking about that first Montrose album.' Because I played almost every song on that album with him live, you know, whether it was down in Cabo or in the Bay Area or whatever, over the course of years. And I said, 'Hey, is this how Ronnie played "Good Rockin' Tonight?"' And I played it the way he did it, and he says,

'Yeah, that's exactly how he did it.' And he said, 'Wow, you figured that out. I haven't seen anyone play it that way since I played it with Ronnie back in the '70s.' And I said, 'Yeah, you know, it was kind of a fluke.' I was watching Montrose at Winterland on YouTube one night, and they started playing 'Good Rockin' Tonight' and I saw how Ronnie played that. And I saw the grip he used. Because it's more of a grip than a chord positioning or anything else. But, you know, having said that, Ronnie Montrose, his guitar sound, the whole Gibson Les Paul through Marshall amps, for me it was the American version of the British sound."

"You know, when I think about that Montrose album," continues Hammett, "I have to say I can't really think of another album like that. When did that come out, '73? That takes it. That really takes it. The only other thing I can think of that is on the par with that in terms of heaviness and energy and progression are the Rush albums. But they're Canadian, so... but I see your point. No, you're right. I mean, it's hard to think of something else that was as heavy as that at the time. The only other thing I can think of along those lines is ZZ Top. But ZZ Top doesn't really qualify because it's not hard like that *Montrose* album. I would put that band Dust in there; remember Dust? And Pentagram. Those are two of those early bands, but they're more along the lines of that Sabbath direction, as is the first Judas Priest. So you know, you're right. I'm just thinking, God, there was nothing that was really heavy coming out. James Gang, Amboy Dukes, Grand Funk, Johnny Winter... I'm trying to think of the more obscure American bands like maybe Yesterday and Today, but even they came out in '76, right? So you really have a point there. That *Montrose* album is much more of a pioneering album than I realized. Absolutely, you have a valid point there."

And so whether it's chemistry or "lightning in a bottle" or what, the pieces really did come together to make something ground-breaking. To reiterate, even if there was already an impressive pile of heavy metal over in the UK, *Montrose* is ground zero in America, qualifier being that we might class as variously too wobbly or stodgy or amateurish, the likes of Blue Cheer, The Stooges, MC5, Cactus, Mountain, Bang and Sir Lord Baltimore.

Further on the explosive makeup of this hot new band and how this could happen, Sammy says, of Bill and Denny, that "they're great players, but they come from such a different place. Denny is still a dear friend of mine. I just talked to him yesterday. I speak to Denny four days a week, and we get together quite often, just go out and talk. Just good friends. Denny came from an R&B background, more like a John Bonham. He's naturally a kind of John Bonham-type player, heavy foot and a real laid-back snare. But he hit hard like a motherfucker (laughs). Denny, we would get pissed-off at him, because we had no money, and every gig he would be breaking drum heads and bust cymbals quite often. He would break the damn cymbal stand right in half. I mean, he smacked them so hard. And we would say, 'Hey man, we can't fucking afford that shit, dude. Lighten up!' (laughs)."

Notes Foghat drummer Roger Earl on Denny, "We became good friends. We did a number of dates and shows with them, with the original band. Denny Carmassi, what a fantastic drummer. I remember I gave him one of my bell cymbals at the time, because he remarked on how cool it sounded, and I had two so I gave him one. Great hands, great feet, again, a great guy and fantastic drummer. But the way he played, he attacked his drums. He approached it the same way John Bonham did, with 24, 26-inch bass drum, no padding in there. You heard the drum—it was just boom, ka-boom. Great style and great attack."

"And Bill Church, a whole different kind of thing," continues Sammy. "He came from a Buddy Holly-type thing, and he played a kind of early American rock style. He wasn't a metal guy at all, but had more… in mentally, in life, he was more like a rock/metal star. He would go out and turn tables over in restaurants and get in people's faces and get drunk and unruly and tear his hotel up. So he was more the metal guy, but he came from a whole different background (laughs). I mean, that's why Ronnie kicked him out of the band after the first album and tour, because he was just kind of unruly. He's a wild man. We called him The Electric Church. I loved him. So, when I left Montrose I got Bill in my band immediately, because I liked his fire and I like his playing."

Next in line is the record's monolithic sledge of a riff rocker "Rock Candy." This one's opened by a Bonham-esque beat courtesy of Carmassi, like Hagar, another of the greenhorns in Montrose. As alluded to, Carmassi was destined for this role—his dad was a drummer, his uncle was a drummer and his brother was a drummer. Denny's main guiding light was the legendary Tony Williams, but given his dad's tutelage, he had heard everybody of note and absorbing what he could.

Quips Hagar on "Rock Candy," "That's such a great line. I mean, 'hard, sweet and sticky'… I don't know how better you can get as far as a rock 'n' roll lyric goes. But yeah, Denny came up with that drumbeat for 'Rock Candy' and Ronnie started playing that riff and I just started singing those lyrics. That's why that song was written by the whole band. That was a jam, at rehearsal. You know, the only song that Ronnie had written was 'Rock the Nation'—the rest we just threw together. At rehearsal for the album, we were practicing all the songs that we had, those six or seven songs."

Says Ronnie, "When the band first met with Ted, he asked what music we liked. We unanimously exclaimed, 'Led Zeppelin! Deep Purple!' Hearing that, Ted insisted that, for a song as heavy as this, we record at Sunset Sound in LA, where Zeppelin had also worked. It had formally been some sort of meat locker or refrigerated storage and still had the recognizable freezer handles on the doors to the rooms. We cut the basic track live, and I overdubbed the solo at another studio."

"With Denny, we went on location several times," adds Bill. "And it was the choice of where we went that made the sound, and that was probably Ted's doing. For example, the drums for 'Rock Candy'—which is probably the best drum sound on the album, right?—those drums were done in the vault at the Sound Factory. It used to be a giant butcher, butchery. And they had these meat vaults, and when they changed it to a studio, it turned out that when you locked drums or anything inside those vaults, man, you got some sound. And that's where Denny did 'Rock Candy.' And he did a couple of drums elsewhere as well."

"Rock Candy" represents Bill's only song credit on the album. "That was the one that I did help write, 'Rock Candy.' They were all put together pretty much the same way. Sammy and Ronnie would work up the lyric and the basic guitar, the rhythm guitar track, and then we would all get together and write parts. So the writing royalties always go to the guy who writes the lyric and the guy who invents the basic three chord pattern. I would like to say, give me writer's credit because I wrote the bass lines, but that's not the way reality is. But all the bass lines on there, I wrote. I mean, they're my lines. The only modifications I made were to add some simple things at Ted Templeman's suggestion, some technical things."

"But we were pretty tight," continues Bill. "It just went along real well. It didn't take that long to do the album. Three weeks, something like that. We went in with dummy vocals, laid down the bass and drums as solid as could be in about a week. And then Ronnie and Sammy piecemealed the rest together, as it were. The rhythm guitar went on the same time as the bass and drums, but everything else went on later. And when I say, everything, there's not a whole lot more than a lead guitar and the voice, right? But still quite the contrary to the Van Morrison band, where we got about three takes. And one of those three takes, that's the song. Consequently, myself, there's one song I actually make a mistake on; it's in the song. When I asked Van to edit it out, he refused and said, 'I want it to be like the band plays live.' He said, 'Did you ever play a gig 100% perfect?' And I go, 'I don't think I've ever played a gig 50% perfect' (laughs)."

"One Thing on My Mind" brings back the funk 'n' blues, but again, cloaked in heavy metal bravado, just the way Zeppelin did it. Ronnie loves the way Zeppelin could mix it up. "Yes, there's only one: Led Zeppelin. In my book, Jimmy Page is, was, and will always be the most prolific rock riff writer on the planet Earth. Prodigious output! Of rock riffs, acoustic, electric, recognizable rock riffs. Nobody has ever done that since. If there was anybody I looked up to, I didn't consider them brothers, I idolized them and considered them icons. I always considered myself at best a second generation guitarist to the big boys, people like Jimmy Page, Ritchie Blackmore, Pete Townsend, Jeff Beck, I mean, that school, that one little wave before I started. And in America, Billy Gibbons from ZZ Top."

When asked about guitar favourites from the next generation, Montrose told me, "To be honest with you, I don't listen to a lot. I guess that's one of the reasons I don't want to describe myself. My tastes are eclectic. I never put on those rock records at home. I love playing it and getting out and playing it live, but at home I would listen to John Abercrombie, Bill Connors, jazz players. I will always put on a Free record, but once again, that's first generation, Paul Kossoff. But I also like classical, world music, and not a lot of second generation heavy stuff. I do respect Joe Perry; he's a great player and he's also a great live take player. I respect Ted Nugent's playing simply because he has an indefatigable attitude on the instrument, and he'll tell you all about himself any time you ask (laughs)."

On his soling style, Montrose ventures, "I had a guitarist once point out to me… because I've never really been interested in fancy techniques. Once in a while I'll do hammer-ons. He made this point, saying, 'You know, you're right. You don't play hammer-ons and all these note flurries. You play one note at a time melodies like you're singing.' And I realized he was correct. I may not be singing great all the time, but I've always concentrated on the melody solos and phrasing as opposed to riff solos and phrasing. That's one of the reasons I haven't been written up in a lot of guitar magazines. It's because I don't believe I have a style. My style is more of a blues rock style. My style is not a style that young tech kids want to pick up."

Notes Bill, on "One Thing on My Mind," credited to Ronnie, Sammy and a J. Sanchez, "'One Thing on My Mind,' the obscure one, was actually written by John Sanchez, my old guitar player from my band, Wheat Straw Blew Grass, from 1968. He actually wrote that and he traded the song to Ronnie for a pair of snakeskin boots. Gave the song, lock, stock and barrel. We were a trio, John Sanchez and me, with Edgar Winter and Sammy Hagar drummer, Chuck Ruff. And we had a single which you can YouTube or whatever; you'll crack up."

The band, previously called Local 205 and then Inspector Vice, had brought Ruff on in 1967 (Ruff has since passed on, in 2011). The guys got to record one single, called "World That's Tight"/"Verily Verily" (misprinted as "The World is Tight"), which is pretty accomplished and complicated proto-hard rock for the day, anything but bluegrass, all the more impressive because the guys recorded it high on PCP. The deal to do the single came about due to the band winning "The second annual 5 state (California, Idaho, Nevada, Oregon and Utah) Battle of the Bands." Adding to the intrigue, "World That's Tight" also showed up on the posthumously released 1971 full-length album by John Sanchez's band Groundshaker, which also included in its ranks Skip Gillette, who would be the drummer on Ronnie's first Gamma album, Gamma 1.

"The album that you hear, the music, that's not really what it was," qualifies Skip. "That was a sleazeball fucking attempt of somebody who got a hold of the half-ass demos that we were doing. It's not a real record. So that shit's not what the real Groundshaker sounded like. The album never came out at the time. It came out 40 years later. A guy got a hold of the partial demos. All the tracks aren't even on those things. It was a really popular band, and everybody wanted it. A lot of big managers, including Bruce Garfield, wanted us. He ended up being the president of Capitol Records. And it was just one of those bands that was really hot. I've been in a lot of bands like that in LA that didn't get signed that were really good."

Montrose closes out with another bombastic slow track, "Make It Last" cutting through simply but effectively. Justly, given Sammy's tale of coming to the new band with songs, Hagar gets sole credit for the track. Still, the fact that he gets sole credit... that wouldn't have happened in most cases like this, namely young kid joins up with established guitarist whose last name gives the band its name. Hagar also gets sole credit for "Bad Motor Scooter" as well as co-credit with Ronnie on "Space Station #5," "Rock Candy," "I Don't Want It" and "One Thing on My Mind."

And let's not forget that Hagar was a guitarist, so yes, quite self-sufficient, proving as much as a solo artist with 20-odd albums to his name, on which he is seen nearly as much as a guitarist as he is front man. This would be a problem, given a leader who wants to be the only guitarist. But in the beginning, Ronnie was all about the team, telling Circus' William Pratt, "What makes this band special is that it's a band, a unit. It's not me, the star, being backed up by them, the band. We work together as one. There is no doubt in my mind that we're going to be the number one band in America some day. We're that tight. Montrose is going to make it because we're one of the only healthy bands around. No drugs, no overdone glitter. Just hard and healthy rock." Also somewhat prophetic and fateful, Ronnie, let on, "I had been going around for five years thinking, 'Boy, am I a terrible songwriter! I just can't write songs.' Then I met this guy, and pow!"

Wrote Rolling Stone's Gordon Fletcher at the time, in a classic example of having nothing valid to compare a record with but having to try anyway, "Ex-Edgar Winter guitarist, Ronnie Montrose's new power trio (plus singer) is a potentially scorching outfit. Montrose is the star and plays Jeff Beck-oriented music, with nods to other great leads. His performances have not yet reached the height of his sources, but he uses his talent to the best possible advantage throughout. For all its derivativeness, the band wraps the music up in a convincingly entertaining package. With Stray Dog and the fiery new Kiss, they prove there's no lack of rookie talent in this year's heavy-metal sweepstakes."

More so getting the point is Circus' Ed Naha, who writes, "Yipeeee! Crotch rock's back. Yup, that super-heavy, ear-splitting, distorted, wunnerful stuff that makes you double over in sheer rock 'n' roll ecstasy when you hear it. Ex-Edgar Winter guitarist Ronnie Montrose has assembled a band that sounds like Mount Vesuvius at a New Year's party… pretty explosive. The drums quake like thunder, the guitar like a jet plane, the bass cuts the air like a dull butter knife and the vocals are raw as hell. The whole thing is a metallic exercise in plodding, avalanche rock and proves to be quite a head-throbbing treat."

"Montrose is loud, boy is dey loud!" chimes in John Tivens from adjunct mag Circus Raves. "I remember when Ronnie M. was in the Edgar Winter Group playing guitar, and he used to open his mouth so wide when he bent notes that you could put your fist right inside. Well, Ronnie Montrose has picked just the right bands to follow in the footsteps of (MC5, The Who, et al), and the drummer's a basher, the singer's a screamer, and they're almost as loud as Ronnie Montrose himself."

And then finally Gordon Fletcher, pulling double duty with Circus Raves himself, gets it much more accurately this time—and one wonders if he's adjusted his writing for a readership who gets hard rock more than that of

Rolling Stone—calling Montrose "a product that brings to mind thoughts of other heavy-metal monsters, though never in a way that denies Montrose their overwhelmingly individuality. This album could give the heavy-metal field a real shot in the arm. Montrose has gotten off to an incredibly impressive heavy-metal start on record; now if they can get out and do their thunder thing onstage there's no reason why they won't succeed."

One can't help but notice the references to "heavy-metal," really flying in the face of the idea that it wasn't until 1975 that writers (and presumably fans) had truly cottoned onto the idea, not to mention the term, for which we can pretty much credit "Metal" Mike Saunders.

Recalls tour insider Ron Eckerman, known for his road work with Fleetwood Mac and Lynyrd Skynyrd, on the impression the *Montrose* album made, "That first Montrose album was incredible, definitely. I'm a very amateur guitarist, but then I was on the songs immediately, trying to learn those licks and everything (laughs). Ronnie impressed me. My friend Mick Brigden was doing their tour management and that's kind of how I got involved with them. Mick was also the manager for Humble Pie."

"I worked with Montrose quite a bit, when Sammy Hagar was with them," continues Eckerman. "That was about '73', '74. I really loved them; they were good. Man, they were so hot. And Sammy was so outstanding. Ronnie was a pretty good friend of mine. I knew him pretty good back in the Edgar Winter days, and when he played with Van Morrison. So I knew him from those two groups, and kind of had a relationship with Ronnie, and he asked me to come help him out. Back then, I had a production company, so I helped a lot of artists out. I drove Peter Frampton around. I lived in a car, station wagon for a year, before he broke, and really didn't get paid for it, you know, just helping him. And then I was with Fleetwood Mac for a while when they were struggling, and they were driving around in a station wagon, right before Lindsay and Stevie joined them. Bob Welch was singing, and the funny thing about that was, we went out to look at the studio, to record the next album, so Bob and I were both kinda burned-out on the whole trip. We walked out to the car and burned one (laughs), and sort of decided that we were gonna quit the band right there. And inside the studio, Mick Fleetwood and Christine were listening to Stevie Nicks and Lindsay, and Stevie and Lindsay were in there putting down some tracks their project. And that was the night Bob Welch and I quit and Stevie and Lindsay joined. So indirectly I had a lot to do with them joining Fleetwood Mac (laughs)."

Asked if he had seen any growing friction between Ronnie and Sammy, Eckerman says, "Not really. They were all getting along fairly well. Ronnie would get kinda down at times, for sure. And I didn't know what it was all about. I was friends with him but I wasn't touring with them. I just promoted a lot of shows for them, and did a lot of lighting through my company Clearlight. But Sammy was great, always up, energetic—man, I love Sammy. And then I watched him when he was doing the Red Rocker thing; we were good friends back then."

But there was definitely friction afoot, says Bill. "Why do you think Sammy never played guitar Montrose? He just flat wasn't allowed to. Ronnie wouldn't allow it, period. You've got the songs that are on the album, and there are obviously two guitars playing on the album, right? You would think sometimes live, maybe the other guitar would happen. And anybody will tell you that has ever seen the original Montrose live, the other thing Sammy was not allowed to do was talk to the audience between songs. Can you imagine him, the way he is? The way his shows are, they're almost all talking, right? He was not allowed to talk in-between the songs like most people do. 'Thank you very much.' No—dead silence. So it was the same thing that Jeff Beck did to Rod Stewart. Jeff Beck made Rod Stewart stand way off to the left, clear to the left side of the stage, and he was not allowed to talk between songs (laughs). And now Rod is a Sir, which I can't believe, and I hate. I can't believe he's a Sir."

Indeed, on the band's session while in the UK to record two songs for *The Old Grey Whistle Test*, even there, Sammy is far stage left, and Ronnie is near stage right, verging on centre stage, while Bill is centre stage left, but back toward Denny's drums. Sammy also recalls how just before one of the UK gigs, supporting Status Quo at Wembley, Ronnie told him not to venture to the right beyond where his mic stand was set up.

Also stoking the flames, says Bill, "Dee Anthony was our manager, and he was screwing us, okay? So we go into his office, on Park Avenue, New York, right? And we're sitting there and here comes Uncle Dee. We called him Uncle Dee, right? And we complained, well, Ronnie was leader, so he talked. Our complaint was that he was supposed to take 20% and he had been taking 50%. And he just turned around and said, 'Well, I always contract at 20% with everybody, but I take 50%. Because, if they don't let me have the 50%, Frank and I, would make sure you guys, nobody would work.' Frank Barsalona, of course, was the only guy who promoted big shows back then. And then he turned to Sammy, right in front of Ronnie—and this is where the split began—he turned to Sammy, and he said, 'Young man, you're gonna be a star.' And of course, Sammy's ego ballooned, and

Ronnie is pissed! And so that was the rift right there. And the band wasn't even together a year at that point. And, well, of course, Sammy got what he wanted, and was in control of everything, and Ronnie controlled everything until the end, although he was kind of an obstructionist in his case. Because nothing ever quite fit after that. They kept changing all the time, you know what I mean?"

Other than this memorable visit to New York, Church says the band didn't have much interaction with Dee, who got to see old age, dying at 83 in 2009. "We didn't hang. They had their own little world. We hardly ever went there. Anyway, I myself, personally, was done with Dee Anthony. Because as I say, he was screwing us moneywise. That was the reason for that visit, quite frankly, that one visit there. He never came to our gigs. He wasn't like a normal manager. The reason for that is because his Mafia partner, Frank Barsalona, is always there, because he's the promoter of every gig east of the Mississippi. But as I say, if you wanted to play, you had to be on his good side."

Incredibly, Montrose's debut record never even made the Billboard Top 100, even if it eventually went on to platinum sales, receiving certification on October 13, 1986, aided of course, by Hagar's long solo career and his recent career apex arrival to the ranks of Van Halen. For the record, the album rose to #133 on Billboard, doing a little better in the UK, hitting #43. As well, the continued hammering at the door by Ronnie through three additional records would send the first album gold, with that level of certification declared on April 13, 1977, just as Ronnie was sinking the ship.

Still, explains Montrose, the band had made a dent in America's hard rock consciousness. "You have to understand, I mean I had just come out of Edgar Winter's Group and *They Only Come Out at Night* had gone platinum and I felt so fortunate to be playing that I couldn't believe I was being paid to play. I was like 26 years old then and that was a big thrill for me. And Ted walks in and goes, 'Do you know that this record is selling five hundred, a thousand copies a day in some places?' We weren't taken very seriously around the Warner Bros. tent at that time because they weren't really convinced that our brand of music was going to give anything back. But we would be in some town touring and I would go into the convenience store and I would be walking in and hear guys at the other side of the counter going, 'Holy shit man, we're going to see Montrose tonight' and I thought, well, I guess they're talking about me. Still, it took about ten years to go platinum. It sold slowly and it continues to sell to this day. Not a pleasant one of those things where it was like boom—smash success. A lot of fans took us seriously but the record company really didn't."

And no question, that lineup had chemistry. Speaking with me in 2009, Ronnie expressed agreement. "Yes, you are right—the same age, the same life experience, the same enthusiasm. I totally understand. And also, if you're talking about the first Montrose album, the four of us there... as I said before, one of the interesting comments about that record was made to me by my friend and old band mate in Gamma, Mitchell Froom, who now produces quite a few very successful artists. I know I told you this, but it's important. He says to me, 'Ronnie, the reason I think that record did great was that it was four young guys who were new at it.' And it wasn't a question of how technically good you were, because I was really just playing a basic rudimentary style, guitar riffs and lead solos etc. It was rudimentary, and he made the comment and it was right. He said, 'The point is that all four of you were playing up to 100% plus of your ability at that time. So you were going all-out. What you did is what you could do.' It was an interesting comment. That first Montrose album was heralded much more in England. I met Cozy Powell when I was over there once and he said (in English accent), 'I gotta tell you Ronnie, that record, it's everyone's favourite over here.'"

As Denny confirms, during the band's brief run, *Montrose* didn't confer the legendary status it would later attain. "No, it didn't (laughs). I mean, Sam and I have been good friends for a lot of years. I knew him before Montrose, even, and we've remained friends for, I don't know, 45 years or something. But once he left, he was opening up for Boston, and he would call me and say, 'Man, these guys are like nuts over that first Montrose album.' And I'm going, yeah? And he's going, 'Yeah, really. It's like, they really like it. That's how they cut their teeth. They're always talking about that first Montrose album.' And I had no idea—I don't think any of us did—that it would become the record that it has and how it's influenced a lot of bands."

But mention heavy metal to Denny, and he draws a blank. "Well, it was a hard-rocking band. We kind of looked at ourselves as like a hard-rocking American band. It was kind of before that whole metal thing. I don't understand the metal thing. But yeah, I don't think we looked at ourselves as a metal band. We were kind of like Johnny Winter 'and.' And Cactus 'and'—it was an extension of that kind of music."

"When the first Montrose album was released," adds Hagar, "only one station in St. Louis was playing us, KSHE, and one station in San Francisco—KSAN was playing us, and that was about it. We didn't get any airplay, and it never even made the Top 200. Montrose was never on the charts. You hear about Pink Floyd being on the charts for ten years, but Montrose was never on the charts, ever, not even in the Top 200 on

Billboard. Yet to date it's sold almost five million records. So it just kept selling and kept selling and that is from other musicians. That's the cult following of people, that's word of mouth. Some musician goes, 'Hey, check this out; I want this drum sound.' And so it still sells great today. I'm really honoured to be part of something that I had no idea what we were doing. It wasn't like boy, I got this idea and we know what we're going to do and we're going to go out and kill. We just got in the studio. I hate to say it, I just got a decent royalty cheque in this day and age where my Van Halen royalties are in the toilet relative to what it used to be; but I'm still getting nice little royalty cheques from Montrose."

Tour highlights for the Montrose album included a trip across the pond in June of 1974 in support of Status Quo, the band logging one date at the Olympia in Paris as well. Noted Ronnie, in conversation with Melody Maker, "We were topping the bill there because for some reason our album had really taken off in France, and the audience brought us back for about three encores. The magazines in France wrote that we were rebelling against English bands, which struck us as unusual 'cause we'd never thought of that before. The first album caught on amazingly considering they'd never seen us and we were brand-new band. When we were there, they wanted to record us in Montreux at the big casino they have over there, so it'd be 'Montrose Live in Montreux,' but it never came together."

Bill Church cites a different reason why Montrose were top of the bill. "You know who was opening the shows for us on the continent? This is a great story. And that was one of the big tours that we did, in Montrose, over here as well. One of the big bands of that year was Black Oak Arkansas, and we opened for them in the US. We went to Europe, and they didn't go to England for some reason, but we met up on the continent, and the roles were reversed—Montrose was headlining and Black Oak was opening. And I asked Jimmy, Jim Dandy, about that, because they were quite big. Their 1973 album was huge, you know? Anyway, he says, 'Yeah, we're all felons, and we've just now been able to get reprieves to get work permits to come to Europe, so unbelievably, it's our first time over. That's why we're opening.' And yeah, we did some big places. We did the Olympia Hall in Paris, which was their big venue back then. All the big venues I played, they tore them all down now, right? The Astrodome, the Superdome... by the way, do you know who played the debut show at the Astrodome? Sammy Hagar, man. The very first rock show ever in the Astrodome, with Joan Jett opening."

"The biggest show, though, was the gigantic show at the Charlton Athletic field in London," continues Bill. "Oh Jesus, what a lineup. Okay, we're the opening act, 10 o'clock in the morning. You've got Lindisfarne, Maggie Bell, Lou Reed, Bad Company, Humble Pie, and the headliner is The Who. I have a picture of us on stage with the crowd in the background, so that we're from the rear, us looking out from the stage. That's one that I actually have hanging in my studio. Playing at 10 o'clock in the morning sucked, but that was the first festival ever played by Montrose. There were eight million photographers at that thing, and there were 65,000 people. Other than that, I believe we played with Uriah Heep and maybe Slade. I think those two, and there may have been another one thrown in there, because we weren't on a standard tour opener."

At Charlton, the band were able to stick around and watch Bad Company and some of The Who, but then had to make their way for a show in Leeds. Still, Bill and Denny as well remember the show as a career highlight.

"Another funny story," continues Church, "we were in London and we had a night off, so we went down to the big club then, which was the Speakeasy, The Speak. And we went down there to see The Crickets. They were gonna play, right? Obviously, without Buddy Holly—he's dead—but The Crickets. So we show up there and the guy... we've never been there in our lives, right? And the guy looks like he's known us forever, like we were superstars. He leads us to this table right in front that is reserved and everything else. About 45 minutes later, the owner of the club comes out and apologizes, because the guy thought that Sammy was Roger Daltrey, and that we were The Who. It was their table."

And Roger Daltrey, or sorry, Sammy, he wasn't getting Ronnie's goat only by being the centre of attention—inevitable given his pipes and the very nature of his job as "front man"—but he also went astray of other band edicts.

"Oh yeah, oh yeah, big power struggle," chuckles Church. "Ronnie had rules. One of the rules was that at no time were wives allowed to go on the road. And it was, well, not lots of times, but the classic one was when we landed for our first tour in Europe. And on the tarmac, Sammy's wife was waiting (laughs). Well, that whole English tour, Ronnie didn't talk to Sammy the whole tour. We stayed on different floors of the hotel, so we would be going to the gig and the elevator would open and I would get on, and then we would go to the next floor and Denny would get on, and then Ronnie would get on, and then it would open and Sammy and his wife would get on. And Ronnie would not even acknowledge them (laughs)."

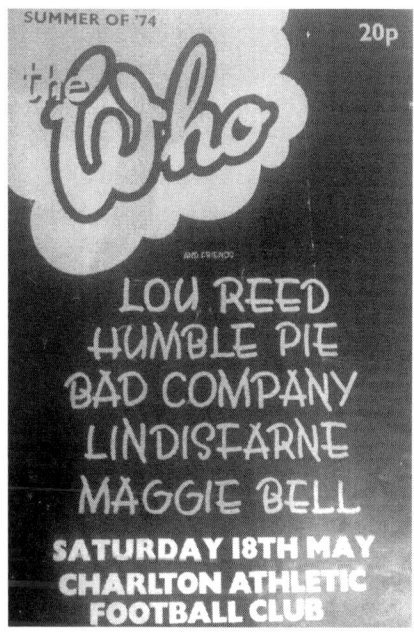

"But the live shows were killer," continues Bill. "Are you kidding me? I mean, we were literally an American type of Led Zeppelin thing. The people we were playing for, it was a little bit new to them, for an American type band. I have always been a live performer, primarily. I mean, I like records and stuff, and even my favourite records in my record collection, I wore them all out so I can't listen to them anymore (laughs). But live, that was always the forte. That was the forte of Sammy's band too. We had a couple of hits, but it was the live show that made the difference. One of the things that we were gonna do after that first album was change the image quite a bit. Because the original Montrose was a semi-European-type glam-type thing, with the clothes and the makeup and that type of stuff. We were gonna try to change that, to be more of an American-based thing. I don't know, like a ZZ Top—they would never be mistaken for being European, right? I wouldn't say like Aerosmith, but maybe like Nugent a little bit. But

I don't know, Nugent, shit, sometimes he goes on stage with a loin cloth. But less dated and less European. Like on *The Old Grey Whistle Test*, you could see how Sammy is just like Robert Plant. He's got a blouse on and all that kind of shit (laughs)."

"The British invasion helped steer what we were doing away from the rambling, jamming, hippie-type music," continues Bill, on what the band were trying to achieve. "But it wasn't just that. As I say, it was visual too. For example, we had rules in the Montrose band, believe it or not. Let's say the band before Montrose, for example, the San Francisco band that me and Ronnie, had called Sawbuck. If you look at a picture of them, it looks like a band that could be from San Francisco, right? Now, one of the rules in Montrose was zero facial hair, period. Gone. Moustaches, beards, sideburns—gone."

To commemorate the UK visit, Warner Bros. pressed up 25,000 flexi-discs at a cost of $17,500 to be given away free to concert-goers. Emblazoned with the flash retro logo in use at the time, this item featured an introduction by Johnny Moran plus three tracks from the album, all on one side, namely "Rock the Nation," "Space Station #5" and "Good Rockin' Tonight."

Back home, the selling of Montrose on the road included dates with Humble Pie, Bad Company, J. Geils Band, Spooky Tooth and Lynyrd Skynyrd courtesy of in-roads made with that band's manager Dee Anthony. Asked if indeed an estimated 33 dates were performed with Humble Pie, Bill thinks that would be about right. "I could believe that. In my archives down in storage, I've got all the itineraries from my career. But I would say probably that. We didn't do overseas; that would just be probably 33 American cities. Oh yeah, big tour, and that was back when they used to have three bands. Those are some drinking bad boys. We were both Uncle Dee bands, and we shared this big giant tour bus. It was a day bus, not a night bus. We didn't sleep on the road in it. They were a raucous bunch. They were heavy into drugs. They weren't like us. We were more serious, I guess... I guess (laughs)."

But then it was back in the studio to crank out what was to be the band's second record—in all of two weeks. Perhaps more time should have been taken, even if in Montrose, time wasn't exactly the pressing problem...

CHAPTER 3: Montrose - Paper Money: "I'm going through a process."

If Ronnie Montrose was not already proving himself to be a sort of second-tier cipher through his work with Van Morrison, Boz Scaggs, Edgar Winter and now a ferocious rocker with Montrose, his second namesake album would have most everyone confused at this man after his muse.

First off, establishing a pattern of firings, bassist Bill Church would be gone, to be replaced by 24-year-old Alan Fitzgerald, brother of a bassist and son of a jazzer and music teacher. "Well, Bill and Ronnie had known each other for a long time, " laughs Denny. "And they had been in a band before Montrose, and so their relationship went back. Just, at that point in time, it just wasn't working out with Bill. There were some personality conflicts and it's just band stuff. I'm sure you've heard the stories a million times. Guys come and go in bands, and that's just part of the deal."

"That's a situation where musically I wanted a change," recalls Ronnie. "I remember, there was a Gamma tour and we were backing up Rainbow in Pittsburgh and Ritchie was there and he came back and said that I had had a really good show that night. And we talked and we realized that neither one of us had done a record with the same lineup in a row. And Ritchie, jokingly of course, said, 'Well, once they ask for money, they're out of there!' But for me, it's just a situation where I don't want to make that same record twice. God bless AC/DC who could do that and make it incredible. But for me, it wasn't my thing. And Fitz, Alan Fitzgerald, was in Sammy's band back in California. Bill Church is an incredible rock bass player, but he said, 'I know a player who can also play keyboards and who's got a different musical sense' and we started changing at that point."

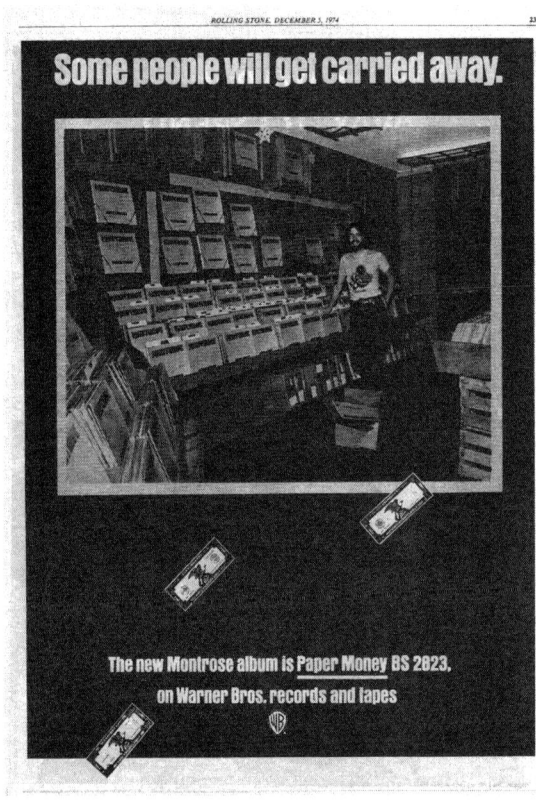

"I was in the band 18 months, my friend," reminisces Bill, surveying the entire trip. "Our first gigs were at rock clubs. We did a whole mess of rock clubs, including the one that is still in Cleveland, the famous one, the Agora. We did Austin, where they did the Austin City Limits, and we did a bunch of a medium ones. Our first big show, our first medium headline show was at Winterland, because both Ronnie and I worked for Bill Graham. In fact, the Sawbuck album was done by Bill Graham's producer and his record company, and then leased off to Epic; he wanted to buy piece of the band. He wanted to buy a piece of Sammy's band for many years too. I knew Bill real well. But we got together, first couple weeks before the album, went in and did the album, then there were a couple weeks off and then boom, we get on the road."

As for Bill's last show with the band? "As I recall, we were somewhere in the Midwest, when we flew home at the end of that tour. So it could have been anywhere. And boy, we played everywhere in the United States. We played six or seven places in Iowa alone (laughs). Now most people don't know this, but there are masters of the second album, the *Paper Money* album, with the original band. I believe the masters belong to Leighsa Montrose now. When I left, they took me out. They edited it and put Fitz in it. And that was the demise of Montrose. They never came close. And of course, six months after I left, Sammy was gone too."

"In the original form, the album was really excellent," continues Bill. "A couple of the songs, specifically, the original version of 'Spaceage Sacrifice,' is really good. They definitely re-recorded 'Spaceage Sacrifice' completely; that's not anything close to the original. The original version of 'I Got the Fire' is really good. And the track that they took off completely, that nobody has heard, 'Takin' a Ride,' was some of Ronnie's most killer playing. And so the material, I liked it, and I like the original album. When they re-edited it and whitewashed it and milquetoasted it, I don't really care for that album, quite frankly. And the other mistake they made is that Ronnie should never have sang on the album. Because in the peer situation, a lot of people, they joke about it—it's a joke. So he shouldn't have sang on it. And if he would've kept the original band together, it would've been the American Led Zeppelin. But onward and upward (laughs). And of course, Ronnie and I, as I say, had already been in three bands together before Montrose: Sawbuck, Van Morrison and our acoustic band, The Corn Brothers. And so Ronnie and I go way back before the original Montrose."

Bill says that "Connection" replaced "Takin' a Ride," lightening the record, but also, "not only that, but the tone quality of the album, the actual, how heavy it comes off the groove and all that, is just not there." As well, there was another potentially heavy song on plate. "When we went back, this time we were gonna record in the Bay Area and have Ted come up there, rather than use Amigo, because Amigo is kind of small. And we wanted to just use the Record Plant anyway, and studios in the Bay Area, that we had worked in, not just Ronnie and me at this point. And so we went in and did all the tunes except we didn't do the Stones cover tune. And we did not do the song that Ronnie sang. I am not on it and never even heard that. But all the other ones are unmastered somewhere."

"And there are songs that were outtakes that are unmastered, like a song called 'Drugs.' In fact, I think 'Drugs' might've been the first song that Sammy and Ronnie ever wrote together. 'Drugs' was sort of like a Robin Trower-type of thing, sort of heavy, but like melancholy and sad." I asked Bill if perhaps this turned into "The Dreamer," and he says, "No, no, way different type of a tune. It was up-tempo. 'Drugs! What I like!' And then the breakdown in the middle where Sammy talks about how he goes into 'You can't quit' and stuff. He goes into this really slow soliloquy in the middle, and then the drums kick in and we go back into the tune. Anyway, I don't like the song, I don't like the lyrics. But that was the one of the ones that was an outtake, and then of course 'Takin' a Ride.'"

Church confirms that this all took place after the tour for the *Montrose* album was completed. "No, we were not touring. We were taking a month off to write songs and get a new album together. And, believe me, it was not called *Paper Money* then. And if I had still been in the band, it would never have been called *Paper Money*. When we were doing it, it wasn't called, 'We are doing the *Paper Money* album.' We were just doing new songs. It wasn't 'til way later, until it came out, oh, they named it *Paper Money*. And of course no pictures on the album, so you knew there were problems."

"The dynamic of the original Montrose band was singular and powerful," continues Ronnie. "It was only after getting together with the four of us in the studio, hanging out and jamming with each other for the first time in about 20 years that I rediscovered and realized how awesome a trio that band was! The band was never the same, not only after Sam was gone, but the band was never the same when Bill left too. It was Sam's friend, Alan Fitzgerald, who came in when we all decided we wanted more from a bass player. Bill's a damn fine bass player, a wonderful rock player, but at that point we wanted keyboards and more harmonic structure. But the band, really, in my opinion, was never the same after the first album. Because it was the original four guys, and the dynamic of those four guys interacting together that had the power."

Look for a reason to sack Bill, and it comes back to the pathology of Ronnie wanting to blow things up. It would happen with the band in totality two records later, it would happen with Gamma... heck, it happened earlier with his leaving of Edgar Winter's band.

"Ronnie, even though he was my enemy for a long time for breaking the band up, he and I for many years were close," shrugs Bill. "We were fishing buddies; we fished everywhere. We were real close friends. And he snapped. The night he called me up, and he's half crying, and he goes,

'Church, I don't know what to fuckin' do. Jesse and Jill are leaving me.' And I go, oh man. I mean, I was there when Jesse was born, right? And anyway, so, we talked. The very next day, he calls me up, and he's just almost like a wired person—'Well, I've decided I'm making changes in the band and you're the first one to go.' That was the very next day. He had snapped. His wife left him, snapped, and he was never, ever the same again. And you know, it sounds funny but to this day, even after all the reunions we've done and everything else, and all the years I spent with Sammy—I spent a decade with Sammy; did 11 Hagar albums—to this day, nobody has ever really told me why Ronnie threw me out (laughs). Sammy says he doesn't know. Actually he says, 'Church, why did he throw *me* out?' And I go, 'Well, the difference was, you didn't give a shit. You were hoping for it' (laughs). It was something different. But he snapped when his wife left him and he was just never the same."

"We were all great friends," adds Bill, asked about Jill. "I mean, they had a kid, and probably what caused all that to happen was simply that Ronnie went away for a year-and-a-half to New York with Edgar, and he didn't bring them with him. And so things happened. But in my opinion, that's what caused Ronnie to snap. He went from being my best friend to my worst enemy overnight. I think that's what did it. Because that's when he changed."

"I don't believe he had children with his subsequent wives," continues Church. "You have to realize that I didn't talk to him for 15 years, maybe? In fact, I didn't talk to him until Sammy one day came up with the idea, hey, let's get together a reunion as part of my set with the Wabos, and you guys, the original Montrose, could play four tunes as part of a reunion. And so we used to do it three, four times a year, right? But up until that point, for 15 years I didn't talk to him."

Asked for a favourite memory from those years, and Church tellingly fills his answer with Van Morrison and Sammy Hagar memories instead. "That's a good one, because I've got lots of them, you know? I would say as an individual moment, my most favourite thing was when I did Carnegie Hall with Van; that would probably be the one individual moment. But there's been so many others that are just a lot of awe-inspiring things. Doing the gigs at Madison Square Garden with unlikely people. We did Madison Square with The Who once. We actually did Madison Square Garden with Kiss once, and we got booed off. Yeah, well, it was all 12-year-olds, and after we were done with our set, they were all out there yelling, 'We want Kiss! We want Kiss!' And I went out into the lobby, and there were as many adults smoking cigarettes in the lobby as there were kids inside watching Kiss."

For the *Paper Money* album cover, the Church-less Montrose would go with stark red and black print on dull grey, as if the band hired a photographer to shoot the aluminum side of Space Station #5 or Starliner. Although this wasn't the first idea, says Ronnie. "*Paper Money* was originally going to be a really intense weathered deco kind of enamelled inlay cover, with either a money clip or one of those old cigarette cases or desktops—it was really supposed to be that. And the proposed cover looked too graphic arts. It looked wrong and we were really at a deadline. So Denny was on the plane reading, I believe *The Gulag Archipelago* and it had a silver cover with blue lettering on it. And he said, 'What do you think of this? It's a great cover.' And we sat down with a designer and said, well, let's do this, use this colour, you can't print shiny, but you can print silver. And then we said, 'Well, this is kind of a new type, this Pioneer font.' So it literally became that, just a simple fix."

Montrose's all-important sophomore record, produced by Ted Templeman and Ronnie Montrose and issued October 11, 1974, opens with not one, but two cover versions—and then there are no more for the rest of the album. Lead track is a slightly rocked-up version of an obscure song called "Underground," featuring Ronnie through a Leslie speaker creating a type of chorus effect on this composition that was issued just the year before on Chunky, Novi & Ernie's self-titled debut album on Reprise (produced by John Cale and Ted Templeman), where it was also that record's opener. It's not a disaster, but they also didn't write it. In an alternate universe, "Underground" could have been a melodic hard rock hit, given the spirited playing from the band, especially Denny, as well as the full-bodied production unsurprisingly achieved by Ted Templeman.

Concerning the methodology of assembling *Paper Money*, Ronnie figures, "It wasn't much different at all. We recorded at the same studio, the same crew. I remember that specifically Donn and I were seriously getting into experimentation and working around with different processes and sounds, as we were on the first album, but just as more of an extension, with different writing. I had always been a fan of a band that was on Warner Bros. called Chunky, Novi & Ernie—she later changed her name to Lauren Wood. Irene Rappoport was her name, and I liked the tune they did, 'Underground,' which is why I put it on the record. I think what also happened on that record is that it was the start of the record company saying, 'Well, let's make a pop hit on here.'"

Still, Ronnie remembers that people for the most part, were on the same page. "Ted was totally into it and Sam was into it to a degree. I was finding my way as a guitarist and a musician and an instrumentalist, and Sam was finding his way as a lyricist and, quote, rock star, working as hard as he could to find out what it would take him to get there. So there wasn't really any bucking. Obviously we had personality differences, but everybody does."

Next is "Connection," a 1967 Rolling Stones song that opens with the line, "Everything is going in the wrong direction." Unfathomably, it's an acoustic ballad with piano (courtesy of Marc Jordan, likely picked for the session by Templeman), and, as I say, a second cover, with *Paper Money* off to an inauspicious start indeed. Lyrically, the track decries the grind of going through airports, accompanied by tired almost country music. The "connection" to a Ronnie Montrose already tiring of the road is readily apparent. Sammy says that Ted dug his vocal performance on the song so much he leapt up and ran smack into the glass door separating the booth from the control room.

As the pensive "Connection" fades, we are confronted with "The Dreamer," the album's heaviest track, like Sabbath, like extreme BTO, like "Rock Candy" and "Make It Last," but smothering in a slow grind, an effect underscored by a laboured tribal drum beat. Signalling that we are in another world from the swagger of the debut, there's a pastoral break where Alan Fitzgerald gets to fiddle with his synth.

"He just likes covers," figures Denny, who doesn't think they were there because of any sort of inferiority complex from Ronnie about his own writing abilities. "One of the things we used to do is sit around in hotel rooms and play covers. You know, just the four of us or whoever else happened to be in the room. Ronnie knew every song. He even knew the commercials from TV. We would play Rolling Stones, Beatles, anything that we had heard on the radio as kids. Songs that we liked. He always had like a group of songs that he liked. We did the Eddie Cochran tune, 'Twenty Flight Rock.' In Gamma we did 'Something in the Air.' I mean, I don't think Ronnie was a prolific songwriter. He was probably better as a collaborator. So we'd have to dip into the songs written by other people list. But he would have his own take, his own version of how it should be done."

Underscoring the idea of Montrose playing many—and arguably too many—covers is a second KSAN session at The Record Plant. Now with two albums of material to showcase, the band nonetheless play the insipid "Roll Over Beethoven" as well as the similarly tired "Evil." There's also just as many (three) songs from the debut as from *Paper Money*, along with Ronnie's acoustic showcase, "One and a Half," which will appear on the next record. Fatefully, again, listening to the inter-song chatter, it's plain to see that the band's vocalist is a born leader, and is by some definitions leading this band, much to the ire of its namesake.

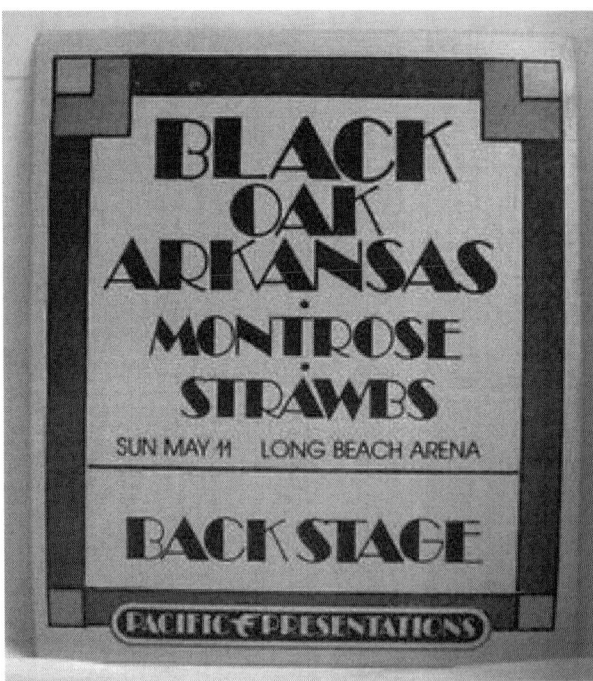

Closing side one of the original vinyl is a spirited, happy, but almost new wavey instrumental called "Starliner," which is again propelled nicely by Denny. Interesting guitar effects and futuristic synths do battle, and there's an amusing break highly reminiscent of "The Song Remains the Same." Still, there goes side one of *Paper Money*: two covers, a humourless heavy metal stomper and an instrumental. Not the right stuff and not exactly substantial, although Ronnie intimated at the time that they had in fact cooked up 21 minutes per side, but had to chop it to 17 because the sound was suffering.

Side two explodes into view with "I Got the Fire," a song that houses within its tight frame all the potential of the *Montrose* album writ large. In fact, "I Got the Fire" just might be the band's crowning song-length achievement, oddly situated on an album that emphatically doesn't deserve it.

"The more hard rocking stuff I enjoyed," muses Denny. "And even 'Connection' was really cool. But 'I Got the Fire' was a great song. That kind of summed up the band: we had the fire. It was just a hard-rocking, straight-ahead, Montrose song."

"Here is a strong song that came alive serendipitously," notes Ronnie, on "I Got the Fire." "We had finished the basic track and I was preparing to cut the solo. Donn had accidentally left the microphone on in the vocal booth, and I was using a big speaker cabinet out in the main room. The reverberation of sound off the door in the main room was so heavy, it literally turned the solo into the wall of sound you hear. A very strong dynamic effect."

"I Got the Fire" is credited to Ronnie alone, with Sammy letting it be known in the press that he of course had written the lyrics, which is pretty obvious—those words of wisdom are almost Hagar autobiographical. But Hagar says Ronnie simply forgot to credit him, no small slight, not because of the money, but more so because, again, this fiery anthem will no doubt go down in history as one of the top five tracks of the Montrose catalogue, maybe on creativity alone, the band's #1.

Laments Sam, of the breakdown in the band's chemistry, "At first it was wonderful. Ronnie treated me really good and it looked like the arm around the little kid saying 'Come on, son, you can do it,' all that kind of thing. And then as soon as I started doing it, he got really kind of jealous and ego'ed-out. Then he tried to hold me back. It would be like, 'Don't do this and don't do that. You can't talk to the audience on stage.' And I'd play him a new song and he would go 'Yeah, yeah, I don't need any new songs.' And you know, Ronnie wasn't a songwriter and he would go to other people to get songs. And I would go, 'Man, what's going on?' It was the first time I had ever experienced an ego. And I didn't realize it, what it was. I was… what the hell is going on? Why doesn't he like me? I felt rejected, like it was a whole different kind of thing. I thought, the guy doesn't like me, man. What am I doing wrong? You know what I mean? I was hurt. And then he finally quit the band and said, 'What are you going to do?' And I went, 'I'm going to start a new one I guess (laughs). I ain't going to go on welfare, pal.'

So that was it; that's how we ended it. And I didn't realize that until years down the road that he had an ego; that's all it was. It's that as soon as he saw me growing and writing the songs, he thought I was going to take over his band, I guess. It was very strange I was naïve—that's all I can say."

Money problems didn't help matters either, with Sammy recalling in his autobiography how the band ran out of cash flow in the middle of the first record's tour, stranded at a Holiday Inn in Little Rock, Arkansas with Ronnie's credit cards all maxed. Sammy adds that the band was getting paid $500 a night per gig, but the road had been piling up expenses at the rate of $600 a night.

But back to *Paper Money*, next up is "Spaceage Sacrifice," which feels like a sleepy-time follow-up to "Space Station #5," with similar oblique lyrics, but dominated this time by angst and loneliness. Musically and lyrically completely antithetical to Sammy's ebullient nature, conversely, one can see parallels between Ronnie's growing weariness with the social and accommodating aspects of the music business, especially at the pace at which he was forced to participate, and the hard rock realm to which he was expected to pander.

Comments Ronnie, on yet another non-heavy metal track from a band that one record back was making the best metal in the country, "This one is the only one out of all the songs on this CD (referring to *The Very Best of Montrose*) that I can honestly say we had recorded a better take on! We had booked a couple of nights at the Record Plant in Sausalito, CA, and were cutting demos. We didn't pay much attention to quality at the time, but when we listened later to our performance, we couldn't believe the spontaneity that track had. Unfortunately, we couldn't find a way to fit the sonic quality of that performance in with the rest of the album. Not that this performance isn't up to par—just that we knew a better one got away."

"Metal to me was... yeah, I didn't like that," reflected Ronnie, again in the modern day, forever ambivalent. "I haven't really appreciated being called a heavy metal band because metal, to me, is Metallica. Metal is the heavy stuff, Megadeth. There's metal, there's grunge, and then there's... I just called myself rock. And I think Aerosmith is not metal; I think Aerosmith is rock. They've become much more polished rock over the years but it's rock. And Kiss is rock. Kiss is not metal to me."

Nor did Ronnie think he was metal standing there in 1974. "No, I never would; not in my mind. In my mind we were hard rock. To me there's a big difference in the attitude, the chord structure, the lyric, the whole thing. Black Sabbath was metal. I didn't listen to them a lot. A friend of mine played 'Iron Man' for me and it was so deep and dark and heavy that in fact, yeah, you've just refreshed my memory. That would be what I'd call metal."

"I have to tell you. Just as a side note for me. I used to take offense at people saying, you know, 'The first Montrose album, that's the best!' California dude going, 'Dude that record fucking rocked!' And I would think, 'Well don't you understand what I'm going through here.' I'm going through a process. I'm doing each record for what it is. I can't continually do the same thing. And then I realized, that for me, the first Led Zeppelin album, the first albums that I hear, the first time that I heard ZZ Top, those records resonate with me as the best records I've heard from. So now I understand. I'm looking at it from a fan's point of view, and it's typically the first record that I was exposed to by a group that really blows me away. It isn't that people are telling me that they don't listen to anything else I've done or they aren't interested, it's just that that deeply touched them. I'm more appreciative now."

"We're Going Home" is just as mournful, fatalistic even, as "Spaceage Sacrifice," made all the more eerie by the addition of Mellotron, provided by Nick DeCaro. Ronnie takes credit and commandeers on lead vocals. "This is my one and only lead vocal performance on these albums," notes Ronnie. "It was personal to me, a song about childhood and reflection of things past, present and future. I'm very pleased at the amount of deep emotion I was able to put into the solo."

"He wanted to sing a song, for God sakes," says Hagar. "You know, 'We're Going Home.' He wrote it himself and sang it, and then he wanted to do an instrumental. He just really wanted to shut me out. He was trying to make it without me, and that's what happened to *Paper Money*. He co-produced the record with Ted Templeman. You know, we have one record that was a flop. It was a long-term success, but Montrose - *Montrose* was a complete flop by the time we started our second record; it hadn't sold 50,000 records. And he wants to co-produce with one of the greatest producers of all time, he wants to become a songwriter, and he wants to get outside material, and he wants to sing a song and do an instrumental and kind of shove the singer off (laughs). I mean, it was really true. It was not my doing."

"And I went to Ted Templeman and I said, 'Ted, I've got these great songs; let me play you this song.' And I played him a song called 'Call My Name,' which is just such a Montrose track. And he goes, 'Oh God, that would be great, but...' he says, 'You know Ronnie; he's just got his own ideas right now.' And I said, 'Wow, I don't get it.' I really didn't get it. But I think he was just trying to take control and not think about success. That was Ronnie. That's when his ego started jumping in. He wouldn't let me write. I was writing all the stuff before then. You know, he would co-write it with me; if you look at 'I Don't Want It' and those songs I wrote before I even met him, he would put a riff or something on it, a different kind of riff on it, and he was my co-writer. That was okay with me; don't get me wrong. But on *Paper Money*, he didn't want to do that anymore. He was looking elsewhere for material."

Sammy and Denny had in fact cooked up a few new songs for the record at Sammy's basement studio at his Sausalito home, but Ronnie wasn't buying. Some of this material would show up on Sammy's debut solo album, *Nine on a Ten Scale* (although according to an adamant Bill Church, everything was new there). And once in the studio, the tension mounted, allayed occasionally by the guys playing basketball.

The band give it the ol' college try to raise the rock quotient of *Paper Money* on the album's closing title track, where Sammy and Ronnie manage to collaborate, the two adversaries putting together a tribal-rhythmed hard rocker that is a little sparse but heavy enough. Sammy's lyric decries the hollowness of materialism, but also rides the line of rock star boast, or, if a sense of irony is grasped, the tongue-in-cheek imagining of what it must be like to be a rich rock star. On stage, however, the song really came alive, with the band speeding it up and Denny driving it savagely. Its airy architecture also allowed Ronnie to do what he loved best, which is extemporize and explore his inner textural Jeff Beck.

"In hindsight, both Sam and I've discussed on a couple of occasions that we may not have paid enough attention to this one," reflects Ronnie. "I still really like the lyrics and message but feel we could've gone further with the music, again, 20/20 vision in hindsight. It's a good one, nonetheless."

But it was all too little too late. Even though the record doubled the sales of its predecessor, and reached #65 on Billboard, the legend of the debut could only take seed and begin to overshadow the set of songs on record #2. After all, studious neo-headbanger types couldn't help notice how much louder and fully-formed this band looked on the first record, now that Kiss, Aerosmith, Blue Öyster Cult and the New York Dolls were getting all the attention. Still, aiding greatly in the positioning of the band as scorching hot, Montrose went on *The Midnight Special* and performed ripping versions of "I Got the Fire" and "Paper Money," two of the album's heaviest songs made even heavier by nerves and the adrenaline-juiced speed they produce.

Gamely trying to sell the record, Warner staffers wrote in their official record label bio, "What America's been needing, among other things, is a band that plays clean, powerful rock 'n' roll music without frills, distractions or hyphenated modifiers; a straightforward, energetic outfit. Two albums' worth of searing hard rock and enthusiastic in-concert audience reaction indicates the name of the solution is Montrose. Montrose's second Warners album, *Paper Money*, was released in November 1974 and was produced, as was their first LP, by illustrious Warners staffer Ted Templeman. Templeman's commercial and creative expertise (honed over successive album projects with the Doobie Brothers and Van Morrison) lent just the right touch of definition and control to Montrose's original rock. *Paper Money* further explored the band's taste for the futuristic ('Spaceage Sacrifice,' the instrumental 'Starliner'), for lighter ballads ('We're Going Home') and, as always, made a heavy commitment to relentless rockers. The group followed up *Paper Money* with another transcontinental tour. On record as well as on the road, Montrose is proving to be more than a stable currency; the band's value continues to appreciate as they continue to serve the audience's demand for distinctive contemporary rock 'n' roll music."

For Ronnie's part, in what basically amounted to the sabotage of a good thing, he says that "*Paper Money* basically happened because it was my intention. It was at that point, during *Paper Money*, that it was really clear to me that I wasn't going to be making, quote, the same album five times in a row just because the first one was successful, and so it was where my music was leading. Even though there was still heavy stuff on there, that's just the way it was. I remember Creem magazine or Rolling Stone, whoever reviewed it, that they said it was a stumble but not a fall. And I remember that quote because that was one of the things that inspired me on more just to go the way my creativity took me and not go the way that all business logic dictates you should go."

And so, obviously, this shows that even back in the mid'70s, Ronnie was pretty much intent on following his muse. Underscoring that fact, on the promotional trail for the band's third album, *Warner Bros. Presents*, he had said, "Sure, I'd like to have a hit with this one. But not at the expense of the music I want to play. I have music going around in my head all the time, and to a certain extent, I have to honour the patterns it forms. I don't want to be just another flash guitarist. I still love *Paper Money*, though. If you play really loud guitar-bass-drums music all the time, it ceases to hold any meaning. When you do it, you should make it count, which is really all we want to do. Don't worry, we can still rock and Kiss with the best. The album I just finished contains three of the hardest songs you'll ever endure. People always want to know why someone leaves a group. It just wasn't happening with Sammy and me anymore. And why not, we weren't married or anything. It was actually better for both of us to go our own ways."

Added Montrose, on his place in guitar rock history as of '75, "I'm not like Beck, if for no other reason than he's got an eight year lead on me. His fingers are that much more educated than mine. He's been places already that I have yet to go or probably won't go. But in eight years, my fingers will have been somewhere else. And that remains to be seen."

Reviewing *Paper Money*, Billboard, not exactly a bastion of heavy metal thought, seemed to agree with Ronnie's creative instincts, proclaiming. "Rock music seems to be moving back to the basics these days, and with their second set, Montrose show that their initial fine effort was no fluke. For the most part, the band engages in a brand of rock that, for lack of a better name must be dubbed heavy metal. Yet they are more subtle than some of the top name bands of the genre. Mixing original hard rockers (including a fine instrumental) and a fine rendition of one of the Stones' earlier cuts, the band rocks through eight cuts highlighted by the frenetic yet controlled vocals of Sammy Hagar and the guitars of Ronnie Montrose. Outside chance for an AM hit on several of these cuts, and if this happens, Montrose could well become one of the major bands of the next year. Dealers: Play in store. LP should draw questions."

Providing a further post-mortem and in general, a justification of the band's left turn on *Paper Money*, Ronnie told me, "Nothing happened on radio with *Paper Money*. 'I Got the Fire' got some medium play, but not much. But this is the path I've been on. By the time this is being read—I'm 63 this month; I'm going to be 63 in two weeks—so this is 40 years ago. I told my son one time, I said, 'A lot of lifetimes we live.' And he said, 'Yep, there sure are.' And I said, 'Yeah, it takes a lifetime to live them, doesn't it?' I don't know how to answer that. I just… I decided that what I wanted to do was what I wanted to do, and a lot of people have faulted me for that, not sticking to my guns, but I didn't want to be a band that kept doing the same thing and didn't have… and the frustrating part for me was I didn't want to be that. I love Angus and Malcolm and I love AC/DC, but every AC/DC record is an AC/DC record. We love it, and that's why we listen to them. But I wanted to be more on the Zeppelin line, doing acoustic, doing electric, just stretching out, but I had nowhere near the ability, musically, guitar-wise or writing-wise that lord and master Jimmy Page had. It wasn't something that I was capable of doing but I was still in my meagre way trying to go there. And then every record after that was something I just kept wanting… and of course I had the record companies telling me, 'You've got to get this, we've got to get a single, we've got to do this.' It's the same story you've heard from every musician."

Sammy, always one to understand the business because he was enthusiastically inquisitive, offered the following survey of Montrose's place in the scene at the time, in conversation with Sam Dunn. Addressing the importance of touring over radio for a hard rock act, Hagar explains, "For the '70s, for metal bands that didn't have Top 40 pop hits like the Carpenters or people like that, Captain and Tennille, it was like, if you put on Top 40 and you put on FM radio, it was like whoa, two different worlds. But the Top 40 people were selling all the albums. So the FM group of people—Montrose, Black Sabbath and the Led Zeppelins of the world—you had to go on tour. The whole record company scene was that they were going to put you on tour, and on your third act, if you did an album, tour, a second album, tour, third album, you broke. That was the consensus of all the record companies. They stuck with a band like Montrose. They wanted to, anyway. The original Montrose broke up after the second record, but you could count on the record company backing you for the third album. Third album, you were going to break. You were going to sell a million records or go gold at least and you were going to become at least a headliner in a lot of places across the country."

"Like I say, Montrose broke up on the second record. Everyone was looking at us for the third record. No one even cared about the first record and what it sold. I mean they did, they would love it if it exploded, but no one ever exploded on their first record other than if they had a big crossover pop hit or had some real gimmick. But even Bowie and Kiss, they didn't explode on their first records as far as I know. They went out and worked and opened for people and busted their balls out on the road. The road was the way you did it, because there was a cult thing to where a band would come to town and you'd have 500, 600 people that were saying I want to see this band."

"But metal bands didn't come up through the clubs," continues Hagar. "Montrose didn't, anyway. We never played clubs. I mean we maybe played five club dates in the three years I was in that band. Even when we were starting we didn't play clubs; we opened for someone in an arena. And so it was arena rock, heavy metal, FM radio... all that stuff kind of came out of that era, and it was smart promoters like Bill Graham who found a venue, some funky old piece of crap venue, and he got it real cheap and he could pay the band nothing and charge a low ticket price and pack it."

"But Montrose, like I said, we put out an album, went on tour, came home three years later, as far as I'm concerned. We came home for two weeks and made *Paper Money*. Had written those songs on tour and… man, we never took a break. And Montrose, we never had a radio hit. On our second album, 'Connection,' the kind of ballad acoustic thing, did really well in Texas. Montrose was starting to break, but I tell you it was St. Louis, San Francisco, Paris. We had three markets where we were a legitimate 5,000 seat small arena headliner, and maybe even two nights in San Francisco. We ended up doing two nights in Winterland, we ended up doing two nights at the Olympia in Paris. We never headlined St. Louis but KSHE was breaking; 'Space Station #5' was starting to break on that station and 'Rock Candy.' I remember I got pictures of Montrose with us in KSHE with the T-shirt with the pig with the headphones—that was their emblem—because we went there and they treated us like kings, man. They were giving us T-shirts."

"There were a few places in the south," continues Hagar, always cognizant of the game. "I remember in Greensborough there was a station. Now that I'm thinking. Atlanta was kind of a little metal spot, and Texas; there were a few places where we got played. But as far as charting singles, Montrose was zero. Never made the charts, never made the album charts, never made the airplay charts. I think it was pretty much word of mouth, and playing in front of 10,000 people opening for Humble Pie. I mean, can you imagine? It was Montrose, Spooky Tooth, Humble Pie. Or Montrose, J. Geils, Humble Pie. Montrose, Peter Frampton, Humble Pie. It was just always a three-act show like that."

"And one time in Montrose—just letting you know how the pop world didn't fit in—it was Montrose, Linda Ronstadt and the Stone Ponies and Humble Pie. And I kind of dug Linda Ronstadt. I thought she was hot. She came out in these little cut-off things, barefoot up there like a little country girl, little straw in her mouth. And I don't know who the hell booked that show, but she was a pop act. She had a big hit on the radio, a lot bigger than us, and had sold a lot more records than us, I'm sure. But we came out, killed. Walked up, I went back out to see her, and the second song she comes running off the stage crying with her head in her hands, and the band quit. And they left the arena. But that was the difference between metal and pop right there, man. That just said it all. It didn't belong together. It was oil and water. It was really becoming apparent that there was a separation. In the '50s there was no separation. Even in the '60s, no separation. You know, pop, rock, Beatles, Stones, Elvis or whoever, it was all on the charts and that was what there was. There wasn't kind of an alternative scene that I can think of until metal."

"And Montrose was different than everything because we were half glitter rock, half punk rock, half metal and R&B. I mean we were such… Ronnie was such a punk before punk was happening. He had an attitude, he didn't want to talk to the audience, he wanted to spit on the audience and get in their face. And I was coming from an R&B place, so it was really… we didn't fit in almost anywhere. We got booed off the stage sometimes. We would open for a band… Little Feat at that time in Europe, they were real big in Amsterdam and we were on tour and they were opening for us in Germany and England and France and our big countries, and we went there and got booed off stage after the third song. I mean we opened for a lot of people and didn't even get an applause. We played 35 minutes of hell, loud and high energy, and stopped and it was over."

On top of decent tour receipts, hard rock bands could count on a boost from the likes of Creem, Circus and Hit Parader for a degree of favourable print press.

"Well there you go. Magazines like Creem, and there was another one I can't remember, but there were two in America that were like the two. And I mean you rushed out to the newsstand to buy the newest issue to see if you were in them guys. I mean it was so important for the metal scene for these people that didn't have a place on the radio too much. There was no MTV or anything yet. Metal didn't really have a home. There were a few stations around the country like the KSHEs and the KSANs that would play it, but they would play it next to an Otis Redding song. I mean KSAN in San Francisco, you would hear an Otis Redding song and then you'd hear a Montrose tune and then you'd hear Led Zeppelin and then Van Morrison, and it was like whoa, it was very eclectic. Which was really cool, by the way. So I think those magazines... and then of course Rolling Stone. If you made any blurb in Rolling Stone, that was the real thing. But the heavy magazines like Creem, they had Aerosmith, they had Kiss, and before Van Halen they had Montrose and Grand Funk or whatever, Zeppelin. I mean that was our vehicle. We'd say man, we made the cover of Creem, boom, we've made it. Like I said there wasn't a very commercial side for metal in those days. It was very, very uncommercial music as a matter of fact."

But the legend grew, and really, thanks to nothing other than that first record.

"Yes, little by little we became like a cult band," agrees Hagar, "to where a lot of bands today—Van Halen and the band The Cult and Boston—Tom Scholz the first time I met him says, 'The first Montrose album, it's the bible.' Everybody say it's the bible. So I'm going, it's great to be part of that but at the time we didn't know what we were doing. And Ronnie was so insecure that he told us on the making of the second record we're too late in this whole game, we have to change otherwise we're not going to make it. Metal is over. That's what he was saying. Hard rock, loud music is done. We barely made it under the wire, but I don't want to go on. So he fired me and he fired... and he started trying to change because he thought metal was over. And then a few years later here comes Van Halen and Poison and Mötley Crüe and everybody else. Same thing we were doing and it makes it big, but we never made it. Montrose never made it. Like I say, we headlined San Francisco and we headlined Paris. We were huge in Paris for some reason, and we did okay in London and okay in Germany, but that's it. Everywhere else we were an opening act. We never headlined ever."

So Montrose was five years ahead of its time.

"Sure, by, say, 1979, that was like the peak of bands like Van Halen coming on the scene. Mötley Crüe was coming onto the scene soon. I know in '79 I was rocking as hard as I ever was. I think there was becoming a big division between pop and metal, and a lot of the bands were writing hit songs and crossing over, possibly. And real metal was probably kind of dying. The record companies were saying, hey, you can sell a lot more records if you get on this station in this format. And Rolling Stone was big and strong and powerful and they certainly weren't a metal magazine by any means. They were just a media, political, whatever the hippest thing in rock is, that's what they were into. So I think everyone started seeing how you could really make it instead of just coming out of the garage. Metal was garage, you know? And it's almost like the speed metal thing that happened later with Metallica and all those guys, that was pretty much… they were just doing what we did in Montrose. That was going in a garage, cranking out and playing this loud music. So maybe it hadn't seen its second really big resurgence yet, but I think a lot of bands were crossing over. I don't know what would have happened to Montrose, but Aerosmith certainly crossed over. They got themselves a big pop hit. Kiss crossed over, they got themselves a big pop hit. Van Halen was crossing over. They were getting semi-pop hits. But Ronnie was wrong because this is 2010 and metal is still out there rocking and it never, ever really went completely away. You take a band like Iron Maiden who was big, kind of went down a little bit, and Iron Maiden's probably bigger now than they ever were anywhere in the world, and they're a pure metal band. Don't call those guys pop—they never crossed over."

"But like I said, Ronnie thought we were doomed," continues Sammy. "He thought we were way too late and we were never going to make it. He obviously felt snubbed and he kind of wanted to be respected as a musician more than me. I just wanted to be a star. But I gotta say, if you checked into a hotel dressed the way we were dressed, whoa; walking down the street… you certainly didn't stop driving a car across city to city. In those days we used to drive a lot in the station wagon. You didn't stop at a truck stop and walk in dressed looking the way we did—you'd get your ass kicked. So yeah, you know, you felt like an outcast for sure as a singer/songwriter."

"But I think there was a community. Like when we'd play with Aerosmith and J. Geils and Humble Pie or those guys, we all had the same vibe. We could hang out together, and backstage it didn't seem as competitive. I think we had a little family about the heavy metal guys. I remember when Montrose played in London the first time, everyone came out. All the English musicians came to see us, because I think they probably thought these guys are American, it's spreading. I think Led Zeppelin and those guys were looking like wow, it's starting to work. I never understood Ronnie saying it's too late, we're over. I'm going, 'You're crazy! I can see it starting to build.' And when I left Montrose, for instance, as a solo artist I didn't want to continue on because Ronnie had my head a little screwed-up. So I kind of went a little more singer/songwriter instead of putting together another heavy metal band. Because I actually… he had me believing it."

"So I felt a little more isolated and removed from the whole scene when I became a solo artist. That's kind of when I took a hard left. Montrose seems like, like I said, everyone would come out and see us, but it was all that same ilk of people. It was the metalheads and metal bands. I remember Rod Stewart coming to see us in London, and he was a hero of mine to the bone. And the Stones—Keith and Mick came to a gig in Amsterdam we were doing with Little Feat to see us get booed off the stage. Not cool."

As Sammy alluded to, by 1979, he was long-gone out of Montrose and himself ensconced as a prolific second-tier solo act, and, as he says, rocking fairly hard, or at least as hard as Montrose would through the last three-quarters of their catalogue. Sammy would leave the band in February of '75, after the boiling-over pressures between himself and Ronnie over the course of the band's European tour for *Paper Money*, with new vocalist Bob James arriving three months later.

Laughs Ronnie, of Sammy's exit from the ranks of Montrose, "We have a longstanding joke now, because I did fire him from the Montrose band for some of the same reasons that I left the Edgar Winter Group. He was onto his own thing and had many more things that he wanted to do as a band leader than he could do in our format. Same thing that I did with Edgar. One of the running jokes is that it took Van Halen a lot longer than it took me to fire him! Another one I love is one that Sam told when I was playing on his last album, *Marching to Mars*, Sammy said, 'People keep asking me, like, what happened to Ronnie? And I tell them, shit, Ronnie fired me, fired everybody else… I think he fired himself!'" But there was something in Sammy that was a classic breed of front man and vocalist. He had the voice, and we all loved Free and we loved Paul Rodgers, and Sammy's the first to admit that was one of his major huge influences. So he had that, and he had that thing that all he wanted to be in his life was a rock star. That was it. I mean that was his calling in life and he wanted to sing and dance and be somebody. And he did a good job of it. Still doing it."

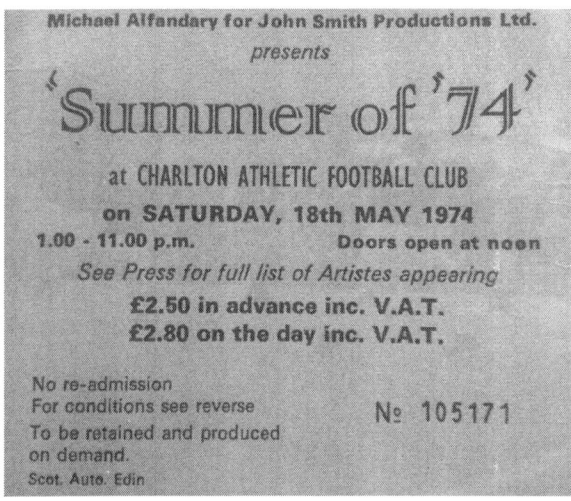

For the record, Sammy says that the final straw with Ronnie came after Hagar had been heralded essentially as the second coming of Robert Plant in some Belgian press review amidst UK and continental touring dates as part of the Warner Brothers Music Tour, in a package with Little Feat, Doobie Brothers, Tower of Power, Graham Central Station and Bonaroo. Rather than appreciate that he had his own power Plant inside the band, when the band got to Paris preparing to perform two tour-ending shows at the Olympia Theatre, Ronnie turned to Sammy in the car—Sammy, Alan and Denny were all in the back seat—and said he was breaking up the band and asked him what he planned to do with his life now. After the shows, with Sammy sick as a dog from food poisoning, Hagar didn't even fly home on the same plane as Ronnie, already plotting to take Denny and Fitz to start a new band. Denny and Sammy actually jammed on a few of Sammy's new songs, but then Ronnie lured the guys back, given a re-signing of the band to Warner Bros., something Hagar suspects was premeditated and already in the works without his knowing.

Adds Denny, "There it was—it's Ronnie. You know, Ronnie was changing direction. And he was the leader of the band, and he was taking it in a different direction. That's all I can really remember about it. Him and Sam were starting to have problems with songwriting. You know, the first record was great, because they collaborated a lot. And then for *Paper Money*, it seemed like with the songwriting, there were two different camps. They weren't getting along, Ronnie and Sam at that point. The honeymoon was over."

"One thing that I want to make clear to everyone," says Hagar on the subject, "as much as we ego-tripped and argued until I got thrown out of that band, he encouraged me as a songwriter. Ronnie was not a songwriter—he had a couple of riffs but no songs. He let me write songs. I also had no idea, on a business level, about things like publishing. Ronnie told me to start my own publishing company and he allowed me to do that. Most guys on the level that Ronnie was at that time would have seen a young guy like me and said, 'I will publish your songs and I will be the writer.' He didn't do that to me and the songs that I wrote on the first two Montrose records supported me through the hard times when I left that band. I had about four to five years of hard times when I went out on my own and started my own band. I was trying to have a family and everything else and that is what got me through. And I will never forget that as long as I live. If Ronnie was ever in a bad situation then I would do whatever I could to help him."

"Montrose opened up for us in '74 and '75," recalls Ted Nugent, who knew a good thing when he saw it, and through his rise in the late '70s, was at a vantage point to watch it whither. "I will never forget that I would see Sammy on the side of the stage. We all of course loved Montrose because they came from that same black school of rhythm and blues. 'Bad Motor Scooter' is a rhythm and blues song, except that it is uppity like a rock song; 'Rock Candy' my God, almighty. Anyway, every night after they opened, on the side of stage would be Sammy, Bill, Ronnie and Denny watching our entire show every night. We became good friends because we all came from that school of black soulful music. We all come from the same work ethic that you practice and make the music tight and authoritative, honest and sincere. I've been onstage jamming with Sammy dozens of times. I've jammed with him, and he with me, and I've been onstage with Van Halen, the Waboritas and even with Montrose. There is a mutual admiration society between us. We have the same work ethic and the same musical ethic."

Glam-rocking boy wonder Ronnie Montrose with The Edgar Winter Group, 1972. © Jim Summaria

Montrose, 1973. Left to right: Bill Church, Sammy Hagar, Ronnie Montrose, Denny Carmassi. © Jim Summaria

Sammy Hagar, the Robert Plant of "America's Led Zeppelin," circa 1973, trying to figure out how much he's allowed to emote.
© Jim Summaria

Ronnie Montrose, man of a thousand guitar solo faces, captured live in 1974. © Jim Summaria

Sam just doing what a front man does, while Ronnie looks on, not so sure. © Jim Summaria

MONTROSE
DENNIS CARMASSI · JIM ALCIVAR · RONNIE MONTROSE · ALAN ("FITZ") FITZGERALD · BOB JAMES

Record company promo photo for the *Warner Bros. Presents* lineup of 1975. © Warner Bros. Records

Ronnie on his 1978 *Open Fire* tour, Oklahoma. © Richard Galbraith

Business-to-business-type ad in Billboard from 1977, announcing the gold certification of 1973's *Montrose*. © Warner Bros. Records

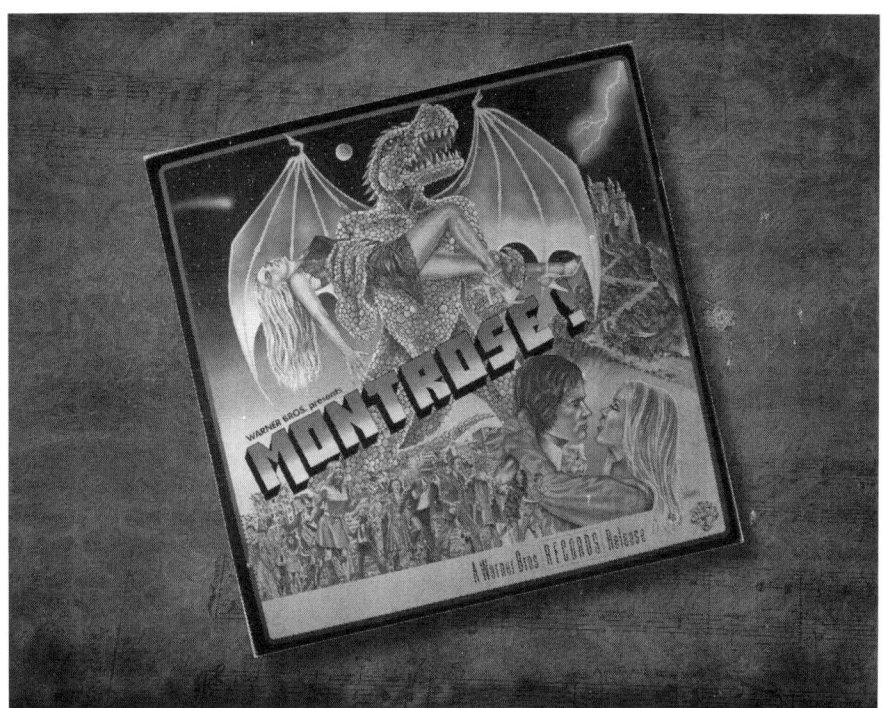

CHAPTER 4: Montrose - *Warner Bros. Presents:* "Where's Ted? Where's Ted?"

Changing lead singers in a band is obviously a risky proposition bordering upon reckless. But for a guy like Ronnie Montrose, it merely falls within a pattern of disdain for the expected, disdain for convention, fearlessness of the consequences. What's more, Montrose would add a fifth member, in keyboardist Jim Alcivar, and Ronnie would take the reigns and produce his third album himself, eschewing both the continuity and great sounds Montrose could have carried on with through the services of the respected Ted Templeman.

Drummer-around-town Michael Kelley and soon-to-be Montrose singer Bob James were just two huge Montrose fans working in a record store when the phone rang at work one day.

Says Michael, long-time friend and manager of James, "Bob has always been a very unique individual, in terms of the way he thinks, in terms of the way he looks at things. He's a very unconventional thinker. And he has a type of wisdom that is... let's put it this way, he's not a linear thinker. As for how I got to know him, in the late '60s, in the South Bay area of

Los Angeles, there was a band I used to see called The Symbols of Tyme. And Bob was in that band and that band also featured Dave Pack from Ambrosia. Bob is 17, maybe 18 and he was already playing. The original configuration of the band Swan, which Bob returned to after Montrose, was Shatterminx, and before that, the original name was Ethan Frome. The way we found Bob is that we had auditioned a singer called Robert Fleischman, something of a local legend. And Robert, at the time was in a band called Wolfgang, and because of other bands using the name, and confusion, they ended up changing the name of the band to Shatterminx. But Robert was the only guy we had ever heard in our area that was as good as anybody you could name. He was a guy who had a voice like Plant and Gillan, and he could sing all of that stuff."

"So we had Robert come over to play with us, at my house. And, I mean, he was phenomenal. We were almost kind of hysterical trying to listen to this guy, because he was so good. He really was not interested in working with us; he had other commitments. So he said, 'You know, I understand what you guys are doing. I know the perfect guy for you.' He said, 'I've seen that you guys were kinda wanting to be heavy, but you also have this progressive thing. This guy's like a cross between Robert Plant and Jon Anderson of Yes—his name is Bob James.' And that was it."

"Of all those guys in the band, I was the little kid," continues Mike, asked about his first impression of James. "Those guys were four, five years older than me. Because at the time, I was either 14 or 15. Very precocious. But the other guys were all like 18 or 19. And we couldn't reach Bob initially. He was very hard to get a hold of. And then when we did reach him, he wasn't very receptive. But we were determined (laughs). So we kept calling him, and finally he consented to coming over. And the thing I remember is, me being a young teenager, where we were playing was in this addition built onto my garage. So he walked in the house, out that door and down the steps into my back area, where you enter into this like other music room. And I noticed that he had left a beer can on my front porch. And I think it was Olde English. And it just kind of freaked me out. Like, what? It seemed kind of gangster-ish, back then, for me. I don't even know this guy, but he leaves a beer can on my fucking porch. But the first thing that struck me was that he was quite small in terms of his stature and he was soft-spoken."

"Plus Symbols of Tyme were a band that were kind of associated with what we called the low rider crowd or culture. Low riders were kind of like the bad boys of the era, and were mainly Hispanic. And there was something about that. That I knew The Symbols of Tyme were kind of associated with that scene. There was something about Bob that struck me a bit like that, and so I was a bit iffy in the beginning. But he was a nice guy, albeit a little aloof. But we played, and he was exactly what Robert Fleischman said he was going to be. He has this voice... I mean, we were equally as shocked when we heard Bob sing. And maybe even more so, because Robert at that time, Robert Fleischman, was really just a siren. He had this incredible wailing Ian Gillan/Robert Plant kind of voice. But Bob was more yin and yang. Bob had this really beautiful Jon Anderson-esque... I don't want to say feminine, but he had that wispy quality that Jon Anderson had."

There was no place for Bob to be writing in Shatterminx, says Mike, because the band already had an expert in that field.

"Yes, the band was really the brainchild of the guitarist, Michael Culiani. Michael was really the architect of everything. He wrote the music, he wrote the lyrics, and to this day, still probably one of the most brilliant lyricists that I've ever encountered. His major influences were Pete Sinfield of King Crimson, and Keith Reid of Procol Harum. We're talking 1972, and the songs were all really long, ten, 12 minutes, lots of different time changes and movements, and the lyrics tended to be kind of theatre of the mind with lots of metaphors. And Mike would just hand Bob a lyric sheet and start playing and Bob just basically picked it up. I don't even know if Mike had vocal melody lines. But Bob just kind of jumped in and we were amazed at the quality of his voice in terms of the dynamic range, like being able to be very soft and sensitive, kind of like Jon Anderson. And then if there was a moment where we really needed him to turn it up like Gillan or Plant, he could go there."

So flash forward a couple years, explains Mike, and Bob James was about to move up in the world. "Yes, so Shatterminx is like '73, '74, and for some reason or another, it just petered out. And Bob and I were working together at a record store in Santa Monica. And that's when we were playing together in this other band, Taken Alive. The concept or this label 'tribute band' didn't even exist then. We weren't really a Montrose tribute band per se, but by today's standards, we probably could've been. Because we did a lot of material from those first two records. We probably did eight to ten songs from those first two records as well as some other things by bands that were very obscure at the time, like Stray Dog, Trapeze, The Sensational Alex Harvey Band and A Foot in Coldwater."

"We just went out of our fucking minds for that record," continues Kelley, referring to *Montrose*. "I mean literally. When we were working at the shop, we basically listened to little else. I mean, we listened to that record, I imagine, like, six, seven, hours, just constantly. Occasionally we'd play something different, but we were blasting that thing constantly. We just loved the concept of it and the heaviness; plus the songs were really great. I mean, everything about it. We loved Sammy, we loved the sound, we loved the songs."

"The first two albums with Montrose just knocked me out," agrees Bob James. "I wasn't really quite sure what the reason was, but the sound was phenomenal. And so the thing that really got me started on this band Montrose, was the fact that Ted Templeman was their producer. That's the whole thing that secured me, as far as being interested in the band in the first place. It wasn't necessarily the musicians or performances or anything, which I considered all excellent, but it was the sound. But as Michael says, we worked in a record store, and I was like with a local band. We were just kids and we loved music."

Kelley had a special place in his heart for the band's slamming drummer, and he wasn't the only one who was taking notice. "Yes, me being a drummer, I was really impressed with Denny Carmassi. He was phenomenal, scary good. Every drummer that I knew, where we were living at the time, the South Bay area of Los Angeles, myself, Marc Droubay, who eventually became the drummer for Survivor—plays on 'Eye of the Tiger'—Bobby Blotzer, who became the drummer for Ratt, Leonard Haze, drummer for a band called Yesterday and Today that eventually became Y&T, we were all Denny Carmassi fanatics. And he was and still is a singular player. His meter was flawless; like a machine. He had the heaviness of a Bonham. He was playing big drums like Bonham, and had that really big sound like Bonham. Bonham was still something of an enigma and a little bit of a mystery at that point. People tried to mimic him, but not really successfully. But when we heard Carmassi, certainly the first thing you think of is Bonham. And yet he was somewhat like Terry Bozzio; very disciplined, almost machine-like. We used to say if Bruce Lee would've been a drummer, he would've been Denny Carmassi. Carmassi was very muscular. He was like a tank, really. If you look at the video of them on *The Midnight Special*, playing 'I Got the Fire' and they do one other one, Denny is just... I mean, the cameraman obviously picked up very quickly that this was a guy we want on camera."

Speaking of "I Got the Fire," and given an obvious level of Montrose expertise, I wondered what Mike and Bob thought of *Paper Money*. "We were a little puzzled," laughs Kelley. "Like, we really, really, really liked it, but we found it a little puzzling that they had taken this seemingly failsafe formula and changed it pretty radically. The dynamics of that second record are vastly different than the first record, which is all crunch from beginning to end. We really liked 'Underground,' and the thing that was funny about that was that was actually the title of the lead song on the demo by Shatterminx that Ronnie heard. No relationship—two totally different songs but the same title. But yeah, *Paper Money* seemed like more of a progressive record. It was almost like a conscious decision to go more progressive and certainly more eclectic. There's a couple things that are very much like the first record, like 'I Got the Fire' and 'The Dreamer,' but then all the rest of it is very different from the first record."

Picking up the tale, Mike says, "So yes, Shatterminx, at that point... again, I don't know why, but they kind of lapsed into a state of being non-active, and so Bob and I were doing this Taken Alive thing and having a lot of fun. We were really excited about the prospects of seeing Montrose on the *Paper Money* tour. And I don't know how this came about—I do recall seeing something about it in the *LA Times*—but we had heard that Sammy had been fired from the band and we were devastated. It really felt like somebody had died. We were so upset about it. And so we had this big wake, continued our marathon at the store, playing the albums back to back. This was The Warehouse, on either Santa Monica Boulevard or Wiltshire, downtown Santa Monica. Bob was the assistant manager, and Bob would post a sign saying, 'Do not remove these records from this turntable.'"

"And that was the point," continues Mike, "when we were playing in this band, Taken Alive, and doing most of those two records. And, you know, it really was my idea. It wasn't immediate, but within a few days, I started thinking, I wonder what's up with those guys? Are they trying out new singers? What's going to happen? And so I called Warner Bros., and you know, first you get a switchboard operator, and you've got to kind of tell her what's going on. She figures out that the call has to go to Ted Templeman's office. So they ring Ted Templeman's office and I repeat myself. It was a woman I was speaking with. She says, 'Oh, hang on, Ronnie Montrose is right here.' And my mind is reeling. Usually Bob and I worked together, but that particular day, we somehow did not have the same shift. He wasn't going to come in until just about the time that I was due to leave."

"So in a split second, I'm thinking, oh my God, what am I going to say? I can't hang up the phone. I was kind of scared. And so Ronnie says, 'Hello, this is Ronnie Montrose' and I just winged it. I said, 'I'm a big fan and I'm a singer. And I understand that Sam is not in the band anymore. I'm wondering if you guys are looking for a singer?' And there was no... it was just seamless. 'Oh, well, do you have a tape?' And I said, 'I do, but it's a couple years old. But it's good. It's a decent tape. I'm happy with it.' And he said, 'Well, give me your information and I'll send a courier over there to pick it up. And I'll let you know what I think of it.' So, okay. So I give him the information, hang up, and I'm just... even right now, I'm kind of shaking my head, because for us, Montrose were gods. And so for this to happen was just so surreal."

"So I called up Bob, flipping out, and he didn't believe me. He didn't believe it at all. And to backtrack slightly, I had actually broached the subject with him, and he completely blew me off. He says, oh, there's no way. There's no... that's impossible. There's just no way. So anyway, I finally convinced him what was happening. I said, 'You've got to get your ass out here, because Ronnie is sending over a courier to get this tape, and he's going to call back, and I don't want to talk to him again. Because he thinks that I'm you. But I used your name. You've got to be here.'"

"So luckily I had the tape in the store," says Mike. "We had a cassette player, so it's something I'd listen to there. So this courier shows up, walks in, and says, 'I'm here to see Bob James; I'm making a pickup for Warner Bros.' I say, 'Bob is out on a delivery, but I have the tape. Here it is.' This tape was Shatterminx, three songs, and as I recall, the first track was 'Underground,' which was kind of Zeppelin-esque, very heavy, aggressive, up-tempo. And then I think there was 'Set to Sail' and then 'All of Us

Children,' and those were very progressive rock, Zeppelin meets Yes. The bass player played cello on one of the songs."

"The courier puts the tape in a large envelope and takes off, and I think what happens was, Ronnie called back right away. Like I couldn't believe it. Within I would say no more than an hour after the guy had left, he called back. He couldn't have had the tape for more than 15 or 20 minutes so I'm thinking not a good sign. I put Bob on the phone and stood there taking in the moment—was this really happening? I could only hear Bob's side of the conversation: 'Thanks, yeah, that was a couple of years ago. Yeah, I can still sing like that. Tomorrow morning, 10am? Warner Bros.? Sure, I'll see you then.'"

Picking up the tale of his strange audition process, Bob recalls, "We eventually talked, and he said come on over to my office. Of course, it wasn't his office. It was Ted Templeman's office at Warner Bros., in Burbank. Ronnie said, you know, learn this song or that song, like 'Bad Motor Scooter' or whatever. I said fine. So I showed up and he was there, and yeah, I walked in and I said, 'Ronnie?' He said, 'Yeah. Bobby?' And I said, 'Yeah.' He goes, 'Step into my office.' I said, okay, fine. So he broke out an acoustic guitar and started playing 'Bad Motor Scooter' or something. 'Okay, sing.' Okay. So I started to sing, and it was like ten minutes, and he said, 'Okay, I'm shipping you to San Francisco. We're going to Wally Heider Studios, San Francisco, and we're going to put down some tracks' and blah blah blah."

Adds Mike, "We were really excited, because we were under the assumption that he was going to walk onto some soundstage somewhere, and Bob was going to play with the band. And we thought, well hey, there's no downside to this at all. Because you're gonna get to play with our favourite band. But that's not what happened. It was Ronnie in Ted Templeman's office with an acoustic guitar. And basically right then and there, Ronnie said something to the effect of, 'As far as I'm concerned, you've got the gig. I'd like to know what the rest of the band thinks, and how it feels with the band, so I'm going to fly you up on the weekend. But as far as I'm concerned, you're in.' With this incredible news I was both thrilled and sad: my best friend had just seen a dream come true by joining our favourite band. We both said that it was like him joining Led Zeppelin—totally unreal. But at the same time I knew this meant the end of Taken Alive and that I'd never get to play those great Montrose songs onstage with Bob again."

Addressing the idea of whether Ronnie had ever considered local firecracker David Lee Roth for the band—Denny says Bryan Adams was actually mentioned as well!—Mike remembers, "As huge Montrose and Hagar fans at the time, Bob and I both wondered whether Ronnie had auditioned anybody else for the gig. We openly discussed this at the time he got the job and Bob said that he never heard any mention of other singers being considered or auditioning. Not that it couldn't have happened, but Bob had never heard any mention of it. As it so happens, there is a live Van Halen tape from right about the same moment in time, recorded at a Pasadena gig, where Roth himself addresses the issue during some between-song banter as he introduces 'Make It Last' from *Montrose* with the remark, 'Yeah man, I heard Ronnie Montrose just fired his lead singer. The guy's got an ego. I wonder if the new guy's any good?' This doesn't sound like someone who has had any personal contact with Ronnie Montrose."

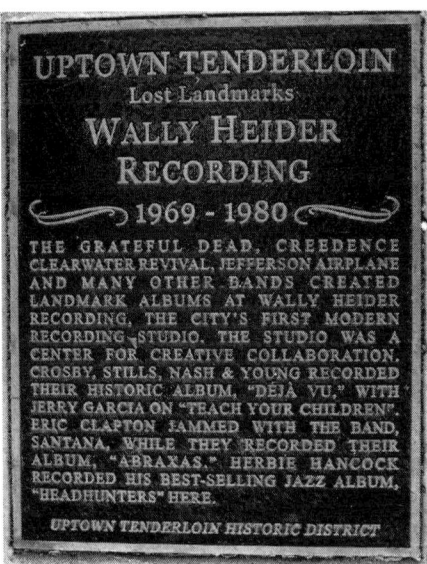

"And then they flew me out to San Francisco and I did some recording with them," confirms Bob, who reiterates as the months went on, that he never got any indication that anybody else was ever considered. "We did a few tunes off the first two Montrose albums and that old Rolling Stones song they did, 'Connection.' No one ever mentioned to me anything about Ronnie looking for other vocalists—ever. They stuck me in a vocal booth and I sang a couple of songs and then that was it. He said, 'Okay, you're in.' That's the way it happened. After that, you know, we were rehearsing at Winterland, Bill Graham's place. There were two or three or four floors in that place and we had the whole third floor, I think it was. Just carte blanche for rehearsals. We went up there and started jamming it out and writing songs. Ronnie with his big amplifiers, and Denny and Fitz, and then we had Jim Alcivar, our new keyboard player. Yeah, it was a blast; it was great. We were just getting ready for our first tour, and we only had like a month, after I joined the band. We had one month. Ronnie said, 'We've got one month to get this shit together—let's go!'"

Mike seems to recall that Bob's performance on "Connection" in particular "figured very heavily in Bob cementing the deal to be in the band. Because apparently there were some performance issues with Sammy and that song. But Bob said they were really amazed with his performance of that up there on the weekend, when he went up there to play with them live. That song in particular, they really, really liked the way he sang that. But when he got the gig, it was just like something... well, not in terms of money, but situationally, a Cinderella rags-to-riches story. Bob figured out a way to cover the weekend at the store—I think maybe even I worked for him—but we got that covered and when he came back, he was the singer for Montrose."

And then Mike got to see his buddy live for the first time... "Yes, that was here at The Shrine, and it was just incredible. To see them come out, and they're playing all the songs that I knew from the first two records, but then they're doing, I believe, 'Matriarch.' I'm pretty sure that Bob came back from that first audition weekend with him on 'Connection' and then 'Matriarch.' I think that 'Matriarch' they wrote right there that weekend. I got to meet with everybody, my mouth hanging open meeting Denny Carmassi. Interesting guys. All kind of aloof. Denny was okay to talk to for a little bit. I tried to engage with Denny; we talked drums and this and that. But the rest of them were pretty aloof. And Bob will probably tell you the story about one of those real early shows that Sammy showed up to and Ronnie wouldn't even talk to him. While Sammy was trying to be friendly with everybody, Bob said Ronnie basically just, you know, stormed off."

"But a great weekend that had happened at some point beyond that on the timeline, was a triple bill in San Francisco at Winterland. And Bob said, 'Hey, come up and hang for the whole weekend. Because we're going to do a couple of nights.' I think it was two nights. And it was UFO with Schenker, Montrose and Journey. And that was funny too, because UFO was a band we had also covered. And then the biggest gig I saw was at

The Forum, and it was Kiss at their absolute height, '76, with Montrose opening. I was sitting either at the front like the very, very front row dead in the middle of the stage, or first couple of rows, and I was just dumbfounded to look at all this stuff. I wasn't a Kiss fan, I never liked them, but to see them up close like that and see them with my best friend opening was really very special."

"It worked out pretty good," continues Bob. "Ronnie used to call me at my place and tell me he was really excited about having me with the band. Because he didn't want to be involved with Sammy anymore. I think he fired him, because Sammy, you know, was doing interviews, and Ronnie was telling Sammy, this is my band, you can't do interviews. I only do the interviews. So I think that's why Ronnie got pissed-off. You know how jealousy works, with those kind of people."

"There was a lot of talk at the time about why Sammy was fired," ventures Mike. "Ronnie said, hey, you know, we're out, and all of a sudden he's doing interviews. And I said I don't want you to do interviews. And Ronnie told Bob, you know, the name of the band's Montrose. It's not Sammy Hagar and it's not Bob James. Remember that. Ronnie really didn't like the idea of anybody in the band being the spokesman. It was his show, it was his thing. And the story also is that a lot of Sammy's vocals, purportedly had to be sung line by line. In terms of like Sammy not being able to just like do a full take. So they were flying in a verse, flying in another verse. That's what I remember at the time. It was weird for us to hear these things because you've got to remember, Sammy was our hero. We really, really loved the guy. Loved those first two records. So to kind of hear the band speak sour grapes about Sammy was a little weird. We took it with a grain of salt."

"It goes back to Denny Carmassi and Sammy Hagar," replies the band's first and only keyboardist, Jim Alcivar, asked about his entry into the ranks of Montrose. "Denny and I played for years together in just local bands, writing, a little bit a club work. And that went on for quite some time. And towards the end of that thing, we were recording, living in Petaluma, California and recording, stumbled across a singer down in San Francisco, brought him up and sang on about three or four songs on a little demo tape we were doing. Sounded really good, we were happy, and it was Sammy Hagar. And at that point in time, Ronnie was looking to put together Montrose, and he stumbled across Hagar singing in a club, approached him and they all got on well. And then it was a question of, 'Well, do you know any good drummers?' And Hagar was knocked out by Denny, and Ronnie snuck in on a gig we played up somewhere in north California, and he was knocked out, and got Denny."

"So there's Denny and Sammy becoming part of the initial band," continues Jim. "And I guess Ronnie knew Bill Church from way back when. And so that put that whole band together. A couple of albums later, I guess they started to reshuffle, and Ronnie and Sam were having difficulties, and they got Bob James to sing. And I have the feeling that both Sammy and Denny were pushing Ronnie to get me into the band, thinking it would be like 'interesting.' I write songs and play keys and all that fun stuff. And it was one of those, overnight, I get a phone call from Denny, 'Fly up here, and we're going to do an audition.' And I went into, I think it was Wally Heider's, and it was the first time I met Bob James. And we played, oh dear, 'I Got the Fire' and some other song. And it was just fast and loose. We didn't really put much effort and time into it, and after it was all done, Ronnie comes up to me and says, 'Can you travel?' I said yeah. 'Okay, you're in.' And that was it."

"Great guy, always was," offers Jim, asked for his first impressions of Bob (along with offering a slightly different rendition of Bob's audition!). "He always struck me as sort of your younger brother. And just, I don't want to say naïve, but that's actually in a pretty good sense. No attitude, no ego, he tried real hard, and always worried about, did his hair look right?, and just overall easy, nice guy to get along with. And he sang great. He was really, really good. He got the job with Ronnie by, Ronnie took an acoustic guitar and Bob down to Ted Templeman's office, and said, 'I want you to hear this singer. This is the guy I want.' Plopped him down and Ronnie strums on his acoustic, and Bob sang some songs for the Ted, which was a terrible place to audition, some cold office, and he was great. And he says, 'Done, you've got yourself a singer,' and off they went."

Adds Denny, "Bob... he was young, and he was really pretty inexperienced. You know, Ronnie rode roughshod over Bob quite a bit. Sam was a little more his own man. I think Bob was probably intimidated by Ronnie. And, you know, he was good singer and he was a nice guy. He was an easy guy to get along with. When you look back on it, yeah, there was definitely a different direction. I remember Ronnie used to like Kansas and bands like that, that had singers that could sing in those really high ranges."

As for Ronnie's view of the two new guys? Well, he didn't know much about Bob's background, that's for sure. "No, I have no idea. I know he was a local Southern California boy who was a big Montrose fan. I remember he tried out... we were sitting in Ted Templeman's office, and his enthusiasm was so great that I thought, 'OK, let's give this kid at chance.' Jim Alcivar, I don't believe he was in any other recording bands. I know he worked around California with demo bands. And he was actually in the club band that Denny Carmassi was playing in when I went in and hired Denny that first time I met him, and asked him to join Montrose."

As part of the pudding that would become *Warner Bros. Presents*, again, Ronnie was again bringing forth covers. There's a reason for that, says Jim. "This album was hilarious. It's the first one for me. We were living out in San Francisco, and we go down to LA to record it. We barrelled in there, and we were recording, and we get about three or four songs in, finish that, basic tracks, and then suddenly, okay, now what? And we're looking at each other going um, er... We had to cancel studio time immediately and rent a little rehearsal room down the corridor, and spend like a week or something, and started experimenting, putting some songs together quick. Because we didn't really have enough to do the whole album. I'm pretty sure, 'O Lucky Man' was just, we all liked the song. We were always open to outside songs that sounded good, especially as long as we could make it our own. Well, the earlier Montrose did the Stones' 'Connection,' which I thought was a great rendition."

"This was a transitional record," notes Ronnie, "because Sam and I went through the split. It was a situation where I started looking for singers. It was one of those things again where it was like, 'Let's get it going! Let's do a record; we have to keep the momentum going.' And I look back to it now actually with fondness, because of all the changes I've gone through. I look back on it and say, yes, this is now a situation where I am taking over on the production front. And while I knew it was my first production with an engineer who hadn't engineered a record before either, I look back on it and go, well, I could have done better. I look back on it and say, yes, this is part of the process I was on."

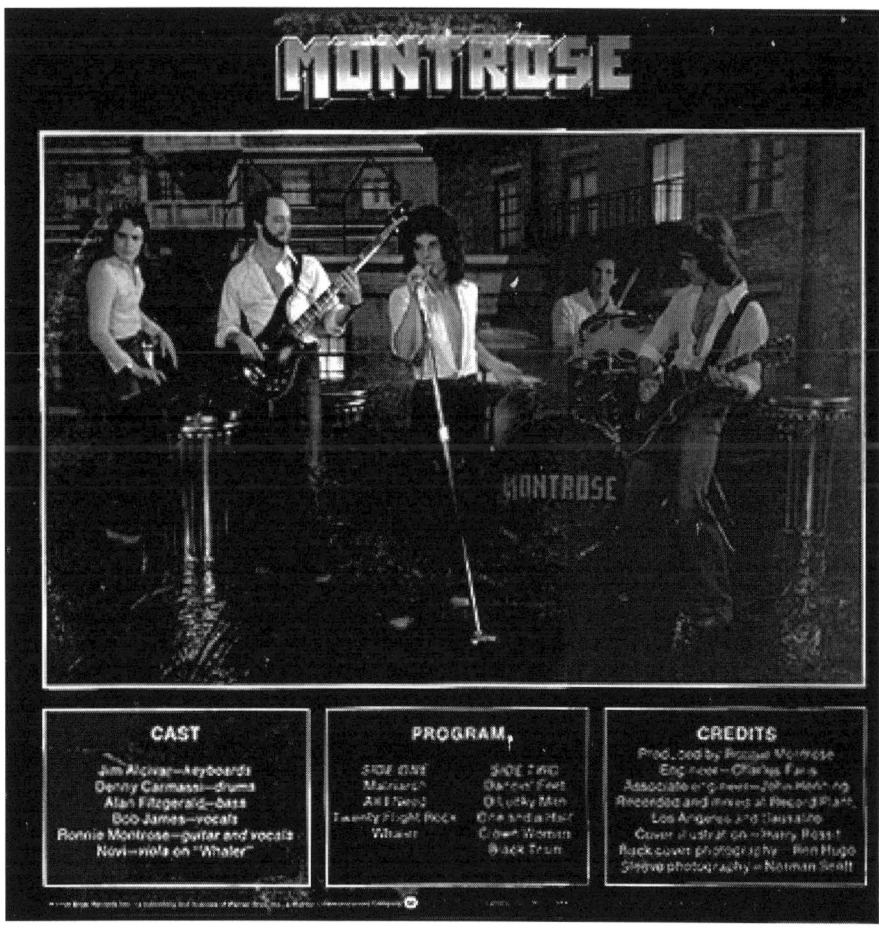

Warner Bros. Presents, recorded at The Record Plant in LA and issued in September of 1975, opens with a stunner of a track called "Matriarch." All of a sudden, not only is Ronnie Montrose back in the heavy metal zone, but he's positively British about it, writing a Rainbow song better than anything on the Man in Black's debut, and thereby Ronnie is rising before *Rising*. A Purple homage, I had asked Ronnie, who chuckled, "Wow, yes, that song, I've always liked. Without a doubt, amateurs imitating professionals." Hardly amateurs, for Denny turns in a groovy, slashing performance, Jim Alcivar and Alan Fitzgerald provide percolating critical mass like Jon Lord and Roger Glover, and new singer Bob James taps the sorrowful medieval blues phrasing of Ronnie James Dio, not that he'd ever heard of him.

There's also twin leads and a tasteful, memorable axe solo from Ronnie that ascribes nicely to the philosophy he had once explained to Steve Rosen: "Just starting slow and building up the speed— that was an invaluable lesson. A guitar player just sat me down once, grabbed me by the collar and warned, 'If you want to play fast and clean, learn to play slow and clean. Then just work your speed up.' But don't try to bullshit your notes. One thing I can say about a solo, and how to play one, is to make it like breathing. If you're going to play lead, sing it out first; then you'll know if it's going to be effective or not. If you start singing the line and have to gasp for breath, you've overextended yourself. Make your solo as vocally oriented as possible. Just as if someone were singing it, so the sound grows more human and natural."

"Matriarch" is credited to the entire band, but even on a track like this, the core of the song came down to Ronnie and Bob, who explains, "Ronnie came up with the guitar stuff, and he called me up and said, 'Hey Bob, listen to this and come up with some lyrics.' And I was like, okay, cool. So I came up with that 'Matriarch' lyric. I mean, Ronnie and I wrote several of those songs, hilariously enough, over the phone. He'd play me like guitar tracks over the phone, and he'd say, come up with some lyrics. And it sometimes ended up, Ronnie told me, 'You know, we should give credit to all the guys on these songs.' And I didn't know any better, so I was like, okay, cool, that's fine. I mean, I didn't think that was a bad idea, and no one ever really gave me any credit for doing that. But I was just a kid; I didn't know any better. So it's like, okay, fine, yeah, give them all credit."

"The way that he and Ronnie wrote," reflects Mike, "was quite peculiar, but apparently quite effective. The bulk of what they wrote, they did on the phone. Ronnie was staying at the Oakwood Garden Apartments, which is here in the Toluca Lake area, between Universal City and Burbank. It's corporate housing, and a lot of entertainment people are there."

Continues Bob, "But I'm pretty sure that song, and also 'Whaler,' was written when I was shipped up to San Francisco by Warner Bros. and was sitting in my hotel room just writing lyrics, being creative. There's not much really to say about it, except for the fact that I was being creative as a writer, and I was only 22 years old. So it was a really fun thing for me to do." Asked if there was a level of trepidation or nervousness attached to the situation, Bob told me, "No, I got an A+ in all my English class from my teachers for creative writing. So I think that's where that pretty much stemmed from. When you're a kid like that, you have all these ideals and imaginary things that you come up with, and that's pretty much where that stems from—actual creative writing."

Adds Jim on the subject of songwriting, "If you look at the credits, I almost feel like it's an emotional reaction with Ronnie, where we would all get in a room together. Sometimes we'd just kind of hash out a song right there on the spot. And that becomes sort of a group project. For those, we didn't literally sit down, okay, you write lyrics, you write the music and here's the melody. Things evolved. You'd have a line, a riff, and we'd play against that, and it would either develop or fall flat. And depending on the amount of effort and ideas contributed, then Ronnie would dole out credit and royalties based on how he felt. We never argued one way or another about that one."

As confounding as "Matriarch" is, not for its heaviness but for its Anglophile qualities, "All I Need" is equally the head-scratcher, only now because the band turn in a type of proto-power ballad, made starkly poppy by Bob's obvious and disconcerting comfort with soft rock. Yet there are proggy bits, textures, and a rocked-up chorus to the thing, Denny playing nicely ragged, the effect not unlike Bad Company.

Notes Ronnie, "I was experimenting with my fingerpicking technique and came up with this riff. Bob James had these lyrics, and they fit together quite nicely. I remember playing Winterland one night right after this was recorded and getting an ovation for the chords, even before the song kicked in!"

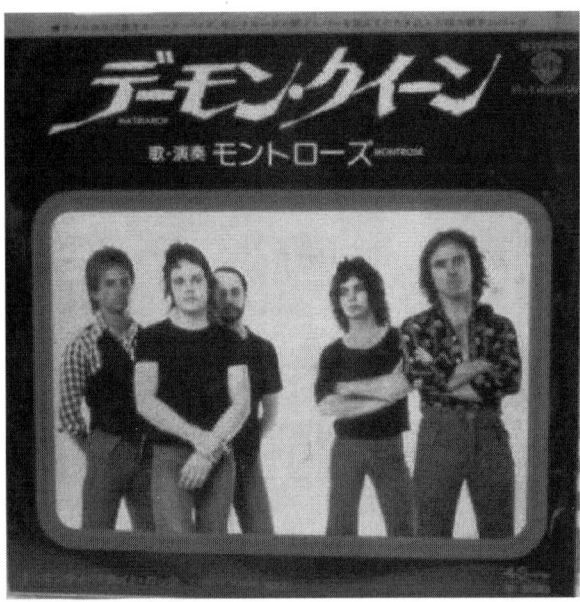

"I really love 'All I Need,'" adds James. "It was a very important song to me; it meant a lot. It kind of tells the story of a guy being in a rock 'n' roll band and being on the road. And even though you're in a total working type of situation, you know, you're there but you're not just there for your audience, but it's nice to have girls to be interested. Evidently, I was only 22 years old, so it was like, yeah, I like girls (laughs). There's a live version out there of 'All I Need' that is phenomenal, where I finally got to sing it the way that I actually wanted, more like Paul Rodgers. Which people always told me... I talked to Steve Marriott from Humble Pie. We did a couple shows with him and he's like, 'Oh, you're gonna be the next Paul Rodgers.' I'm like, oh yeah, sure."

Next up is the band's spirited cover of "Twenty Flight Rock," and one instantly thinks of how Montrose transformed "Good Rockin' Tonight," namely from old original rock 'n' roll into metal with blues roots.

"Like most people my age," says Ronnie, "I was a huge Eddie Cochran fan and still am—he was not only a great singer, but also a great rhythm guitarist. I loved this song and was thrilled the band was into covering it. It always went over big when we played it live. I feel we did it justice and still enjoy playing it even today."

This is the first song on *Warner Bros. Presents* where we really get a good look at Ronnie's production job on the record. And somewhat poetically, on a track that plays up Jimmy Page's idea of strapping new riffing onto old blues standards, it's pretty obvious that Ronnie is emulating his "lord and master" when it comes to production as well. For indeed, even if the production on *Montrose* was clearly better in a number of ways, *Warner Bros. Presents* is more Zeppelin-esque, with its dry sounds, its room ambience and its boxy drums. And if I dare venture any further, what Ronnie does here ranks with the best of Jimmy's jobs, sort of in that *Physical Graffiti* to *Presence* zone, if not as satisfying as *In Through the Out Door*.

"Great, I'm glad," responds Ronnie as to this assessment. "At the time I thought there were serious problems with what I had done, and then I get e-mails and your comment, from fans and friends who say they love that record. The record was a situation where I was trying to... I went down into the Record Plant and was working on just whatever tunes that we had available, and using an engineer who hadn't really cut a record before. And it was one of those... everyone has peaks and valleys in their life. You do for writing, for everything. And that was a valley for me. It was a valley of just an experience chalked up, you know? That which doesn't kill you makes you stronger."

As for whether it drove him crazy producing, Ronnie says, "Yeah, it really did. It was very taxing. I was feeling the pressure of not only putting out the music but also to be on the top of my game playing it and technically, as a guitarist, getting the tone that I wanted but also the situation of making sure everything else was correct at the same time. I have to add, it just blows my mind the conjecture that came from that title, *Warner Bros. Presents*. People were saying, 'What is this? Are you under contract from Warners to do this?' And no, it was specifically done because of the artist who did the cover, as a film spoof. That was the only reason, but we got a lot of different takes on it."

In fact, some versions of the front cover art lack any reference to Warner Bros. presenting, with fans having to go to the spine and the record centrepiece to divine the name of the record. Additional to the movie set shot of the band on the back, courtesy of Ron Hugo, the esteemed Norman Seeff, who had done the debut album, was brought back for an artful soft focus shot of the band filling one side of the lyric insert. Says Mike Kelley, "Bob had told me that they actually filmed what you see on that back cover shot. It was done on a movie set, and Bob says they actually filmed a movie. They played the entire record on this movie set and filmed it. Ronnie just decided, no, forget it, just shelved it. Bob has long wanted to have that released."

"You know, big drums, big sound," reflects Denny, asked about his ties to Bonham, which can clearly be divined from pictures of his kit as well as his approach to a song like "Twenty Flight Rock." "Obviously, everybody, a lot of guys grew up influenced by John Bonham and Carmine Appice. That was a special era of drumming." And as I say listen to "Twenty Flight Rock" or "Dancin' Feet," and you can clearly hear those celebrated Bonham tones... "You know, on the first Montrose album, I didn't know much about recording drums. I'd only played on one other album up to that point. I knew how to tune my drums, but to actually get the sound, that was Donn Landee and Ted Templeman. And on *Warner Bros. Presents*, we were probably influenced by that, but more so experimenting with room mic'ing. Because the first record, I remember Donn would use like a lot of close mic'ing—until we went to Sunset Sound for 'Rock Candy.' That was more of a bigger sound, because it was using the room. And I think that's what we tried to do on *Warner Bros. Presents*. To try to use more of the room and not so much close mic'ing."

For Bob James, it was pretty significant that there was no Ted Templeman this time. Really, for the whole Montrose franchise it was significant, because having Ted and Donn on board might have lessened the feeling of radical change, given the switch in singers and the addition of a keyboardist. There's even a theory that Ted was resentful at being sidelined by Ronnie, and that what he did so gloriously with Van Halen not three years later was in part to show Ronnie what could have been had he not been so divisive.

Not so, says Bill Church, good friend of Ted's since the beginning, who says, first off, Ted was anything but sidelined by Ronnie. "What had happened was because he was a staff producer at Warner Bros—he wasn't an independent at that time; he was a staff producer—he was on the line after the *Montrose* album basically bombed. By their standard back then, it wasn't what they were expecting. He was on the line with *Paper Money* because not only was the band now different, but now the second album better be way better, right? And, of course, the second album was a... well, I won't even pass comment on it. It did not cut the mustard. Ronnie fired me and Sammy, but he didn't fire Ted. No, no, after *Paper Money*, Ted was going because he is not going to want to ask for things that aren't selling. First of all, Warner Brothers is not going to let him. And now, I suspect that he's glad that he didn't produce that bomb (laughs)."

Meaning *Warner Bros. Presents*. Plus, on top of that, things between Ted and Ronnie had been going south already on *Paper Money*. "Yes, as I explained before, the original masters were already done. They were already in the can, so Ted had to come back out now and replace stuff, me with Fitz, and replace other stuff, and redo a new song and all that, with Ronnie co-producing. So at that point, you could be pretty much assured that Ted, if you were to ask him, I bet he would tell you that at that point he put in as little effort as he could."

But this all does indeed have a link with Van Halen, although in Bill's view, it has nothing with showing up Ronnie. "Now after *Paper Money*, as I say, Ted is really on the line with Warner Bros., and then so he had to go out and literally do a stopgap. He went out and made a really incredible choice. Got a band that had exactly the same lineup as Montrose, know what I mean? Prime guitar player, three-piece band with a front man, American, from California, oh, and I don't have to tell you their story. But yeah, Van Halen happened because Ted was on the line at that time, with Joe Smith, president of Warner Bros. Records."

"I really was disappointed by that, actually," begins Bob, on losing Ted's helmsmanship of Montrose. "Because I had absolutely no clue, no idea what was going on. I was very excited about working with Ted. I mean, the guy's a freaking genius, first of all. Once we started doing the recording here in Los Angeles, it was like, 'Where's Ted?' Ronnie's like, 'No, I'm producing' (laughs). For an engineer, we worked with Charles Faris, who unfortunately has passed away in the past few years from cancer. But Charles and I ended up being like the closest friends on earth. I just absolutely loved the guy, and we became best friends on the road. All kinds of stories. He became our sound man and we were on the road for two-and-a-half years. It was just a knockout. Playing live, whether we opened the show or we headlined, our audience would not let us off the stage. We always got at least one encore, if not three. And yeah, it was crazy. We were a total kick-ass band (laughs)."

"Charles was hired personally by Ronnie, from New York" continues Bob. "I think he met him when he was with the Edgar Winter Group. And he hired Charles as an engineer because he was comfortable with him. Ronnie pretty much had to take control of all things, which was fine, because he had the experience, working with Edgar Winter and then starting his own band, hiring Denny and Sammy and Bill Church. And so yeah, those guys had a good thing going on. But I just loved the original band and I loved the sound. Like I said, it was really the production that knocked me out. It wasn't necessarily the band or Ronnie Montrose or anything. It just sounded so phenomenal. But Charles had a lot of good things going on, being an electrician kind of guy and into that aspect of it. I'm not saying he's the best engineer and I'm not saying that he was actually ever allowed to let loose, while working with Ronnie. Because Ronnie was just that kind of guy. He had his own ideas, unbeknownst to the rest of us (laughs), which probably we would've had much more to say about things, but that's just how it worked out. But it was kind of earth-shaking for me to find out that Ronnie decided to be Mr. Producer (laughs). And, you know, I was just a kid, 22 years old. 'Where's Ted? Where's Ted?' And Ronnie's like, 'No, there's no Ted. There's no nothing. It's me. I'm handling this situation.' I'm like, uh-oh."

"So I and the rest of the guys in the band, including Denny and everybody, couldn't figure out why Ronnie wanted to become Mr. Producer. But he gave it a good shot, and he did a lot of great guitar tracks. Ronnie always told me, he said, 'Bob, you know, I'm not the greatest guitar player. I know my limitations' blah blah blah, and he tried his best. But in the end run, we were all kind of disappointed, because we didn't have that Ted Templeman sound when it was done. So that was the most disappointing thing between me and the rest of the members of the band. Because they are obviously all excellent musicians. Denny, to me, is the most killer kick-ass drummer on earth. But I was kind of wishing for more heavy guitars going on in some spots, maybe 'Whaler.' But production was up to Ronnie at that point. I don't think Warner Bros. was really excited about this (laughs). I'm sure if you talk to several musicians or writers, you'll hear that working with Ronnie was actually really difficult. I'm not putting any blame on the guy. You know, it was a heads-up kind of thing. He of course played with Edgar Winter and stuff. I mean, those guys came out and saw our shows. In Chicago I hooked up with Linda Blair, an old friend of mine. It was a crazy time; just wonderful."

"Well, it's Ronnie's band," sighs Denny. "Ronnie kind of fancied himself as a producer. He thought he knew enough to where he didn't need somebody like Ted. But Ted is a very valuable guy, man. That's a guy that really brings a lot to the table and has a lot of wisdom and experience. You just look at his track record; he wasn't a one trick pony. He could produce anybody. And so that probably wasn't the smartest decision. To get away from Ted. But that had already been starting on *Paper Money*. You could see the cracks in the relationship already back then. You know, you've been around for a while. You've heard the stories about Ronnie. We don't need to get into that. He was a difficult guy to get along with, for people—he was difficult. So that's about all I can say about it."

Charles Faris, says Jim, "was an engineer for Eventide, made all the harmonizers and delay lines, so he was good at electronics and tech but not terribly proficient in the studio. We had some tuning problems, but mostly when I listen back, it could've been mixed better. Sonically and level-wise and whatnot. But that's how you always feel. But what I also think is happening is that Ronnie is coming from a place of just bass, drums, guitar, singer. Hard-up-against-it, in-your-face rock. And suddenly he's wandering down this little path of, oh, now we've got some keyboards and synthesizers and sound effects, and we brought in a girl named Novi, to play a viola on 'Whaler.' So it was sort of his introduction into a little bit more sonics than just the straight rock set-up. So I think he was learning too. Again, there could've been some things mixed better. But I still get compliments on that album which sort of surprises the heck out of me."

Speaking of "Whaler," this near seven-minute track closes side one of the original vinyl. And yes, here Ronnie pulls out al the production stops, on a mournful song that evokes the death knell of a busted ship hopelessly drifting at sea.

"'The Whaler,' naturally, is the one I prefer the most because it's a lot more key-oriented," points out Alcivar. "And it's a lot more orchestrated. And that really is more what I do, rather than sit down and go, 'Now I'm gonna play my pianos and organs and stuff.' To this day, I like hearing a song and going, okay, well, it has this little cello part going over here, and these little strings doing the pizzicato. It's more like colour painting with a brush and bringing in different ideas and chops in and out and whatnot. As opposed to your 'Matriarch,' which is gonna be following Ronnie's lines and just doing chords and basic rock stuff that you hear all the time. Or 'Twenty Flight Rock,' which has very simple and slight rock 'n' roll piano running through it."

As a reminder, Montrose covered Chunky, Novi & Ernie's "Underground" one record back. Here Novi Novog reappears, this time as a performer, as an encore performance as it were to another great guest cameo, namely on the Doobie Brothers' "Black Water," from the Ted Templeman-produced *What Were Once Vices Are Now Habits*.

"I wrote that song in my hotel room," recalls Bob. "It's really funny, because it was a big hit in Canada. And we were in Canada and we were headlining a show over Styx. They were pissed-off, because we were headlining the show over them. But it was because of 'Whaler.' I can't remember if they refused to do it, but they were like, you know, we're supposed to headline. Canada just picked up on that song like crazy. But it's not necessarily a song about a whaler. The song is actually about a young man trying to do his best in any type of situation where he needs to get to work and do the best that he can. It has nothing to do with killing whales, that's for sure. Because I love animals; I'm an animal lover. It had to do with a young man doing something that he needed to do, to cooperate with whatever needs to happen as far as him being successful, to get his shit together and work (laughs). And so it was kind of exciting as far as concept was concerned. And then Ronnie brought in Novi; oh, she was excellent! She was exciting. But people took that lyric several different ways. But you never know when you write lyrics. You kind of expound on certain situations, you get a bit creative, and that's pretty much what I did. The song was not about killing whales—that's for damn sure."

Over to side two, and fans starved for a second hard rock original from Montrose get it with "Dancin' Feet," a funky metal rocker distinguished by an erudite and jazzy bass line from Alan Fitzgerald.

"Alan Fitzgerald was an excellent bass player," notes Bob. "He was kind of a space cadet, but I always loved him. He ended up being keyboard player and bass player for Night Ranger. And he did an excellent, excellent job. He added, I don't know, just something really different. He was super-smart. Very intelligent, great human being, nice guy, but yeah, he definitely was out there. The funny thing about him was, like, when I first joined the band, he was a bit difficult to speak with because you could ask him a question, and he would not answer it until the next day. Airport to airport, when we were on tour, we were like constant—the Montrose that I was with was a constant working band. I mean, we were working, working, working. There was no sleep, no nothing. But when we did get a chance to talk, it was like we would be in an airport in, say, Chicago, and I'd ask Alan a question, and he wouldn't answer me. I was like, wow, that's weird. And the next day, in the next city, he would answer the question. I'm like, 'What?! I asked you that question yesterday.' And he'd be, 'Oh yeah.' That's just the kind of guy he was. But super-talented, great bass player, great musician, wonderful guy. But he didn't really sit in with the rest of us."

"We were just a working band," continues Bob, "and all kind of short guys, you know, 5'7", stuff like that. Ted Nugent used to call us The Munchkin Band (laughs). Because I don't know how tall he was, but compared to us.... I thought that was a funny statement. But Ted, I never thought that he was that great. I always thought that Ronnie was a much better guitar player than he was. But he seemed to work his way up in rock 'n' roll status better. But I don't have any idea how that worked. I definitely thought Ronnie was going to come out on top. There was no doubt in my mind at that time."

Ronnie remembers 'Dancin' Feet' as "an infectious party groove song! David Roth and Eddie Van Halen told me later that they loved to play this song at their jams and parties. I would play it live, and other guitarists I was touring with would specifically come up and insist that I throw in all of the riffs in between the chords like I did on the record… so I did!"

Adds Bob, "'Dancin' Feet' was a situation where I had wished… I love the lyrics and it's a real fun song, but again, it didn't come off the way it was supposed to come off. It didn't sound like a real dancing kind of song. It just depends on who you are. I mean, you can dance to it but I was thinking, gee, 'Dancin' Feet,' this song should be a little more danceable, don't you think? It was funny, because we were at The Record Plant in Los Angeles, and we had Joe Walsh recording his stuff next door to us. During my break of doing vocals, I would be walking by and hearing Joe Walsh in the next door studio doing his stuff."

"'Dancin' Feet' was kind of a weird song," laughs Jim. "I wouldn't want to claim that one for copyright or anything. I know I was kind of blown away by the whole experience of it all, so I was just happy to do whatever, anything they wanted me to do. Both me and Bob were pretty tickled with it all."

"O Lucky Man" marks another example of Ronnie finding a fairly obscure song to cover, and once again, no mind paid to fit for the band, not that there were any rules. Nonetheless the Montrose arrangement of this singer/songwriter-like Alan Price song is raucous enough, the band creating a noisy pop filled up with energetic drumming (underscored by fills, ride cymbals and open high hat sizzle), multiple keyboard tracks, distorted chords and a typical stadium rock guitar solo. The song is one of many Price had written for the lengthy and experimental UK film *O Lucky Man!*, issued in 1973 and starring Malcolm McDowell.

"It was pretty much Ronnie who came up with the songs," notes Bob. "He liked the fact of changing modes from the original Montrose. We had other songs that Ronnie and I had talked about, but he was interested in doing these other songs, I think, pretty much because of the guitar track he wanted to create on the tracks. He was fond of changing some of these older songs, and felt comfortable adding his own Ronnie Montrose style to them. I think the songs that he chose for *Warner Bros. Presents* were great and I think the lyrics were great."

Next up is one-and-a-half minutes of straight-up instrumental Led Zeppelin *III* called "One and a Half," featuring an alternate "drone" tuning where the two E strings are tuned down to D. As soon as one hears those flagrantly Pagey acoustics, it becomes hard to ignore how much *Warner Bros. Presents* resembles in construction a Led Zeppelin album. There's the middle eastern-tinged epic rocker, an acoustic instrumental, a Bonham-esque drum sound (and slight nods to Bonzo from the drummer himself). There's widdly riffs, there's the *Presence* vibe of "Dancin' Feet," and as direct as "One and a Half" is the conceptual idea of "Twenty Flight Rock," where Ronnie takes an old rock 'n' roll number and applies a whole new heavy metal riff to it while keeping the frame. Sure, there's keyboards, Bob never tries to evoke Robert Plant (whilst Sammy sometimes did), and "All I Need" and "O Lucky Man" don't fit the script. But there's enough here to draw comparisons to a certain band at the height of their powers, issuing just seven months earlier, *Physical Graffiti*, arguably the greatest rock 'n' roll album of all time.

Granted "Clown Woman" doesn't quite fit the conspiracy either, although take off the jazzy piano work and what's left is a murky blues rocker drinking at a tavern near the intersection of *Presence* and Mick Taylor-era Stones.

"That was Ronnie's idea," shrugs Bob. "I think the song speaks for itself. It was a trying song for me to get through. At the time, actually, I think I was tired when singing the song. To me, it really wasn't getting anywhere. But I was thinking, I've got to do my job. I've got to get this done. It was just kind of hard spiritually. Because it's a song about a girl that wears too much makeup. Whatever. Blah blah blah (laughs); I don't know if anyone ever got that. But it was also an added song to the album."

Says Ronnie, "I wanted a steamy, sultry slide guitar feel for this one. In the '70s, I was aware of many women who wore so much makeup and had fingernails so long it was a challenge for them to dial a telephone! Which isn't meant as a put-down—I was just amazed by their commitment to a look that was so high maintenance."

Warner Bros. Presents closes as slammin' as it opens, with the album's other uncompromising heavy metal number, "Black Train." This song was written by singer/songwriter Kendell Kardt, ex-of-Rig, who recorded the song in its much lighter and acoustic original form with both Jerry Garcia and Ronnie as part of the session. Its poetic and relentlessly dark cautionary tale about the evils of heroin fit well with Ronnie's vehement anti-drugs policy for his band. The song was to appear on Kardt's shelved *Buddy Bolden* album.

Recalls Jim, "Jerry Garcia and Ronnie were kind of fiddling around working with this guy. And I think that's where Ronnie heard it, or picked it up. And then it struck his mind, oh, we can do our own version. That's usually what this came out to. We would do covers only if we could make them different. And we were the only ones who would play it a certain way. And from what I understand, our version of "Black Train" is a lot harder than the guy originally wrote it."

Says Kendell, "I met Ronnie in 1971 and invited him to work on an album project of my original songs which was slated to be released by Capitol Records. Bill Graham was my manager at the time. I believe he recommended Ronnie. We got along well and he played on all the tracks for that record, which however, was never released—too bad; it was a good record. In addition to lead guitar, Ronnie also played lap steel, mandolin and acoustic guitar. It was a pleasure to work with him. Several years later, after Ronnie had started Montrose, he asked me for permission to record 'Black Train' with his band. The song was written to memorialize a friend who had died of a heroin overdose. As for Ronnie, I'll simply say he was very intense, but in a good way. He radiated a cheerful confidence that was good to be around. As for Jerry, I was very impressed with his overall level of musicianship, a quality that wasn't always evident with the Dead. He was a 'star,' of course, which meant he usually arrived late to the session with three or four roadies in tow—and he had some killer weed for 'social' occasions (laughs). Overall, it was a great time to be living in the Bay Area in spite of professional disappointments—and I survived, with some wonderful memories."

"I think it's a great song," adds Bob. "Like again and again and again, I don't think it was produced properly. But I think it's a fabulous song. Speaking about a person who is an addict and going through that type of situation, that was pretty much Ronnie's decision on that song. I have absolutely no idea why he chose that, but I just went along with it."

Warner Bros. Presents would stall at #79 in the Billboard charts, marking another under-performing record for the band, even if Montrose were causing significant damage as a live act. Writes Creem's Joe Fernbacher, amusingly about the record's two heaviest tracks, "Dancing outa his rock abattoir, Ronnie runs roughshod through the void with a Deep Purple-intoned piece of purulence laconically tagged 'Matriarch.' Emblematic of all cosmic indolence and frenetic lyrical imagism, this song spills over the edge of the world into the heebie-jeebie hallucinatory world of Jim Starlin's 'Warlock' Marvel books. Creeping along close behind is a necropolis mass transit commercial 'Black Train,' whose underlying deathblow guitar larceny is highly reminiscent of Savoy Brown's 'Hellbound Train' and Black Sabbath's classic hymn to uselessness, 'Into the Void.'"

"Coming off a flat second album, Montrose could've gone in several directions," muses Rolling Stone's Andy McKaie. "Unfortunately, for their purposes, and considering their limitations, they chose the wrong one. Instead of reenergizing themselves to the raw, hard-rock fervour of their debut, they've reemphasize the core proficiency that made their second LP, *Paper Money*, lifeless. While the new members elevate Montrose to a previously unattainable level of professionalism, the results are slick and spiritless. This, combined with the seeming refusal of leader/guitarist Ronnie Montrose to unleash anything resembling the rhythm and lead barrages that made the debut LP so attractive, makes this release utterly pedestrian."

As for Mike Kelley's assessment of the record featuring his best buddy at the mic, "First of all, I couldn't believe the huge change, once again, in direction. With me and my friends, we thought, oh, keyboard player—maybe a nod to Deep Purple here. But I really loved it. I love the diversity of it, and what I was really shocked by was how progressive it was. Like the song 'Whaler,' that sounded just like Shatterminx. When I heard that song, I thought, oh my God, this is Shatterminx. Because Mike Culiani, the guitar player and writer for Shatterminx and later Swan, lived and worked in San Pedro, and he was actually a dock worker here. And Bob knew that culture very well as well. So when I heard 'Whaler,' I thought, oh my God, this is a total Shatterminx song. It's got the spirit of San Pedro and the fishing industry and all of that stuff."

"Actually, in the early days of Bob's tenure, Ronnie liked a Shatterminx song called 'Silverwind' and expressed a desire to cover it on the album. Ronnie and Mike spoke by phone a number of times and Mike said Ronnie was quite congenial and inquisitive, asking for instance, 'How do you play the chords for 'Silverwind?' As Montrose got deeper into pre-production, Ronnie decided against using 'Silverwind' but it was on the table for a time. It's another example of Ronnie's interest and openness with regard to doing covers. So I loved the album, but I wasn't crazy about the production which I thought sounded kind of hollow and mid-rangey. I thought that it lacked that crunch and wall-of-sound quality that the first two records had."

Shedding a bit more light on why Ronnie was producing, Kelley explains that "at the time, Bob told me that Ronnie didn't want to work with Ted anymore—he wanted to do it on his own. Now fast-forward however many decades later, and I met Ted in October last year, and we spoke about a lot of things. We talked about that record and Bob James and I asked him about that, and he said, 'You know, I just remember that I was busy with other things.' But Ted is a very diplomatic guy. So again, who knows what the real truth was at the time?"

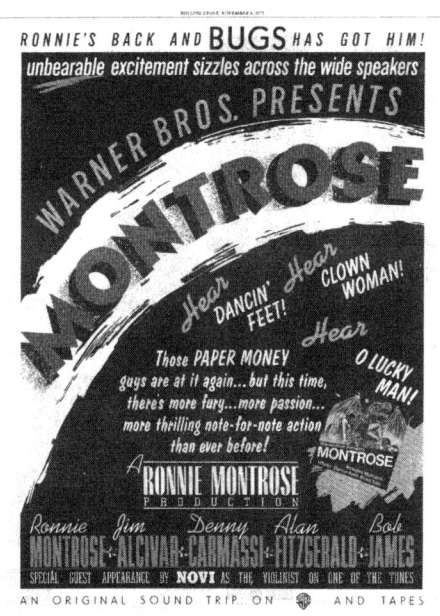

But as Bob James often comes back to, recording aside, Montrose were a live act working often and with passion. He might have been enjoying himself, but less so the boss. "Right about now, it really gets gruelling," Ronnie told Rolling Stone's John Grissim. "The gigs have been good, but after two months into the tour, the last thing I wanna know about is standing on stage. The thrill of rock 'n' roll at this point is absolutely gone. There's nothing left. Musically, I feel weird because a lot of people conceptualize me to be a typical heavy metal rocker. You know, hardcore, fuck 20 chicks a night, snort coke and party all night, beat people up or whatever. But I'm not. I don't even drink."

And yet even this version of the band, working their way through a switch in lead singers, could do no wrong live, even as they were testing the crowd's patience with old rock 'n' roll covers over and above those on the records, as well as quickly dropping the songs from the Sammy Hagar records.

"Our first gig was like totally packed, like 7000 people," says Bob, suggesting this was up San Jose way. "And I had absolutely no idea what I was doing (laughs). And no booze, no drugs, no nothing. I think I was allowed to have a beer. And it was funny, because when we first walked out of the dressing room down to the stage, I believe I was with Barry Imhoff, from our management, Fat Man Productions. And when I walked down, I smelled marijuana, and I said, 'I smell smoke. I smell marijuana.' He looks at me, and he goes, 'Jesus, are you out of your goddamn mind? Haven't you ever been to a concert?' And I was like, holy shit. It just stank of weed. But anyway, we just hit the stage and the lights came on, bam, bam, bam, everything. We came on with 'Matriarch' and there's Ronnie playing and Denny doing 'Matriarch' going nuts. And I couldn't move until like after the second song. And then after I realized what was going on, we just went fucking nuts. We went fucking crazy. It was great. Really fun stuff. I gotta tell ya, it was a total kick-ass band."

Jim Alcivar suggests that the first gig or at least a very early gig would have been at their home base of Winterland, "which was a fabulous venue. Upstairs, through a locked staircase was a whole rehearsal room that we took over and commandeered. Every once in a while, they would haul all the junk down to the stage and we'd play on the stage, and that made that place ideal. And it was all Bill Graham-owned and he was our manager, so it was all very convenient."

Asked if Winterland would hold 7000 people, Jim says, "Pretty darn close. Bill was a master at cheating the fire marshals. He could fill a building and get away with it, without any problems. Yeah, it was not small; it was a great big ice rink, and several tiered balconies all the way, even behind the stage. It was huge. And just thinking, I don't think we did any shows before making the record; I really don't. And I'm guessing too. It would not make sense, because we'd want to come out with our own thing. For songs, we'd do covers and we did 'Bad Motor Scooter' and whatnot just to keep the flow and the fans happy. But at that point, we'd also want to be doing the new stuff off the new album. It would surprise me if we did any shows before."

Bob also figures Winterland, commonly estimated at 5400, could hold 7000. "Absolutely. Oh, Winterland, I mean, when we played that place, the lines were around blocks and blocks, waiting to get in. I mean, when we played there, they couldn't fit enough people in there. It was insane. Live, early on, we did most of the songs off our first album, plus we probably did 'Rock Candy' and 'Bad Motor Scooter.' Actually, Sammy came and saw us, I think, first time we played Winterland. He was out in the audience. And later, actually, we did shows with him with his new band, a few other gigs in California. He came into our dressing room and we chatted for a bit. Good guy. We were just cool with each other. Like, what can you say? (laughs). We were good. Those guys were probably pretty much in shock at that time, as per what was going on between them. So I don't think that either one of them really had much to say to each other. All I knew about the firing was that Ronnie didn't like Sammy doing interviews; I knew that much. But I stayed out of their personal or business type of situation. I really actually didn't care (laughs). It was none of my business."

A highlight of the *Warner Bros. Presents* tour cycle would have to be the band's show at the Cotton Bowl in Dallas, July 6th, 1975, at which Montrose shared the state with Trapeze, Joe Walsh, The Eagles and headliner Rolling Stones, who had Billy Preston along as a special guest. Otherwise, the band found themselves grouped with other hard rock bands of the day, busting their asses trying to make a living, most prevalently Foghat and Black Oak Arkansas.

Asked if he or the band had any rituals or warm-up routines before hitting the stage, Bob says there was never any time as it was usually pretty much straight from the hotel to the gig. "A couple of times I put a pillow in front of my face and screamed," says Bob. "I'm sure if you talk to a lot of lead singers out there, they probably have done this. It's a little secret (laughs). You put a pillow in front of your face and you scream and you kind of get your voice going that way. It gets you warmed up. What else you gonna do? Kind of a fun thing. But I tell ya, when we first got together, it was a match made in heaven. I mean, me and the band... the rest of the guys were just so happy to have me in the band; it was just wonderful. Management and everything, everyone treated me like gold. And it was just a wonderful, wonderful thing. With Bill Graham, F.M. Productions, Fat Man Productions... Barry Imhoff had a side deal going with Bill Graham at that time. He was kind of managing us, but Bill Graham wanted to make sure that we were like on big stages. Those guys put us on every huge show imaginable. It was a crazy working band. And like I say, we could never leave the stage. Whether we were opening the show or closing the show or headlining or what, people just would not let us go. It was insane."

Mike says by this point he wasn't seeing much of Bob, even when he was back in LA, going so far as to say he had become reclusive. "Well, you know, I was playing, he was playing, and when he came back, he would just kind of hole up in his house. I think he was renting a house; he was in an area called Walteria. But when he would get home from a little tour break, he basically just wanted to stay at home. We would go out and maybe have dinner or go for a walk or something, go see a movie or whatever, but I could not get him to go to any gigs at all."

But there's an interesting crossing of paths with Van Halen at this juncture as well, says Kelley. "Yeah, fast forward to 1976 and there is a bit of a Montrose/Van Halen connection. Through drummer Skip Gillette, who would later play on the first Gamma, I was introduced to Eddie Van Halen at the Starwood in early 1976; we were both there to see Skip's band Straightjacket. Eddie talked about how his band Van Halen were going to be making their all-originals debut there in a couple of weeks and wasn't sure if he could do it. He felt very nervous and intimidated at the prospect of playing at the Starwood. At Eddie's invitation I came back to the Starwood to see Van

Halen's first all-originals gig in Hollywood. Though I knew the band's name from Gazzarri's and the local cover circuit, I'd never seen them or even heard anything about them. I really had no idea what to expect. By the end of their opening number, 'Let's Get Rockin'' I knew I was seeing probably the greatest rock guitarist alive. I stood there shaking my head and laughing as I said to myself, 'Holy shit! *This* guy was afraid to get up there?!'"

"Eddie and I talked for a bit after their set and I ended up going to see many of the early Van Halen gigs at the Starwood, during which Eddie and I would talk. At one point the subject of Montrose and Bob James came up, and I told Eddie the story of how Bob got the gig. By this time I had also told Bob James about Eddie, insisting that Bob had to see Van Halen when he was on a break from Montrose. Eddie was keen to have me bring Bob to a Van Halen gig and asked if I might be able to get Bob to jam at a Van Halen rehearsal. I said I'd do my best and did, lobbying Bob to come with me to see this incredible guitarist. But Bob was always too burned-out from the road to go out clubbing or jamming; when he came back home on a break he just wanted to chill. But when Bob finally heard Eddie, he was dumbfounded and said, 'I should've listened to you and jammed with those guys!'"

When I asked Ronnie to assess *Warner Bros. Presents* from a vantage point decades, later, he tells me, "I'm now looking at them as a body of work that is the past. And I'm looking at the connected lines of where each one goes so that none of them, even the first one, defines anything other than where I was at that moment. And it's always in motion. And it's always growing and changing and evolving. So I look at them as part of the past, part of the journey. I don't think I changed that much in terms of guitar, but if anything, my writing might have changed. I was certainly experimenting more with the guitar tones, and 25 years later I still am. That's part of the process; that's what I enjoy. With *Warner Bros. Presents*, that was an unfortunate record on all counts because I was trying to produce when I wasn't capable of producing at the time. I didn't have the ears or the chops, but I wanted to do it because I wasn't happy with everything else that was going on."

For his part, Denny Carmassi was never as excited as he was back in '73, on that first genre-defining, earth-quaking record for the original band... "No, absolutely, there was definitely a special chemistry between the four of us. Unfortunately, when you are 25 years old, you don't realize this. There is a certain bonding that we went through together. To this day, I'm still friends with Sam and Ronnie. After the lineup started to change, it just wasn't the same. They were a great bunch of guys and they all brought something to the table in they're own way, but the chemistry was shot."

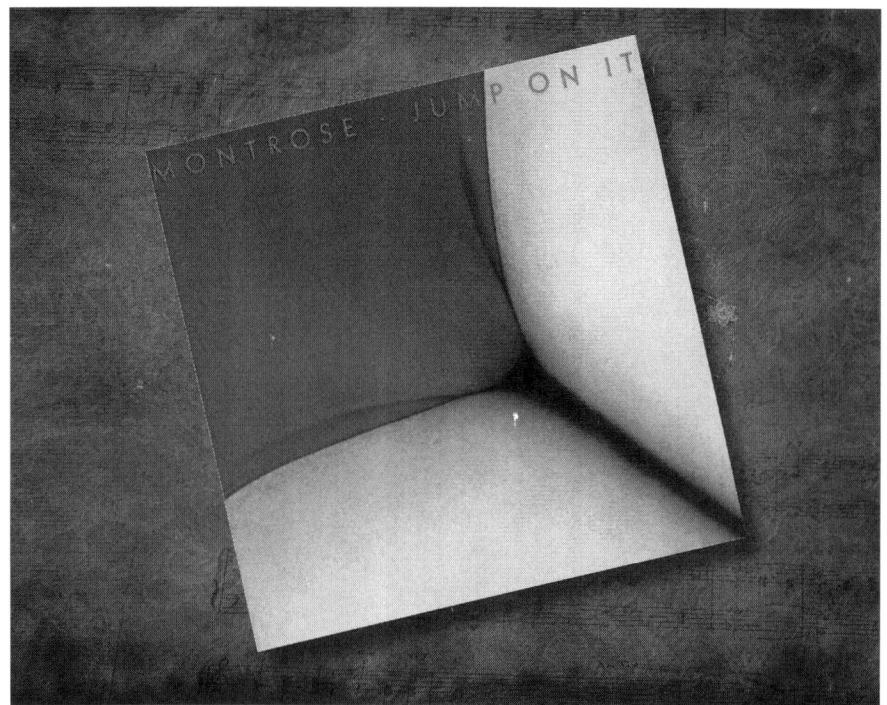

CHAPTER 5: Montrose - *Jump on It* – "Bobby, what's the name of this band?"

In September of 1976, Montrose would return with their second album of the Bob James era and as we might expect, there'd be a further disorienting shift in the band's sound. Gone would be the hard surface Led Zepplin-ness of the band's urgent first stab, replaced by a kind of aloofness that is underscored by *Jump on It*'s quietly edgy album art.

"I remember being approached by the band, and Ronnie Montrose, who was asking for an album cover," relates Aubrey Powell of famed album graphics shop Hipgnosis. "And in those days, we had pretty much carte blanche. Hipgnosis had gained a reputation as very much a laterally-thinking studio and not, you know, going along with just taking a photograph of a band on an album cover. We were known for photo designs and our more surreal approach. And our aim was to do something which, probably these days, would seem rather sexist. But our aim was to be more subtle. We were looking for was a graphic which was striking and at the same time had overtones of sexuality. And there's the red, and of course, it's interesting, Sammy Hagar, when he left Ronnie Montrose used red as his theme, with his guitar and his clothes, and in fact, we did a cover with him where the whole idea was all based on red. We ended up doing several covers with Sammy."

"But the brief was, really, something that was sexy and was hot, like the band, but something that Hipgnosis would not approach in an obvious way. We were not the kind of design studio that would create what I would call a tits and ass kind of cover. Which you could see on many album covers in those days. We were looking for something more subtle. And I'd say that the graphic shape of the lower abdomen of a woman, both on the front and back, created a striking image. And in no way is it sexual at all. It's more to do with the shape, which is a Y shape. It's a very graphic, lovely cover. And they were over the moon about it. It covered the full range of things for them. Most importantly, it was attention-catching, sight-catching. Because of course in those days, you went in a record store and there were thousands and thousands of album covers. These were the days when albums sold tens of millions, and to have something that stuck out from the crowd was very important."

Recalls Jim Alcivar on the picking of the covers, "The first one, *Warner Bros. Presents*, it does bring a movie scene to mind and I think that's how that came out; I really wasn't privy to it. With *Jump on It*, it was explained to Ronnie, as well as us, what was going to be this kind of arty, just this colour panel thing. You really can't tell what it looks like or what it is. It's real, like, you know, French, classy, unusual, and if you really thought about it, you might go, I know what that is. Well, we were out on the road somewhere having dinner and the delivery came in with the cover: 'It's done; here it is, guys.' We opened it up, looked at it, and all went, 'Oh my God!' (laughs). And it's like, okay, there's nothing you can do, it's all printed and pressed and released and done. And you just kind of bear with that, or live with that little mistake. We didn't like it. It was blatant. And I think Ronnie felt the same way. Because he was selling it to us as more like this art thing that is hidden. Sure, sexuality and rock are always hand-in-hand—it's a good combination—but not just blatant. That was blatant, and we wanted to do something rather clever."

"To be honest with you, Hipgnosis had a lot of power," says Aubrey, who doesn't recall any negative reaction, intimating that it wouldn't have mattered much! "We said, this is what you get. We were very expensive. And we were considered by many bands, particularly the more well-known bands like Led Zeppelin or Pink Floyd or Peter Gabriel or Genesis or Yes, we were considered by them to be in a sense, part of the band. We didn't work for record companies, we only worked for bands. Or we rarely worked for record companies. Paid by bands and worked directly with them, and formed friendships with them. And we were considered to be very much instrumental in creating images around their music and around the image that they wish to be portrayed. You have to go back again to look at the '70s. There was no MTV, no VH1, no YouTube. There were very few rock 'n' roll TV shows in those days and also very few magazines. There were actually not that many outlets to gain access to a band."

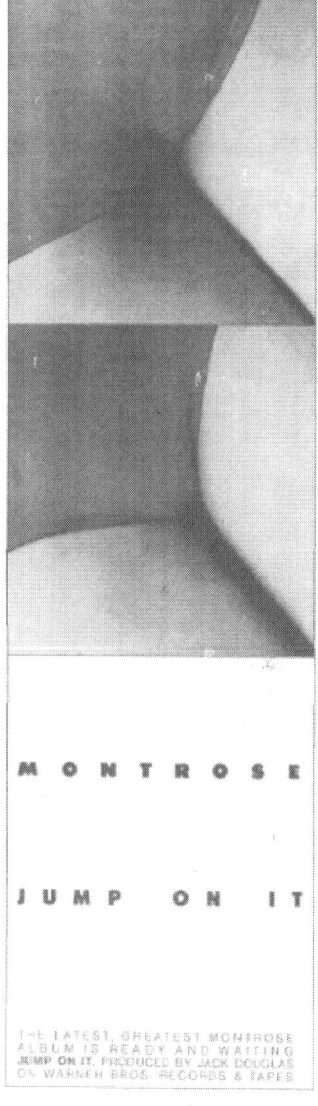

"And of course, the album cover became a representation of that. When people bought an album, it was a ritual. You've got the cover, you peeled off the shrinkwrapping, looked inside for all the clues you wanted to know about your band and the latest kind of information to get about them, and it was very subtle. And there was the ritual of taking the album out—careful not to scratch it—putting it on the deck and then putting the needle down, playing the album, and at the same time, reading the lyrics or looking at the posters inside of the band, or trying to work out what the cover was all about. So there was an incredible ritual around our covers. They played a very intrinsic role. I received no bad feedback from Ronnie Montrose at all. I always remember him being incredibly positive."

DENNIS CARMASSI   BOB JAMES   RONNIE MONTROSE   JIM ALCIVAR

From a fan's point of view, however, line up the Montrose sleeves and there's no continuity, of logo, of colour, of band members. Indeed now two of four had no pictures of the band on the front or back (and Hipgnosis wasn't about to go there, this being one of their trademarks, as is the hand-tinting of black and white photographs, also on display here). So we now had a band radically changing their sound record to record, and no visual branding to help stave off the sense of vertigo experienced by the potential consumer. To be sure, once you got the record home and cracked the cellophane, there were pictures of the band (once more, Montrose utilizing the top-shelf Norman Seeff), but, tellingly, the guys are all segregated into individual boxes.

What's more, Montrose would call in marquee hard rock producer Jack Douglas to knob-job the songs, which were recorded outside of the band's natural environment, over in New York City. And yet the result would be no Aerosmith album, Ronnie following his individual course yet again, with Warner Bros. left at the altar once more with a variety-infused record that would be hard to market.

But things get off to a promising start with "Let's Go," a heavy enough rocker strafed constantly with slide from Ronnie, but atop a tribal beat from Denny and a vaguely disco bass line from session player Randy Jo Hobbs, given that the band's keeper of the fat strings Alan Fitzgerald had now been dismissed from the band.

"Well, Alan was fired," says Bob, "and I don't have any idea why. There were other people that were fired. Our road manager was fired. I don't know, Ronnie just liked to fire people, I guess (laughs)."

Hobbs, an Indiana native, had played with the likes of The McCoys as well as Edgar Winter and Johnny Winter from 1970 to 1976, having also jammed live with Hendrix in 1968. He was found dead of heart failure at the age of 45, in a hotel in Dayton, Ohio back in 1993.

"There were a couple of tracks that did have bass, because I just can't play bass like I should," says Alcivar, who is referring to the fact that much of the bass one hears on the album is reproduced by him on keys. "Randy was pretty much just like 'Let's Go' and 'Jump on It,' just the real hard-edged stuff that really needed somebody pounding on the bass, whereas obviously 'Tuff-Sedge' is not. 'Music Man,' I remember, is me. I don't remember 'Rich Man.'"

"Rich Man" is indeed the third and last track indicated on the inner sleeve of *Jump on It* as containing a Randy Jo Hobbs performance. "That makes sense; he was an excellent player," reflects Jim. "He used to play with one of the Winter bands, which Ronnie knew from way back then. And I guess he was just in New York, and Ronnie said, 'Randy, we need help on a couple of songs.' So he was glad to pop in and do it."

But "Let's Go" somehow doesn't rock as hard as it could have. It doesn't exactly fulfil the promise of Bob's escapist party hardy lyric, with Jack's production not exactly stressing heft. I asked Ronnie if Jack did a good job on *Jump on It*, and all I could get was, "Yes, I think he did. Whereas that record didn't have the open air intense heat of the first Montrose, it had more of a raucous midrange-y kind of tone that Jack got with Aerosmith. It turned out well. We really hit it off. They brought Jack Douglas in because he had just come off of doing Aerosmith—he was Aerosmith's man. So they brought Jack in to do things. But it's still... remember Sammy wasn't involved. It was me and it was... Denny was on one of them and then there was another. And as I've said before, I was talking to Ritchie Blackmore one time backstage at one of the concerts we were doing, and we both realized that it was just kind of comical that we've never used the same lineup twice on an album, and it's just the way it was. So yeah, there was that kind of pressure there and it never really materialized. And as I look back 40 years from now, it's easy to look back and see why. But at the time it's just been the journey I've been on. With Jack, it was just a question of here's the songs we need, let's move this in here and let's pull this... he was just trying to get raw sounds out. Just the basic, raw sound. But at the time I was working with Bob James singing vocals, and Bob James and Steven Tyler are about 20 universes apart, so there's nothing you can do about that."

"I'll tell you what happened with *Jump on It*," continues Ronnie. "At that point I really wasn't interested in producing the next record because I just wanted to get down and play guitar. Jack Douglas had just finished working with Aerosmith and the record company and management said, 'How about this guy?' I met with him and talked with him and it seems right, and we went back East and we cut the record. Stylistically speaking, it was one of those situations where at this point we were experimenting without a bass player. The keyboard player Jim Alcivar was playing a left-handed bass and keyboard parts on the right hand. So we were a four-piece without a bass player. Randy Hobbs—may his dear soul rest in peace—from Edgar Winter's group, came in and played on a couple of tracks. I think *Jump on It* went back to what everybody was trying to get me to go to anyway, which was more of a rock direction, a little more loose."

Specific to "Let's Go," Ronnie commented in the notes we did for *The Very Best Of*, "I remember really committing to building up my slide guitar chops. Earlier on in my career, I was often on the road with Johnny Winter and Lowell George—talk about mentors! After the final take we did on this, I recall producer Jack Douglas walking in and without a word shaking my hand and nodding his head… yeah!"

"We loved Montrose because first of all you had a great singer and Ronnie was a fantastic guitar player," says Douglas, recalling the session. "You had a great band and Ronnie was really a progressive jazz player who was like our Jeff Beck. By the time I got to him, he had a different singer and with a different band. Well, Denny was still in the band. But I think maybe we had lost our way by the time we did that that record. It didn't do all that well. But I had great respect for Ronnie and what they were doing. I thought it was different."

Like everybody, Jack was fond of what Ted Templeman had done for the band, "I loved everything Ted did. I liked that album. It was classic west coast, but by then like there was like a west coast sound and they were doing a lot of their stuff on Trident boards over at Cherokee, and that stuff sounded cool. I think Ronnie wanted to get heavier and join the crowd and thought that with my participation we would get him to the Aerosmith stage. But he never really was an arena show. And you know, you've got to keep the same lead singer, really, to keep things going. And so it just wasn't possible."

And yet Jack doesn't cause there to be heavier songs on the album, nor does he bring particularly heavy tones. And contrary to Ronnie's assertion, *Jump on It* is definitely less guitar-crunchy than its predecessor, and as light in the songwriting as—or even lighter tha—*Paper Money*.

In any event, Bob has fond memories of gearing up for the record. "'Let's Go' was really kind of a fun song. Because when we were rehearsing, we were rehearsing at Winterland. Like I said, Bill Graham was our manager, and we had carte blanche at Winterland. It was like a three-story building and we had carte blanche and we could do anything we wanted. We were just blasting out music. Ronnie had a couple Marshall amplifiers going, and I was like, wow, cool. But that lyric was inspired by… I'd just had a bad night with this dame (laughs) in my hotel room and she stole my rent-a-car. I'm sorry, I always had a problem with women (laughs). I love them to death. I was raised by the greatest woman on earth, my mother, but I don't want to get into it. But I just remember that place as… you'd get your limousines and stuff and it's like, okay, come on, Bobby, we're going to rehearse, blah blah blah. Everybody's there, Denny's got his drums set up, the keyboards are set up, Ronnie's got his stuff, and I show up and go, 'Oh, I've got a hangover.'"

Great performance from Bob on this one (featuring one of Ronnie's credits to the whole band), which is also the case on "What Are You Waitin' for?," track two and really only one of three hard rock tracks on the album. "What Are You Waitin' for?" has a bit of a Deep Purple Mark III and IV vibe to it, crossed with Hendrix. Appropriately, Bob gets to inject a measured amount of blues phrasing into the thing. There's a twin lead, some added percussion, and just like that, *Jump on It* has stormed out of the gate in stark contrast to the opening salvos upon *Paper Money*.

"Great song; it is what it is," comments Bob, on this composition credited solely to Edgar Winter and solo artist Dan Hartman, deceased from AIDS in 1994. "I love the guitar parts in that and I love the vocals." All told, this is one of the busier tracks on the album for Denny, who really doesn't get much of a drum sound on the record. Notes Carmassi on working with Jack, "I learned a little bit from everybody that I worked with over the years, every producer, and every engineer. And Jack, yeah, he was great to work with; I really enjoyed working with him. We did it in New York, and it was fun; it was good. Good shopping in New York in those days. Those are the days where we didn't live in a global village where everything is the same everywhere. You could go to different cities and get things you couldn't get on the West Coast."

As for the odd situation of dealing with keyboard bass on the record, Denny figures that it wasn't much of a challenge being part of a rhythm section like that. "No, not really, because I played with Jim in a band before Montrose. And organ trios are always kind of fun things to be in. I had done that. I had played in organ trios in clubs before. It's a different concept, coming from a different space, with an organ trio, and it was fun for a while. Because Jim could cover that; he was good at doing that. We just kind of worked out what it was going to be and we just played. We didn't have certain patterns or parts that we played—we just played. There's a lot of freedom in an organ trio for a drummer, anyway, so it was interesting. While it lasted (laughs)."

On the subject whether it was true that Ronnie deliberately routined his rhythm sections pretty extensively, Denny says, "Oh yeah, yeah, but I mean a rhythm section has to do that anyway. Bill Church and I, we would even just play songs as a duo, in rehearsal, to get it really tight. That's just part of the gig, man, is to get it tight. But Ronnie wasn't a taskmaster, even though he would suggest that we play together a lot. Because it's a partnership and you've got to get to know the other guy. You're thrown into a situation with people that you don't now, that are from different backgrounds, different parts of the country, and it's a growing process that needs to happen."

Next up is "Tuft-Sedge," a spacey but short instrumental with lots of layers, including most prominently guitars, bongos, and synthesizers.

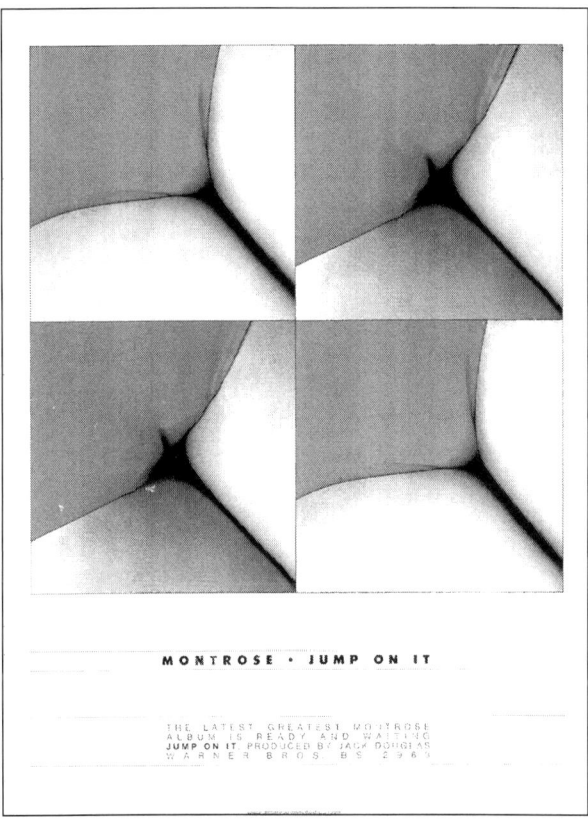

"What was killer on 'Tuft-Sedge,'" says Jim, "was... I don't know if you've ever heard one of these, an Ondes Martinot. It's a French synthesizer, and it's old. It was all tubes, had this little miniature keyboard. You know, not full-depth, and monophonic. And you would hit a note and you could vibrate... if you moved the keyboard side to side to side, you had vibrato. It was the most expressive way of hitting a synthesized note; you could ease into the vibrato fast flow, anyway you felt. And that was on that instrumental. That's that little lead thing that was going through. And Ronnie was so knocked out about it, when he got back home, he found a Martinot for sale and bought it. And that wound up on the *Open Fire* album. And that was the last—other than him trying to get me to repair it once, which was a nightmare—that was the last we heard of it. By the way, that all came through Jack. He's an original tape-flanger. He doesn't like to use the Eventides and the delay lines, he wants to get tape reels out to create flanging effects. Very old school, old tech."

"He was probably the most fun of all of them," continues Alcivar, on Jack Douglas. "He at that point was working with John Lennon and learning about and understanding what in the world The Beatles were into and what they'd done. They had a storage facility upstairs at The Record Plant out in New York, and it was filled up with Beatles gear, from John. They would just toss it up there and he would haul it down when he needed something. And Jack, 'Oh, we've got the Mellotron, Beatles Mellotron, up there. Let me bring it down.' Suddenly this big monster Mellotron would show up, and it was enormous fun to play. It had just an unbelievable selection of sounds and whatnot. And the engineer was all crazy, you know, 'Check this one, check this out!' The introduction to 'Bungalow Bill'… I believe it had this kind of acoustic guitar flamenco style, but you press this one key and there it is. And it's on the Beatles record."

"I used it a couple of times," says Jim, of the Mellotron. "It's got that real buzzy string thing here and there. But not very often. It had so many different voices, so it wouldn't surprise me if there were other things through the album I don't remember."

"I would expect relief," answers Jim, asked how Ronnie would have reacted, not having to produce *Jump on It*. "There's so much to worry about and deal with. And that was why he picked very good engineer/producer types pretty well, I thought, over the years. He could kind of back off from that responsibility a bit and just play. It was a good move."

"All of us, the whole band, was really happy that we were finally going to have proper production," adds Bob. "So Jack, who was obviously a very hot producer at that time, took over. Still, Ronnie, I think, had a little bit too much to do with the production. Jack wasn't pushed around, but it's hard to explain. I'm not saying he was being pushed around, but he was dealing with Ronnie. It took Ronnie many years to finally realize that you should let other people take a little control. Not necessarily business-wise, but production-wise. But he was in a position where he could actually be the hardhead that he was. There were a lot of issues that were obvious. But like I said, I was just a kid, so I kind of stood back and stayed out of it. I just wanted to make it in the music business and did the best that I could."

"We had Kiss recording next door with us," recalls Bob, who took advantage of his time in the city more so than the other guys, notably Jim, who says, "I'm a wallflower. Really, during the recording, that's all it was; 24/7 you were in the studio and then you were exhausted, had something to eat, and out."

"I talked to Paul Stanley and the bass player, Gene Simmons," continues Bob. "And they sat me down, and Gene's like, 'Bobby, Bobby, Bobby, what are you doing? What are you doing? You can't have an orchestra come in. You can't play rock 'n' roll with an orchestra.' Can you picture him saying that? He's like, 'Bobby, Bobby, you know, no, you can't have an orchestra when you're doing rock 'n' roll. There is something wrong here. You have to figure it out.' Those guys have been friends forever. They've known each other for a long time. And I'm like, 'What, what, what?! What do you want me to do?' (laughs). I go, 'I don't have too much control over this.' And then it's funny, because then they ended up doing an orchestrated thing with their own band, after we did it, after Gene was telling me, 'Oh, you can't do that. It's not possible. It's not possible. You can't do that in rock 'n' roll.' I'm going, 'Okay, okay, okay, fine, Gene.' So yeah, talked with Kiss, talked with the guys from Angel, talked with the guys from Cheap Trick. Actually, I ended up being managed by Ken Adamany, who managed Cheap Trick after I left Montrose. And he was my manager for a couple of years. And I was working with Pete Comita, who played bass for a while for Cheap Trick, and we wrote a song called 'Reach Out,' actually, that Cheap Trick covered."

Closing side one of the original vinyl was dark power ballad "Music Man," which has a bit of Elton John or late '70s Alice Cooper to it. It's interesting production all 'round, that Jack and engineer Jay Messina get on the track, including a novel drum sound and a lush string arrangement from Jim's dad, Bob Alcivar.

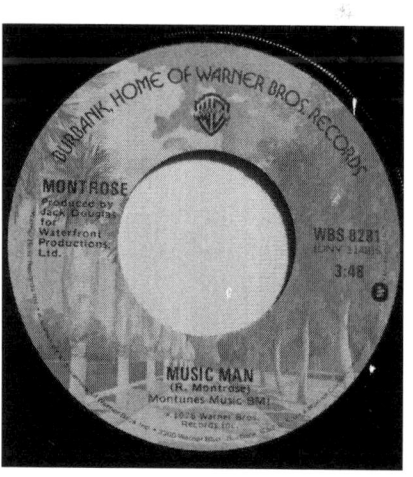

"I wrote this at a time when I was tired of touring and the pressures that accompanied being on the road," explains Ronnie. "What I think I was trying to say (albeit abstractly) in the lines, 'I can't be your Peter Pan, but I'll be your music man' was that I wasn't going to be comfortable staying in the same place musically, going through the motions for the sake of success (whatever that means), but that I recognized that music would always be a deeply important part of my life."

"Funny story about Jack and 'Music Man,'" notes Jim. "I was gonna do bass on the thing, and he says, 'I've got an idea.' And I said what? 'We're gonna speed up the master tape.' We got a Clavinet that he brought in, and he says, 'You're gonna learn to play the bass sped up, on the low register of this thing, and then we'll slow it down and hear what it sounds like.' And so I played through it a bit, just to listen to it, and it was stunning—monster. A Clavinet has a pretty big, deep, bright, biting sound. You drop that about an octave and it's insane. The problem is, my time is not that good, so I'm trying to play a ballad fast, staying in time. Because when you drop down, you amplify all the mistakes, all the timing problems. We couldn't do it. I could not pull it off. I don't know where he got that idea, but it was brilliant."

"But that's one of my favourites, and that's all piano," continues Alcivar. "Again, I'm not a killer keyboard player, and I usually playing soft touch organs and synth. And that's like a nine- or ten-foot Yamaha grand that I had to go play, and I'm going, oh crap. So I'm like, weeks and weeks playing hand scales trying to build up for it. And the session hits, and it was easy at that point. It's always been a hard rock band with Ronnie, but our thing was blending classic instruments with hard electronics. So, you know, the fact that there's actual live strings is sort of a departure. But you can imagine that being a Mellotron also, quite easily. And it's just, again, that evolution. Ronnie was really, really enjoying this thing. He had his guitar, which was never diluted, but suddenly this band's sound is getting wider and wider sonically. It's still got killer drums, strong bass, great singer. But we took the original Montrose and added a huge wall of sound to it. That's kind of what Jack was good at."

Definitely a production tour de force, this one is, and yes, a wall of sound of sorts, although not of quite the same construction as the one Ted Templeman built, to greater creative distinction one might say, on *Montrose*. Concerning the strings, Jim remembers that, "Ronnie and probably Jack were thinking it might be nice to have some orchestra stuff on here. And he came up with the scheme. My father has been writing songs, movie scores and stuff for years and years and years now, and so I got them talking to each other. Ronnie sent him a couple of mix tapes from New York, and basically they just went with it. He got the tapes and wrote out, I guess, parts for a fairly large orchestra. They flew him out to New York and they did a session. And my father, he's scared to death, thinking here's nepotism gone wrong. What if this is horrible? What if they hate it? All that money and time wasted on this thing. And when he was all done with it, they said, 'Perfect, we don't need to change a thing, that's it.'"

"They didn't use a full orchestra, but more than a four-piece ensemble," continues Jim. "A large string session. My father is used to a pretty big sound, and that fell over into *Open Fire*. They wanted a *Star Wars* kind of sound for the intro to 'Town Without Pity' and there's one or two other little bits and pieces that are on there. I think that's it, but almost Gamma as well. He wrote some strings parts that I tried to play. It was on a Yamaha CS-80 or something and it was horrible. When I got done playing all the parts, it sound like a big old pipe organ—it was awful. If you want strings, you gotta get strings. So that was an experiment that we just tossed."

"'Music Man' really knocked me out," adds Bob. "That was a song that Ronnie came up with, and me and him wrote the lyrics together. I thought that was the most excellent production job on that album; it really made sense. And Ronnie just kicked total ass on guitar on that one."

If accurate, Bob's comment would mean that he's missing a credit on this one—both "Tuft-Sedge" and "Music Man" are credited to Ronnie alone. Addressing the idea of ballads and pop as opposed to hard rock, Bob reflects that, "I think Ronnie's idea as far as the relationship to heavy metal was pretty much the same as mine, which is that I could do the heavy metal vocals and all that, but I'm actually really more of a pop kind of singer. I kind of grew up with that, singing pop music that is a little bit lighter and more in the mainstream. By the time Ronnie and I would have our falling out, we were probably going to become pals, given the sort of music that we both actually really liked to do. I mean, you could see the difference with *Jump on It*. We're starting to get more into melody and pop sort of music, which we were both interested in at that time. But we just didn't have the opportunity to explore it more."

Over to side two, and Montrose deliver the record's standout track, made more so by its status as title track, and, as Ronnie says, its marriage to the album's notorious front wrap. "Hard to talk about this title track without mentioning the cover controversy," says Ronnie. "The song was written as a positive message: 'Jump on it! Be a lion! Go get what you want and deserve from life!' Unfortunately, the company that did the graphics used the now-famous close-up of a model's, er, midsection, giving 'jump on it' an entirely different twist."

"I just love that song," says Bob, suddenly not the pop man anymore but, it seems, a supporter of proto-speed metal. "I mean, it really has a lot of meaning. I'm a big animal lover, and that lyric... when you see the lion, when he's on the run, that's basically what it is. I don't know if you watch the Animal Network or anything like that (laughs), but you see the lion standing in his cave, and he sends out the girl lions to go kill the hyenas. And then when they don't, when they can't accomplish it, they get back to the lion, and the lion is sitting in his den, saying, goddamnit, you can't get this accomplished?! And then he comes out and he just rips the hyenas apart. And then he goes back to the cave, and he's like, laughing, I got it done for you. You couldn't do that yourselves?! (laughs). Anyway, that's kind of what that song is about."

Notes, Jim on the song's amusing first few seconds, "I remember Denny was just knocked out with one simple thing on 'Jump on It'—how it starts. It's just like a switch gets thrown and bang! And he loved that. Once that hits, the whole song just runs that way."

More so like Jack did with Derringer, specifically *Sweet Evil* and something like "Let's Make It," or like Tom Werman did with Ted Nugent's equally brisk "Turn It Up," he in fact goes for a really light drum track and performance, barely more than a shuffling bass and snare, before he allows Denny a ride cymbal for the clouds-parting melodic chorus. There's further ear candy such as talk box on the "jump on it," as well as an extended effects-laden solo from Ronnie that keeps lifting and floating until it touches the stratosphere.

With "Rich Man" we are back to a second song written by Dan Hartman, this one a Stonesy, southern rocking ballad, again augmented with string arrangements, but at least full band. Ronnie turns in an uncharacteristic country blues solo, and together he and Jack conspire to massage in more layers than we had been hearing on records one through three. "I love the opening segue into 'Rich Man,'" notes Bob. "I love that part still to this day when I listen to that song. And the lyrics, I mean, they choke me up. I love them."

And the pop continues with both the up-tempo Babys-like "Crazy for You" and morose ballad turned slightly hard rocker "Merry-Go-Round," making for a distinctly anticlimactic side of music for fans of Ronnie as rocker, especially after the fire and excitement of opener "Jump on It." Says Bob of "Merry-Go-Round," "That's another one that me and Ronnie kind of collaborated on. The song pretty much speaks for itself—yes, it was a merry-go-round." Once more, the credit to the track goes solely to Ronnie, while "Crazy for You" includes Ilene "Chunky" Rappaport (Lauren Wood) from Chunky, Novi and Ernie renown.

"Somewhere in the middle of 'Merry-Go-Round,'" adds Jim, "Jack and his engineer took a stereo Nagra tape recorder to Coney Island and turned it on and rode the roller coaster. And they recorded this whole thing, all the racket and screaming or whatever, and that's part of that mix at some key point in there."

Refreshing roller coaster sound effects aside, as the strings fade on "Merry-Go-Round," there's no mistaking the fact that Montrose had turned in a record that was too serious, too pensive and essentially as austere as its stonewalling cover art. Not only do we not get to see on the cover who the band is this time, but there essentially *is* no proper band, given that the bass slot, abandoned by Alan Fitzgerald, has been left vacant.

Wrote Rolling Stone's Charles M. Young, reviewing a record that likely hit the pages of the top music mag in part due to the band's relationship with Bill Graham, "Their latest starts well with 'Let's Go,' an unrelenting road song riding centre line between the absurdist humour of 'You Can't Catch Me' and the ecstatic release of 'Born to Be Wild.' Another tasty rocker, 'What Are You Waitin' for?' places more emphasis on lead guitar over bass and drums. The third song is an almost acoustic instrumental. Sucked in by this typical Led Zep song pattern, the listener is primed for an all-time gut-thumper like 'When the Levee Breaks.' Instead, he gets piano and violins on a self-pitying lament, 'Music Man,' whose sentiments are worthy of Barry Manilow."

Curiously, with this band and so many others, when reported upon by staffers that usually put down hard rock any chance they get, when Montrose doesn't deliver that, they are universally put off. In other words, or turning the tables, one wonders if all of the hand-wringing by label executives over needing pop songs out of their charges was worth it, or indeed, whether it was the wrong strategy. Not that Ronnie—or Rick Derringer, or Frank Marino, or Gary Moore—were particularly enthused by the prospect of delivering slabs of heavy metal, but one wonders, if any of them had done just that, on a consistent basis, maybe one or more of them would have been commercially more successful, like your Aerosmiths and Ted Nugents. In any event, in contrast to *Warner Bros. Presents*' #75 placement on the Billboard charts, *Jump on It* would stall out at a lowly #118.

"But I think it was successful," counters Montrose. "Like I say, all my records now, any record that has bore my name, is part of the journey, part of the path, to get to the here and now, and so philosophical speaking they are all successes. I don't have a single record that I would consider to be a failure. And the point is, had I not made the record at that time I might have looked back and said I failed, because I didn't go with my heart or with my artistic inclination. And believe me, I put a caveat on the interpretation of quote unquote artistic. I'm not in any way claiming that my music is art."

"These records did OK, but not great," concedes Montrose. "Timing is everything. That first album happened to be in a situation where if any record like that would come out, it would just spread like wildfire. I guess we beat everybody to the punch, but not consciously. Like I say, timing is everything. You have to remember too, those were the days when I was coming out of Edgar Winter's band, and all through the first couple of years of touring with Montrose, there was no MTV, there were no music videos, there was no internet or mp3s or CDNow. There were records, record stores, radios and concerts. As you would travel across the country in the early '70s, whether with Edgar or Montrose, everywhere you would go, people would go to the existing concert arenas or coliseum or big theaters sometimes not even knowing who was playing. But it was the place to go and hang out and get loud music. Literally, in the '70s, I'm amazed, thinking back on those days, it really didn't matter who was playing. It was the gathering place for people to go and listen to live music and to see a loud live show. And it was this wonderful music concert escape. So it's not that way today, but it was that way then. I like what today has become in a lot of ways, but it's an amazing thing when you think back to when it didn't even matter who was playing (laughs). Let's go down to the coliseum, there's going to be someone good playing there tonight. How do you know? Well, hell, they always have good shows down at the coliseum!"

"Also, there were venues everywhere," continues Montrose. "Especially with Edgar Winter. Edgar and I would always go out with Humble Pie. Montrose did a huge tour with Humble Pie and Spooky Tooth, as a matter of fact. It was Humble Pie, Spooky Tooth and Montrose; and we went out with Black Oak Arkansas, Montrose did, back in the day. And the thing I was realizing—I was actually having this conversation with someone recently—back then, it was like no matter where you went, whatever town... I've literally played every town that has any arena or has any venue, like a big theater, anything in the United States. All of them. I've played them all. I start thinking about it and I'm talking with my wife and we're talking about this, 'Oh yeah, I've played there, I've played there.' And what it was—I'm now realizing—there was no MTV, there just wasn't any entertainment. There were movies but there really wasn't anything to do. So like I say, people would buy tickets to go to any coliseum anywhere to see... 'Where you going?' 'I'm going out to see a concert.' 'Who's playing?' 'I'm not really sure but I'm going.' And it was an event and it was a hangout and that was part of the deal. It was just a thing to do—in the '70s that was what you did. And then that's how bands gained a lot of their notoriety, because they happened to perform very well in front of people who may not have heard them before."

And within the realm of '70s hard rock, this idea has very much a Midwest vibe to it. "Yeah, but then again, I wouldn't call it the Midwest," counters Ronnie. "I'd call it anything that's not New York, LA, or Chicago. Everything else, as far as I'm concerned, is the Midwest. Any place that wasn't... well, back then, big cities would get a different level of culture. So like I said, what I call the Midwest is way bigger and more spread-out than just the middle of the country. The Midwest was a place where blue collar workers just wanted to hear good, easy... not easy, but music they could relate to, that they feel, and boom and just go out and party to it. And that's anywhere. That's why 'Rock the Nation' hit so hard. Because the lyrics are, 'I just wanna rock the nation.' Everybody wanted to rock the nation."

And hopefully for one of these mid-tier acts like Montrose, they'd get thrown a bone or two by radio. "There were the FM stations, independent FM stations, who always played Montrose and always played 'Rock the Nation' and 'Rock Candy' and 'Space Station #5' and 'Bad Motor Scooter' and 'Good Rockin' Tonight,' which is a song that I arranged... I actually got the arrangement from PJ Proby. But they'd play those. So we'd go in and interview and do things when we were in town and they'd play those songs, but that was about it. What I remember about radio in the '70s... there was a beautiful thing about FM radio that you could go in and we always did radio shows around the Bay Area here. KSJO, there's another one down in San Jose that I went to, and KSAN in San Francisco. And the DJs actually got to be themselves, and they got to play whatever they brought in and whatever they found. Certainly there was criteria that had to be met so people would pay money to advertise on their station, but not nearly… I mean they had freedom, and they were able to be who they wanted to be. And then when I started going to radio stations later and I saw the pie slice of the clock, and you have to play this colour tunes in this section and it was all pre-programmed, at that point DJs became bus drivers."

As *Jump on It* hit the streets, old nemesis Sammy Hagar had earlier in the year issued his first of many solo albums, *Nine on a Ten Scale*, featuring Bill Church on bass and in a lesser role, Alan Fitzgerald on keys. Even more of a nuisance, the Ramones had ushered in the punk rock craze with their incendiary self-titled debut album.

Notes Ronnie, "My reflection on punk rock was that I hated anybody American who even presumed to be a punk rocker. I just hated it, because I understood… it was so much more apparent that when you're living in England, the haves and have-nots are completely on each other's backs. They're right outside your back door. Here in America, you're spread out. There's people who are living in the haves neighbourhoods, gated haves neighbourhoods, who have no idea that the have-nots even exist. And vice versa. In London, when John Lydon sang 'No future,' he knew what he was talking about. He realized that there was… it was a total reflection on an absolute cultural level. I mean, I'm sure there were people who just went along for the ride for the cool looks and the cool hair and whatever, but there was an absolute statement by a lot of punk that we have every right to act out because there is nothing going on here, period. There's no hope for any of us.

We're just going to be sitting here for the rest of our lives doing nothing. And that isn't the case in America. So the American punk stuff just didn't resonate with me at all."

As for Sammy's *Nine on a Ten Scale* record, it was surprising to see a Van Morrison credit on there. Recalls Church, "Van came down the hill, because we were recording at the Record Plant, and he lived up the hill. He came down the hill one night with his 12-string, and said, 'Church, I wrote you guys a song.' 'Flamingos Fly.' And it just so happened that there were two other bands in the studio that night, Tower and the Trinidad Steel Band. Ever heard of them? Trinidad Steel Band was in Studio B. We invited them all over, so the singing on 'Flamingos Fly' is the Sammy Hagar band without Sammy. Tower, horns, the Trinidad Steel Band... all singing 'Flamingos Fly' (laughs). But yeah, Van wrote that specifically for us. He came down the hill with his 12-string, said, 'Church, wrote you guys a song. Church, you're still doing it. Still doing it.' And I go, 'Yeah, I'm still doing it.' He said, 'Well, I wrote you a song.' And actually, the other connection with Van, the first time that I ever met Sammy Hagar, he came to Van Morrison at the Winterland and we were headlining. Sammy's first wife, Betsy, was one of the fanatic Van Morrison fans."

To promote *Jump on It*, Montrose would raise eyebrows by deciding not to fix the situation and get a bassist, but rather to soldier on presenting their new tunes live with the same band configuration that made the record, minus even the minimal guest bass. Most bands wouldn't even entertain such an idea, but Ronnie, as we've seen, was pretty fearless when it came to defying expectations. In effect, the futuristic twist to the *Jump on It* live campaign would presage the idea of a band like Gamma.

"Ouch," laughs Jim Alcivar, asked how the tour went. "Well, from my point of view, not very well. Denny and I had played, yeah, with keys and organs, where the left hand always pounds away at the bass and low end. It's just kind of natural, the way a piano is. You put a big B3 in, and then I modified my B3 with a Moog filter amplifier trigger system, so it would be punchy, like bass, rather than just go 'bong.' And so it's passable that I could spend a lot of my time and effort worrying about that left hand, keeping it tight to the drums, and oh, by the way, I've got solos and string parts and all this other junk going on on the high end. And it got tedious. I was so happy when we finally got a bass player back (laughs). But I thought Ronnie appreciated the keyboard bass, because bass was a large loud thing with his kind of guitar. It wasn't terribly critical, sonically. It just booms all over the place."

And so this was not done with pedals... "I did have pedals, but I've never learned how to do it properly. On a couple songs I could use the pedals, because the parts were slow enough or simple enough, but really I had to rely on the left hand to do anything difficult. I'm pretty sure we were never without a bass before that. Ronnie had a habit of changing members every album, so, you know, whoever is on the album, generally, that's going to be the group that tours that year. And then we came back to do this *Jump on It*, and we drop bass completely, so I got stuck with it. And I don't know how we worked that out. I was really not happy dealing with that. We were in Canada once, touring during the winter, and the B3 froze up in the middle of the song. So all the bass is gone (laughs). Not good."

"Besides having Alcivar playing bass on the keyboards, we had a brand-new stage set-up," recalls Bob. "It was all phenomenal stuff. We had the big ramps going up, and all the equipment and the Marshall amplifiers and everything was hidden behind a scrim. You couldn't see any amplifiers or anything. It was all hidden behind giant black scrims and there were ramps set up and there was this huge microphone stand that I was to use (laughs). Which had like a 10' x 10' base, and this huge chrome microphone stand, at the front of the stage. Oh, it was phenomenal. I mean, it was a really great idea, I thought. And then when we did 'Jump on It,' when Ronnie came out and did the slide guitar thing, he wanted to come up and do the slide guitar on my microphone stand. And I could grab the microphone off the stand, and at the same time, he could use it for his slide guitar stuff. I thought it was an excellent idea; it made for a really good show and was a lot of fun. When we didn't have Alan, it was just the four of us, and so it was really kind of a Led Zeppelin-type show, very simplified. Basically our whole goal was just to come on stage and just kick ass and rock 'n' roll."

Again, Montrose was the quintessential example of a band in the mid-'70s that jumped on isolated dates all over the place, rather than sign on for one organized long trek with a consistent headliner or indeed support act. And so throughout 1976, they shared stages with the likes of Deep Purple, Nazareth, Kiss, Foghat, Yes, Ted Nugent, Jay Ferguson and Rush.

And underscoring the futuristic personnel configuration, sound and look of the band was the curious situation where Ronnie all but ignored his band's back catalogue. Says Bob, "Well, I did a couple songs of Sammy's when we first started, but we were on the road for like two-and-a-half years, constantly. I mean, it was nuts. It was incredible. But later, we didn't do any of the old Montrose stuff. The only stuff that I did with Sammy, that Sammy sang, I think was just within the first couple of months that I was with the band. After that, we never did any of those songs."

"It was a totally different thing," confirms Denny. "It was a totally different band. And yeah, we never went back and did any of the same songs with Bob."

An odd situation to be sure, and yet, "I have absolutely no idea why," shrugs Bob. "I was the singer, so what do I care? (laughs). I wasn't there to cover Sammy Hagar songs, even though I appreciate him and I love the stuff that he did. There were only two singers in the Montrose band: there was Sammy and me. And the actual Montrose band only lasted about four years. Maybe two years with Sammy and two years with me and that was it. After I quit, you know, Ronnie took off and tried to do his own thing. I don't know how well it worked out, but that was it."

But while the guys were still flying the Montrose flag, they were gonna do it sober. "Yes, when I first joined the band, there was no drinking, no beer, no nothing," says Bob. "I was like, okay, cool. You know, I didn't mind that. I'm not a drinker or smoker or anything like that anyways. So I said, yeah, there's no problem with that. I think that stemmed from when Ronnie was with Edgar Winter's band, and I heard—I'm not saying this is the truth—I heard stories that he almost died on an airplane, because he was heavily into speed and drugs and all this kind of stuff, and drinking. And he almost died when he was with that band. But when I first joined the band, I heard the story, and I was like, okay, that's cool, whatever, I don't care. Okay, no beer, no whatever. But when you're out doing rock 'n' roll concerts like we were doing, I mean, these were like huge concerts (laughs). Geez, can I have a shot of beer or a shot of wine? But it wasn't allowed. The Rolling Stones and these bands, I mean, who knows what they had in their rider and what their trash cans with ice were full of? I've no idea, but I'm sure it's full of something. But no, we were not allowed that in the beginning. When we were on the road for a couple of years, it changed a little bit. But, you know, it's hard for a person to go out and perform on stage without, gee, can I have a shot of something?"

A slightly different telling of the story has Ronnie getting busted on the plane trying to bring some acid back from San Francisco to sell in Boulder, and that that may not have been his first trip ferrying illegal substances back and forth. The idea is that the arrest is what got Ronnie to straighten out. Additionally, Sammy had been a recovering junkie, underscoring the situation that Montrose better run a tight ship if it was going to survive—on Sam's part, his wife at the time Betsy was as much a parole officer of the situation as Ronnie was, giving a tongue-lashing to anybody who brought drugs anywhere near Sammy.

Bill Church, now out of the band, confirms that he ran afoul of the drug laws on the Montrose books as well. "Believe it or not, for a period of time, both Ronnie and Sammy, unbelievably, in the middle of the hippie era of San Francisco, both of them were really down on marijuana too. And of course, I've always been a pothead. But anyway, for a period of time, they were both anti-that. Since that time, Ronnie never reverted to drugs, but of course he went to the bottle, right? And then Sammy, he fell off the wagon in the big cocaine years. But they both got on my case all the time for smoking pot. They hated drugs, hated anything to do with them, and we weren't allowed to bring it around."

"Ronnie was vehemently anti-drug and anti-drink, anti-anything," confirms Mike Kelley. "His thing was nobody dare do anything in this band. And especially not before we're playing. Yeah, very strong sobriety policy. There may have been some stuff going on on the sly after the shows (laughs), but Bob told me that nobody dared do anything before a gig. Anywhere where Ronnie would know or anything like that. It was just absolutely forbidden—you'd bring down the wrath of hellfire on yourself."

All told, spanning the career, Montrose played some big gigs, and as we've alluded to, even got to England. "Yeah, we toured with Status Quo," says Denny. "We did that Charlton festival, with The Who and Humble Pie and Bad Company; that was the first time, with Bill Church. We went a couple of times. But management did a good job. Yeah, I thought so. Bill Graham was a good guy. He was a 'for the artist' guy. I have good memories of Bill, and Mick Brigdon was involved. But Ronnie was a hard guy to handle. You know, he wouldn't… He was difficult. For management and record companies. He was a complicated man."

Jim agrees that the band experienced uncommon exposure during its relatively uncommercial run. "You ever hear of the six degrees of separation? Well, how many degrees of separation are all of these musicians? I think it's a far less number, thinking back to all of the people I've played with. You think in terms of the groups. We were with Bill Graham and with Premier Talent, booking agent, and they were the guys that did The Who and the monster bands. I mean, we opened for the

Rolling Stones at the Cotton Bowl. The Who, several times. Aerosmith at The Forum. Kiss, more times that I want to think about."

"Kiss were a riot," continues Alcivar. "because they were so struggling with their persona and their trying to justify themselves, if you will. And we opened for them, and Denny would have the sound guy put a phase-shifter on his drum solo. Ooh, that sounded cool. Well, all of a sudden the next day, we would get the riot act read to us, about, no, no, no you cannot put a phase-shifter on the drums, period. We're gonna do that. You can't do that, we're going to do that. They did a lot of that. They were nervous of being upstaged. By contrast, ZZ Top—we walk in, opening band, and the sound and lights guys come back to us and say, 'Guess what?' I say what. 'You can have everything. You know, full power, no limiting, every light in the house, whatever you want to do. Just have fun, it's yours, go for it.' And that was the sign of a band that really knew what they were about, and what they had, and had no worries or fears. They always took the show. And I really respected groups like that."

Bob James was soon to leave the fold and then Montrose would be no more. As he told Raw Power magazine back in the fall of 1977, in fact for an article about his new band Swan, he left, "because I wanted to do my own thing and Ronnie was doing his own thing. I like moving around and new things. Ronnie Montrose is a perpetual type of guy. He wants to keep moving on; he wants to explore different thing; and that's basically the way I am too. I wanted to move on and play with different people. I don't know if I was the cause of it or not. I'm sure the group would have gone on and possibly done another album and a couple more tours, but I just couldn't handle it anymore. I didn't have enough say, although I enjoyed working with them and being on tour and stuff. But I just wanted to do more, especially vocal harmonies. That's something we couldn't do with Montrose in the studio, because we couldn't do it live. Swan will be doing a lot of vocal harmonies and some of them we won't be able to do live, but I'm not worried about it."

Not complaining, but as part of the conversation, Bob says, "I didn't get complete credit for what I did. On the last album, *Jump on it*, I wrote the lyrics to a Dan Hartman tune called 'What Are You Waitin' for?.' I did a couple others, and I co-wrote 'Music Man.' On the other album, I wrote four songs. It was one of the greatest experiences I've ever had."

"The complaints really don't start to happen until the tour for that record," explains Mike Kelley, on Bob's departure. "There were no problems making the record. I know that they were really happy with the way that it was produced, and they liked the record. I liked the record too, but I liked the *Warner Bros. Presents* record more. It seemed like *Jump on It* was moving even more in a sort of consciously eclectic direction, and that they kind of toned it down and became more pop-oriented. Bob loves that record; he actually prefers it to the first one. I thought it had superior production values to the *Warner Bros.* record, but it didn't strike me as being as strong compositionally. But I thought it was a great sounding record."

"As far as the problems, Bob and I would talk on a pretty regular basis," continues Kelley. "I'd get these late-night post-gig phone calls, and he wasn't doing well. There was a lot of rancour between him and Ronnie, over really peculiar things like, Ronnie wants only certain coloured lights used for himself and he didn't want certain light colours on Bob. 'No, these are only for me.' Bob would step into the wrong light and Ronnie would get upset. Bob would say, 'Well, it's not my call. If you don't want this light on me, I'm standing there singing, and the light guy throws a light on me, and it's on your forbidden colour list, what am I supposed to do? Do I jump out into the darkness? What am I supposed to do here?' He said that became a big issue."

"And yet Bob was told to go for it, command the stage, which in fact, he didn't really do. I mean, even when told to let loose and be a front man, Bob didn't exactly do that, whether it's by nature or an instinct that it wouldn't go over well." Asked what kind of front man his best buddy was, Mike says, "In those days, it was more about projecting a certain confidence or swagger. It wasn't about running around the stage being David Lee Roth and being an acrobat. If you think back to that period, to the gods of that era, you had Plant, and he's no showman. He had charisma, but he wasn't putting on a circus show. Gillan never did much. Even with Paul Rodgers, there was a certain way he would stand, there was a certain way he would hold a mic stand. Bob was really from that school."

But as Ted Nugent was shocked to find out when Derek St. Holmes would open up his mouth and start singing the band's biggest early hit, "Stranglehold," all eyes gravitate to the lead singer. This was part of the problem between Ronnie and Sammy, and it was rearing its head again with the young and good-looking Bob James. And let's face it, the females in the audience, compounded with the fact that, as Ronnie says, people would show up to concerts not even knowing who was playing (not to mention that Montrose were often support)... it's gonna look like it's Bob's band up there.

"According to Bob, he started to see Ronnie as being very jealous," continues Mike. "In ways that were indicative of some kind of envy or jealousy, which Bob couldn't... he was clueless. Where is this coming from? We were best buds. Everything was great and all of a sudden he's being an asshole. And I just remember that it evolved pretty quickly and the calls became more frequent and they became more desperate and Bob had to talk to Bill Graham on the phone a number of times. It was almost like Bob saying, 'Oh, I'm going to jump, I'm going to jump. I'm jumping off the building.' And Bill Graham was like, 'No, please, I'll call you, I'll call you every night, I'll talk to you through this, work with me on this but please do not leave. Whatever it takes. We'll talk every night, but please do not quit in the middle of the tour, because that will really fuck things up.' And then Bob finally said, 'Hey, listen, this is it.' And I don't know if he really did wait to the end of the tour. He quit after the New Year's Eve gig, New Year's Eve ringing out 1976, ringing in 1977. That was the last gig."

Appropriately, Montrose's last show (of the golden era) would be staged at Winterland, Bill's place; support on the night came from Beserkley Records acts Greg Kihn and Earthquake, plus Yesterday and Today, who would now neatly replace Montrose as San Francisco's reigning and spirited second-tier hard rock ambassadors.

"I'm proud of *Jump on It*," begins Bob, charting the course out of the band. "I would have loved the opportunity to continue with Ronnie, but unfortunately, as far as I'm concerned, it became unnecessary to work together anymore. Ronnie was happy about his performance on the album, but I don't know if he was too happy about how it ended up. As far as I'm concerned, I listen to that album and I think it's phenomenal. I think it's the best thing that Montrose has ever done."

"But I know that the guys weren't happy about the final sound. Even though me and Ronnie came out upfront on the recording, on the album, I feel sorry for the guys! I really do. I really feel sorry for them, because I listen to Led Zeppelin albums, and you can hear everything! Seriously. I mean, everybody in the band shines. I thought, and I still think, if you've got a group of guys like that that are so talented, let them all shine. Bring it all forward. That was the problem with Ronnie, unfortunately. I know Denny was totally fed up with his drum sound, and he could not handle it anymore. Because, like I said, the first Montrose albums they did, that were produced by Ted Templeman, the sound was just phenomenal, incredible. And Denny certainly missed that. I know for a fact that he was pissed-off with the production. Because the guy is a super drummer (laughs). He's a superhero, in the rock world. I mean, come on, get over it. The guy is a drum god in the rock world!"

"I loved music," continues Bob. "I was more into the music and Ronnie just became too involved with himself, and, I don't know, proving to the world... something. He's the one that loved Led Zeppelin. But Ronnie always told me, he said, 'Bob, you know, I know my limitations. I'm not the best guitarist in the world but I do my best.' And I'm like, that's cool. That's cool, right? I mean, when we first started, like I said, me and him were the best friends on earth. We were so happy to be together. He was so happy to be rid of Sammy and we were like the best of friends. I would visit him at his apartment in Burbank, California and talk about songs. But I couldn't figure out where things went south with him. But I don't have anything to say about Sammy, as far as what I've heard. I think the only thing between him and Sammy was probably just the jealousy thing. I'll just tell you the truth. I'm not putting the guy down, but he was a jealous guy."

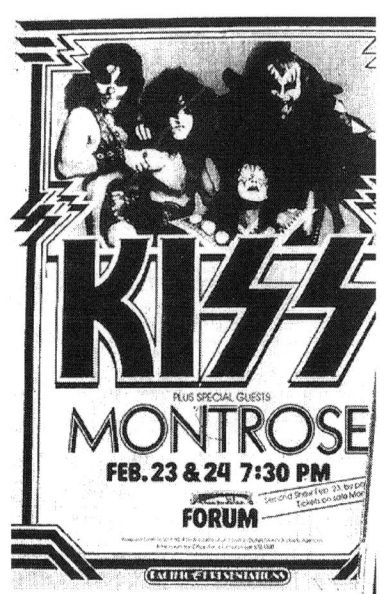

Confirming Mike's spotlight story, James adds, "Yeah, that started turning up later, because my friend, Charles Faris told me that Ronnie didn't want white lights on me, only blue. He was the only one that got the white spotlight. He didn't want me to wear white on stage, only different colours. I'm like, serious? You serious, dude? Come on, what's up? We're a band here. Come on. Plus I kinda stayed away from interviews, because I'd heard all the bad stories between him and Sammy. So I wasn't there to get involved with that situation. I had no clue, and that was not the reason for me to be in the band whatsoever. So I pretty much stayed away from it."

Bob also says that Ronnie had told the band's soundman not to add any echo to Bob's vocals, leaving them sounding rather dry. Denny says that just as he did to Sammy, Ronnie drew an imaginary line that Bob was not to cross, lest he get too tempted to fulfil his role as entertainer by using too much of the stage, part of which was reserved for Ronnie alone.

"It was funny, because one time we were on an airplane, and me and Jim were sitting in the back of the airplane, and Ronnie and Denny were sitting in the front. And Denny came back and said, 'Bobby, Ronnie needs to speak with you.' And I said, oh, really? Okay. So I went and sat down. He took my place next to Jim, and I went up and sat next to Ronnie, and Ronnie, it was funny, because he drew a picture of the band, Montrose. Like kind of stick men. And he drew like a drum set, he drew a person playing keyboards, he drew a person, the guitar player, and then on his little drawing, on the drum set, he wrote Montrose. And then he drew a little stick man on vocals, with a little microphone. And he said, 'Bobby, what's the name of this band?' And I said, 'Oh my God. You've got to be kidding me.' I said, 'I don't know.' I said, 'Montrose?' He's like, 'Do you get it?' I'm like, 'Oh my God. Okay, fine, Ronnie, fine!' You dumb shit (laughs). That kind of tells you the story of where he was at. And I mean, to me it was hilarious. But I'm like, oh, come on, dude. Get over it."

"When I left the band, the guys were pretty much with me," says Bob. "You know, we understand. Because at that point, they were pretty much fed up with him at the same time. They were kind of in the same state of mind that I was. I'd said, I just gotta move on, I can't deal with this, I'm out. And they told me, 'Well, we want to go with you.' And I said, you know, don't do that. Don't do that. I said, look, I love you guys, but no, I just gotta go. This is not working out. But they wanted to go with me, and I'm saying, no, just... no. Stick with what you're doing. Do whatever."

Although good friend of the author's, David Krebs, drew a blank on this one, Bob corroborates rumours that at one point he was asked about joining Aerosmith. The timing is right, given his sojourn in New York around a new band project called Magnet in and around 1979, just as Aerosmith was imploding post-*Night in the Ruts*. And apparently, says Bob, Jack Douglas had nothing to do with the hook-up.

"Well, when I was in New York, when I was working with Magnet on A&M Records, yeah, I met with the manager for Aerosmith," says Bob, who, granted, might be referring to Krebs' partner Steve Leber. "We were at a nightclub, and I sat down and talked with him. He was interested in having me take over for Aerosmith. I was like, no, no, no, that's not gonna happen. Tyler is perfect for the band. That's his band. I said no, I'm not interested, sorry (laughs). But that's when Tyler and his guitar player, what's his name, Joe Perry, they were having some rough times. I don't want to say that they were drug addicts or anything, but they know as well as I do what they did. But I said no, no, I'm not interested. It's not my thing, it's not my place. I mean, that's Tyler's band."

Instead Bob found himself embroiled in a rock folly of a situation called Magnet, essentially a bunch of guys from the past trying to make post-glam pop for no reason, all within a climate of exciting and fresh new wave sounds from The Cars, The Knack, Blondie and erstwhile A&M stable mates, The Police.

"Well, that was just one of the things that I was going through at a time, after I quit Montrose," explains James. "I was doing my own thing here but I was like, I was getting all these offers. I was dealing with a guy named Billy Gerber, whose dad had a lot of TV shows and stuff going on at that time, *The Love Boat* and all that stuff. Anyway, he called me up and he said he was talking to Jerry Moss, from A&M—he's the M in A&M, Herb Alpert and Moss—and says, these guys have a band out there in New York. Let's fly you out to New York and check out these guys. Magnet was Jerry Shirley, the drummer from Humble Pie, and they had Pete Wood, who co-wrote 'Year of the Cat.'"

"The reason we were with A&M," continues Bob, "was that Jerry Moss was good friends with Jerry Shirley. And they had a band out there, and all these people are calling me saying, hey, you know, they need a vocalist. Go out there and check it out. So I went out and checked it out, and he wanted me to stay, and I said, no, I live in California. I don't want to stay here. But anyway, they wouldn't let me leave. So we ended up doing that album in Jersey, at the House of Music, with Stefan Galfas producing. A good friend of mine but not a great producer. But, you know, good friend. So that's kind of how that happened. And then I stayed out there for a while, and we did a small tour. We were working with A&M Records, and they spent like a couple million dollars on us in rehearsals and stuff like that. But at that time, I wasn't really knocked out about the music or anything. You know, you had clubs in New York City like CBGB, and The Police and Joe Jackson were playing these clubs. And it was a brand-new type of music scene. And these bands went in and did their demos for like $25,000 or something apiece. And of course they really hit the spotlight, while A&M Records were spending millions on us (laughs). The album wasn't that great. It was a fun thing to do, and they paid me a helluva lot of money, so it was okay. It was fun. A lot of great guys, great musicians."

"Funny, Peter Frampton, we recorded at his house in New York, and Peter told me that he was always afraid to talk to me. And I said, 'What?! Are you crazy? What's going on?' And he said, well, he was always afraid to talk to me, because he thought that Ronnie would get mad at him (laughs). I'm like, 'Are you kidding? Come on, dude.' So yeah, it was a weird situation with Ronnie. Because he insisted on being in control with so many things. But I think later in his life, he finally realized that he should calm down and that he doesn't need this kind of control. He actually needs people with expertise and stuff like that. But when you get into a position like that, some guys get big heads and they think everyone is interested in me—me, me, me. Well, really it's not."

Wrote Billboard in March of 1979, on *Worldwide Attraction*, Magnet's lone album doomed like Pilot, Ambrosia, Paris, Rubicon, Mr. Big and Sailor, "Great things are expected from this band considering the personnel involved. Drummer Jerry Shirley formally played with Humble Pie, Robert James was former lead singer of Montrose, Peter Wood played keyboards for Al Stewart and co-wrote 'Year of the Cat,' Les Nichol played guitar and co-wrote with Leo Sayer, and bassist Michael Neville is formerly of New York Central. Together, the band create an intense and exciting brand of rock in the Foreigner tradition. Robert James' lead vocals convey a wide range, while the power chord muscle keeps the pace fast and vibrant. Expect the group to build a strong AOR base."

But after Montrose, we never saw much of Bob ever again. Mike Kelley says there's a reason for that. "Well, Bob's projects, you couldn't call them necessarily failed; they were more stillborn projects. Because back then, you'd have these situations where somebody would come along and want to tie him up, and say, 'Oh, we have this project.' So they wanted to get him, remove him from the marketplace, and get him committed to their projects. And in order to do that, they paid him some money. But then when it doesn't pan out, behind the scenes, it gets wrapped up in red tape and it just becomes stillborn. It never comes to fruition, and then you have years go by."

Meanwhile, over in Sammy world, Hagar had followed up *Nine on a Ten Scale* with two records in 1977, *Sammy Hagar* and *Musical Chairs*, and then found himself with a minor hit on his hands with "Plain Jane" from *Street Machine*, issued in September of 1979. Hagar, capable, resourceful, talented and ambitious, had risen to at least the sort of lower mid-tier status that Montrose had occupied, and now Montrose was in fact over with, leaving the similar-sounding Sammy Hagar band as heirs, so to speak.

Having finally arrived as a solo artist, Sammy looked back to the start of his post-Montrose career with a sense of bemusement.

"Back in those days, I was willing to do almost anything," explains Hagar. "My producer, who is my manager now, Carter, the guy who signed me to my first record deal, I listened to him, I listened to the record company, I listened to my manager, Ed Leffler in those days, I listened to everyone, because I was just interested in becoming famous. I wanted fame. I wanted to be a big rock star. And I didn't really know how to do it. I just had my talent, and I felt that it was raw. I knew that it was raw, but I knew I could sing and I knew I could play the hell out of the guitar, and I wrote some pretty good rock songs.

And I just said, 'Somebody help me. Tell me, how do you go from here to there?' And I listened to everybody. So right around *Musical Chairs*, that's when I started spreading my wings a little bit—'No, no, I wanna do this and I wanna do that'—and I started calling the shots a lot more. And that's where Carter and I bumped heads, and that's the last record he produced, because I guess my live, album, *All Night Long* record, no one produces a live record (laughs)."

Of note, that live record, issued in 1978, includes live renditions of "Make It Last" and "Bad Motor Scooter," and in Sammy's band at the time were fully four ex-Montrose alumni, Bill Church, Alan Fitzgerald, Denny Carmassi and the golden-throated one himself.

Says Bill on the quick transition to Sammy's band, "What happened after I was out of Montrose was that Bandana Productions was formed, and Jerry Berg had left Dee Anthony Organization to start Bandana, and he became their manager. And then six months later Ronnie fired Sammy and that was history. Sammy and I had a long-time, lifelong friend who was a bigwig at Capitol, John Carter, the late John Carter. So it was real easy for Sammy to call me up and say, 'Hey, Carter is waiting for us at Capitol.'"

Told about Bob James' assertion that Montrose and Sammy might have appeared on a bill together, Church says, "Negative! Negative (laughs). First of all, never happened, and he never would anyway. They actually didn't speak for quite some time too. And our crook attorney... Sammy and Rob were already in legal problems over who owned what and this, that and the other."

In a sense, there's a parallel with Sammy's trajectory to the career path taken by John Mellencamp, where he takes in all this advice, plays all the games correctly because he wants to be huge, and then he grows into himself and becomes who he is. John Mellencamp, Sammy Hagar... this couldn't be more different that Ronnie Montrose's approach to the business.

"Yeah, you get a little taste of success," reflects Sammy, "and it's usually... I know it almost sounds egotistical, but it's not. You get your first taste of success, and you go, you know what? That was my idea. That's what I wanted to do, and all the stuff that everybody else has been telling me what to do was not successful. Like when they were saying, 'Hey, go in there and cover "Dock of the Bay."' 'I don't want to cover "Dock of the Bay!" Man, Otis Redding killed that song. You want me to compete with that?!' And everybody told me no, it's going to be successful, it's going to be successful. And the record company got all behind it and they spent more money on that than they spent on my whole damn album, and when it was a stiff, I said, 'See? I told you. I'm not putting it on my record.' And things like that. And so that's the Mellencamp story. Every artist has probably had that moment, if they started out the way we did, where we said we just want to be rich and famous; tell us how to do it (laughs), and we'll do it, you know? And if it doesn't work, you say OK, I want to do it my way."

And so to reiterate, fully four records in plus a live album, in 1979, Sammy had made his first record that was not fuzzy of focus like *Paper Money*. As well, just like Ronnie did with *Warner Bros. Presents*, Sammy would try his hand at production.

"Yes, *Street Machine* was the first record that I produced myself. Producing yourself is very, very difficult, when you are young like that. So I wished I would have had a great producer on that record, because I think I wrote some great songs. But because I was producing myself, I don't think the songs... they are diamonds in the rough. But when you listen to it, I think you hear the real Sammy Hagar. That was the first real pure Sammy Hagar record. Pure Sammy Hagar record—wrote them, produced it all myself. And so therefore, it's a very unique record, and I think it's a special record. Like I said, I think it's the first real pure 100% Sammy Hagar record. Diamonds in the rough. Some of those songs could've been fantastic, with Keith Olsen or Ted Templeman producing them."

"He helped me out sound-wise," says Sammy of his engineer on the album Peter Henderson. "He helped me make them sound good, but he wasn't even... he had no production credits. He wasn't a producer, he was an engineer, a sound engineer. Him and I butted heads a couple times, I remember. Because I was even willing to compromise the sound a little bit. He was willing to spend time with the drums, and he kept changing drum heads trying to find the right drum heads, and I'm going, 'Man, that's unimportant—just put a microphone on it—let's go!' I was rocking. I just wanted to rock. And he was slowing me down, thank God (laughs).

He was doing the right thing, and I didn't want to be slowed down. I just wanted to rock on that record. I didn't know what I was doing. I was in there producing as I went (laughs). It wasn't like I had a plan. I would just say, 'Oh, let's try this; oh, hey, I want to do this.' I always wanted to hear a guitar solo with guitar on one side and guitar on the other side, two guys. And I just did everything pretty self-indulgent, but pretty basic."

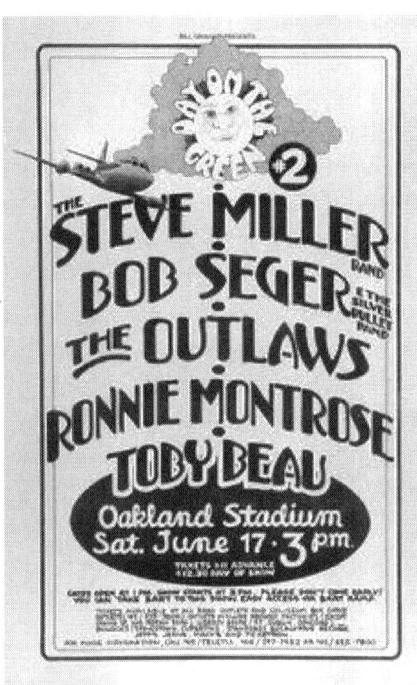

"'Child to Man' was real special," continues Hagar, offering a glimpse into what he thought of his path from Montrose to here. "I think it was a real departure for Sammy Hagar, to come out with a kind of grown-up song. All my songs are more like 'Growing Pains,' which was kind of like the bridge to 'Child to Man' from all my previous stuff, like 'Bad Motor Scooter.' I wrote very teenage songs, teenage lyrics, you might say. I wrote about those times in my life. But that was my first writing, so those were special times for any kid growing up—man, your teenage years are wild. You're just growing every day. So when I first started writing music in my 20s, I was writing about my teenage years. So I was always writing really young lyrics. And when I wrote 'Child to Man,' I thought that was kind of a grown-up, adult-y kind of song for me. And 'Never Say Die' was even like that. Just about growing up. And even at the age of whatever it was, 1978, I had to be 30 years old, I was just starting to grow up (laughs), with my music. It's kind of interesting."

And Hagar was rewarded with a couple of hits, sort of, in effect scoring at a level similar to what he was used to with Montrose. "Well, they were hits for me, the types of hits that I always had. They weren't giant Top 40 hits. I thought 'Plain Jane' should have been a bigger hit. Like I say, I think if I would've had a real producer on that song, that song was a hit. That song had hit written all over it lyrically, musically, arrangement-wise, anything. But it didn't have enough fairy dust on it, and it had a lot of fat. Someone should've trimmed that song down, made a concise little three-minute Top 40 single out of it; I would've had a huge hit with that song. I really believe that. 'Planet's on Fire' and 'Trans Am' were friggin' rock classics, man; they were #1 at rock radio, I'm sure. It was the closest thing I had to real legitimate classic rock, although when I say classic, there wasn't classic rock then, but classic rock-ish. You know, those were classic rock songs like 'Cat Scratch Fever' or 'Whole Lotta Love.' 'Trans Am'… they were rock 'n' roll fuckin' staples at that time."

OPEN FIRE The first Ronnie Montrose solo album.
Produced by Edgar Winter on Warner Bros. records & tapes.
Bill Graham Management.

As for Sam's nemesis, Ronnie Montrose, well, he went instrumental guitar, striking a death blow for Montrose and simultaneously a death blow for his prospects of selling any records, just as Hagar was in ascendance by trying to appeal to the widest possible audience. *Open Fire* was issued in January of 1978, and found Ronnie reuniting with Edgar Winter, brought in as producer (plus providing piano), while Ronnie explored his inner Jeff Beck. Continuing on from *Jump on It* were Jim Alcivar and in a minor role, Jim's father Bob. Alan Fitzgerald was back, and on drums, Ronnie worked with Rick Schlosser, who had been part of Van Morrison's *Tupelo Honey* with Montrose.

As Ronnie told John Wardlaw, "I had just basically gotten tired of working, touring on the road with a vocalist and the whole process of doing vocal-oriented music. Attempting to write vocal-oriented songs to me felt like going through the motions. And if you are going to go through the motions, you might as well just do any gig that caused you to do repetitive motions like banging a hammer or serving fries. I mean it just didn't make sense to me at the time, so *Open Fire* was what I wanted to do. I was following my muse and I was very fortunate in having good people around me and it turned out to be a pretty good recording in my opinion. A lot of vocal-oriented rock fans and fans of the original Montrose band hated that record. There were reviews from people who said that the album sucked and there were reviews from people who said finally he's doing something good. You know, you don't please everybody."

Ronnie appreciated the fact that some top-shelf musicians had noticed the record and gave it the thumbs-up. Legendary drummer Tony Williams even took Ronnie along for a tour of Japan in July of 1978. Billed as the Tony Williams All Stars, the band included Tony, Ronnie, Brian Auger and Mario Cipollina, with special guest Billy Cobham. The set list included three *Open Fire* compositions, "Rocky Road," "Heads Up" and the title track, which showed up on Tony's album, *The Joy of Flying*, issued by Columbia later that year.

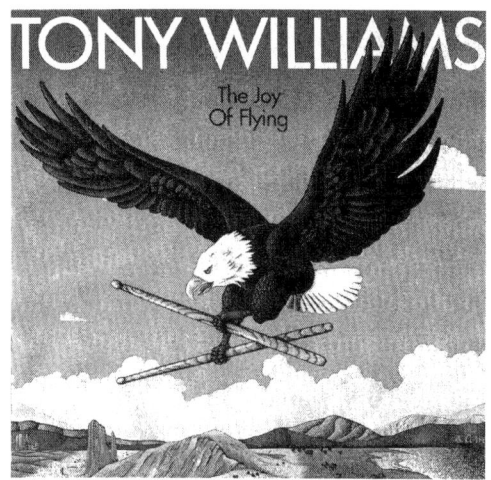

"Oh, I'm sure he just wanted a change," says Denny, now out for a spell, only to return. "He wanted to do something different. You look at Ronnie's career, and he was kind of all over the map. He had a blues rock trio, and then he had more of a pop thing, probably trying to crack that hit single thing. And then he was probably tired of that, and he wanted to do something different. But 'Town Without Pity' was really good, man." The latter comment referred to Ronnie striking for himself a bit of a minor instrumental hit with his remake of the Gene Pitney classic.

"*Open Fire* really was Ronnie's, okay, I want to do something different," explains Alcivar. "I want to do an instrumental. And it's funny, I think Warner told him, if you do an instrumental, you're out. You'll never do another record with us again. And he goes fine. And that was his purge, to get all the acoustic playing in. 'Town Without Pity' was just this... he loved that song and wanted to hear it done. Bottom line, it wound up being with Edgar too, and Edgar was a phenomenal piano player. And it was this big mishmash of more and more synths. That's where that other French Ondes Martinot came in. And that got Ronnie really down the tech path. We built this thing called a Pulcivar, that you could put guitar or keys or anything through it and it would chop up the audio, either left or right or pulses. We'd get this weird sequence sound that was based on any instrument through it. And that whole thing was fun."

"It was wonderful, the tour was excellent, great players, but of course a disaster in sales," recalls Jim. "It's hard to sell instrumental anything. It was a dangerous thing to do. Simply because nobody expected any record sales, and they were right. It sold well enough, but nothing, none of the bands really sold that many records. And I'm sure *Open Fire* was probably the most dismal, if you will. But I have no idea at all about specific numbers. That's accounting, and I get hives when I think about accounting."

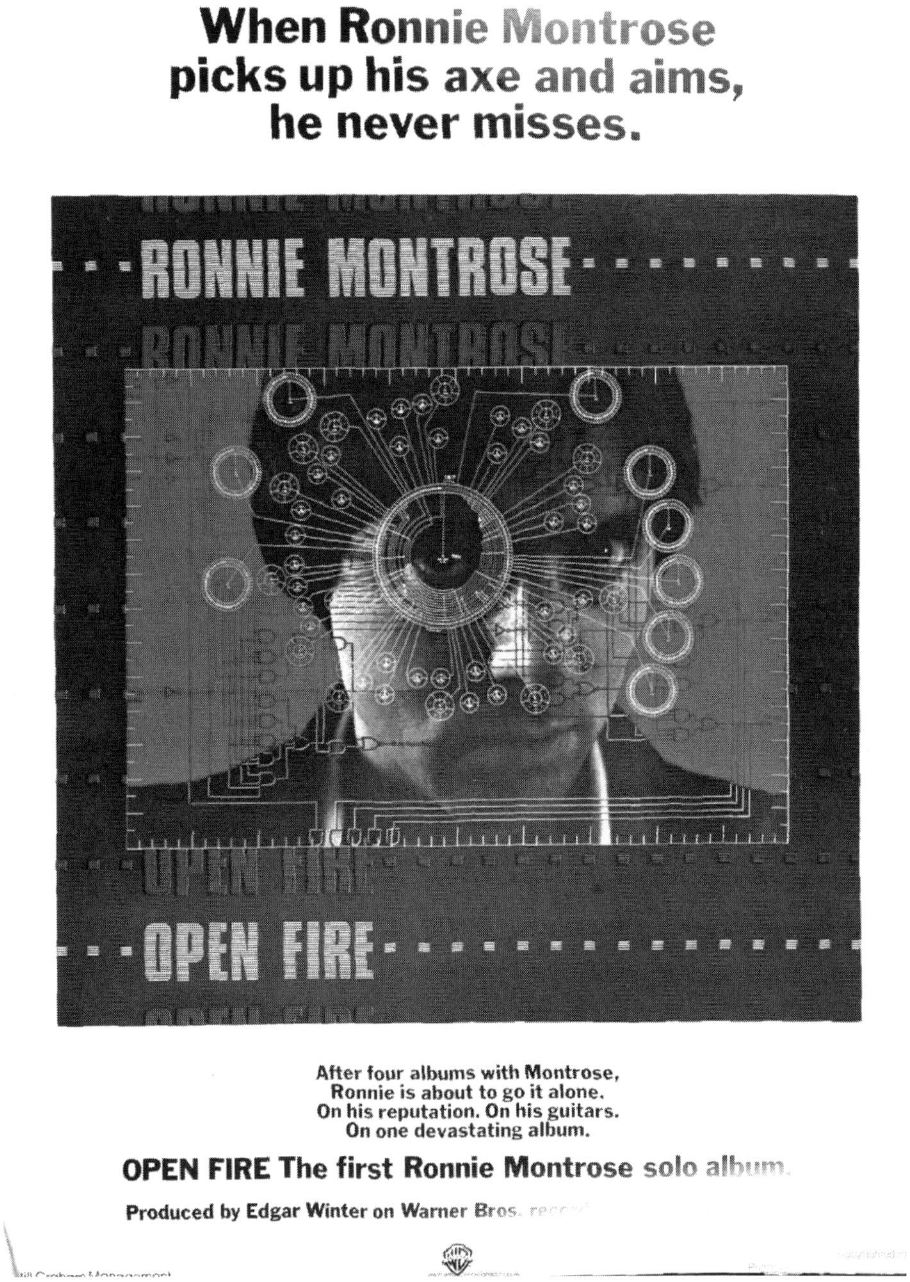

When Ronnie Montrose picks up his axe and aims, he never misses.

After four albums with Montrose,
Ronnie is about to go it alone.
On his reputation. On his guitars.
On one devastating album.

OPEN FIRE The first Ronnie Montrose solo album.

Produced by Edgar Winter on Warner Bros. records

Buddy of the author's, Jim Collins, was witness to an early date on the spring tour live, checking out the band in Kansas City on March 31st, 1978. As he recalls, "The encore was 'Starliner' from *Paper Money*. The set consisted of most of *Open Fire*, with 'Starliner' and 'One and a Half' being the only 'Montrose' songs performed. People were yelling for 'Rock Candy,' 'Space Station #5' and 'I Got The Fire' throughout their set, even though there was no vocalist anywhere on the stage (sigh)."

Donna Palatas of the Kansas City Star reviewed the show, which featured a little something called Van Halen warming up the crowd, followed by Ronnie and then headliner Journey: "Montrose took the stage next with an entirely instrumental set spotlighting lead guitarist Ronnie Montrose's proficiency on both electric and acoustic guitar. The guitarist's credentials with driving bands such as Edgar Winter's brought expectations of a hard rock set, but Montrose was surprisingly sophisticated instead. Ronnie Montrose's guitar lines were more melodic than heavy metal, with a group of synthesizers adding to the fluidity. It wasn't until the group's encore, from the 1974 *Paper Money* LP, that the band lived fully up to its heavy metal image. Representing the band's current style was the anguished blues of their new single, 'Town Without Pity.' A projected backdrop on stage of a city landscape of lights made the music not only a song, but an atmosphere, with the dramatized guitar work right out of a Philip Marlowe detective movie. The feelings that Montrose rung out of his wailing guitar were so clear that the addition of vocals would only have been in the way."

It was all a strange turn of events, this *Open Fire* business, and Bob James just shakes his head at what could have been. "After I was with the band, my name never came up again (laughs). If you watch his interviews after that situation, he never mentioned me again. He never did, in his live concerts, anything that we did together. He was totally pissed-off because I'm the only person in his whole life that ever told him I quit. Bye. Later. Later, dude. Not interested. Oh man, that pissed him off. Like you wouldn't believe. I'm probably the only person in his life that has ever done that to him. Like I said, the guy had it made. He was huge. He had everything at his fingertips, literally. It was crazy; I mean, he was a knockout. He didn't care. He no longer cared. As far as Ronnie was concerned, it was Ronnie, Ronnie, Ronnie. Marsha, Marsha, Marsha (laughs). He got to the point where he didn't care about any of what made his career. It could've been freakin' huge, but the guy, I'm telling you, the guy just went south. I don't know how exactly to explain it. I am not a psychiatrist. I'm just a regular guy. But we had a shot at all this stuff, and like I said, it just went south—and it had everything to do with him."

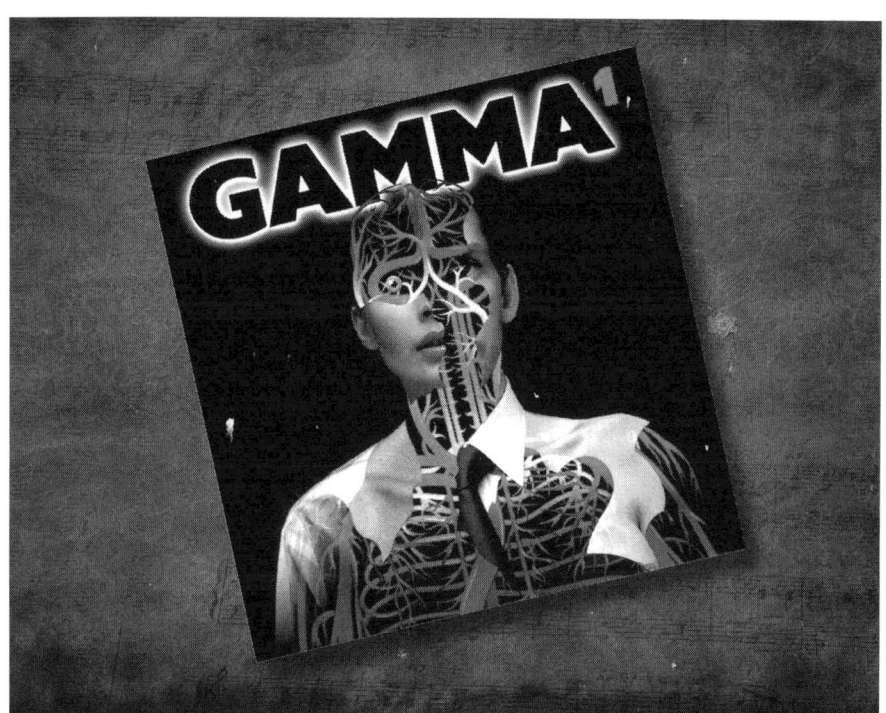

CHAPTER 6: Gamma – *1*: "And he's hungry, Ronnie. He's hungry!"

Having wilfully flung himself into a world of diminishing returns (final destination: obscurity), Ronnie, fortunately for us and his own commercial prospects, decided to get back on track with a conventional band, vocals and all (imagine that).

But the act was fresh and forward-thinking, with Montrose embracing technology and finding interesting ways to strap it to the rocket that was his guitar-playing and riff-writing. And then, most intriguingly, floating atop the musical melange would be a singer in native Scot Davey Pattison who would anchor the band in bluesy roots older than even the first Montrose record, let alone the arch-'70s pop delivery of Bob James.

"I had just finished my *Open Fire* record and I wanted to do a group again," says Ronnie providing his sense of the history of the band. "I just wanted to get that instrumental out of my system, so I finished *Open Fire*, the whole tour and the whole deal. We toured with Journey and Van Halen, wanted to change record labels, make a new start. At first I went through quite a few different things, but I was looking for the right singer because I just wanted to work with a singer who had the thing that I wanted to interact with, to the point where I actually contacted Andy Fraser from Free, but he was down in Jamaica doing his thing."

"I had called up at his place in London Jimmy Dewar who was one of my favourite singers, from Robin Trower, and Jimmy told me, 'I don't think I can do this. I'm doing this and that,' and he'd been doing Robin Trower all his life and he just wasn't into it. Jimmy recommended Davey, who was up in Glasgow, and who was just playing in club bands up there. He said, 'Ronnie I know a wee lad in Glasgow; he's hungry, Ronnie, and he's good—he's a great, great singer. And he's hungry, Ronnie. He's hungry!' Jimmy said he was one of the best undiscovered singers around and he was definitely right."

Alan Fitzgerald   Davey Pattison   Ronnie Montrose   Skip Gillette   Jim Alcivar

GAMMA

"So I met Davey and talked to him and flew him over to the United States and we just started writing. And since I had just done the *Open Fire* record, I was really into combining guitars and synthesizers and doing that kind of tech thing but still with a rock feel, but with as much tech as possible because that just happened to be where I was that. And certainly I was glad to have Ken Scott as our first producer, who had his Beatles history and his Supertramp history, who I loved just for the production. So we did the first Gamma record and had fun with it."

"Before Gamma, I'd started in bars just like everyone else, playing other people's music," Davey told John Wardlaw, adding a slight twist to Ronnie's telling of the first meeting between the two. "I got a break in 1977 thanks to Jimmy Dewar and Bill Lordan who passed on an album I had been working on with Matthew Fisher of Procol Harum, to the management at Bill Graham's office. My man Montrose liked it, and I have been here ever since. I can never thank Ronnie enough for giving me the chance. I have been fortunate to work with two of the best guitarists in the business. It is difficult for me to compare Gamma with Robin, because I am very proud to have been a member of both bands." Asked by John for influences, and Pattison adds, "So very many. Little Richard, Ray Charles, Solomon Burke, John Lee Hooker, Muddy Waters, Howlin' Wolf, Donny Hathaway. Man I could go on for days on that!"

"Gamma was a logical progression after doing the *Open Fire* record," adds Ronnie. "I was working with Bill Graham management at the time and it was obvious to everyone concerned that albums like *Open Fire*, while they were good for me creatively, were not going to be commercially successful. So I didn't have any problem, at the time, doing that. Seemed natural. The last two Montrose albums... I felt like I was in a real rut here and so by doing the *Open Fire* record I was ready to do another vocal album. It was a logical progression."

"Went with Elektra," continues Ronnie, picking up the tale. "Elektra had Queen and there was a big vocal in that. We were on tour a couple times and we did a lot of shows with AC/DC. And it was just a lot of fun. Gamma was rock enough, with my guitar, with Davey's bluesy vocal, and with Jim Alcivar's synthesizers and keyboards that were pretty much way stepped-out at the time. It was all those elements that actually worked pretty good, but still the ingredients weren't there to make... like I said hindsight, you look at the ingredients and the ingredients have to be there, and they weren't there."

"Gamma really was the combination, okay, we like this *Open Fire* thing, but we need a singer," adds Jim Alcivar. "And by great miracle, Ronnie was in touch with Jimmy Dewar, and Jimmy knew Davey. And says, 'I got a guy for you.' And I don't know if they sent tapes back and forth, but Davey shows up, and he was just a dyed in the wool blues singer, blues rock. And just, you know, heart of gold, all about feeling, sings like a bird. Just effortless. You could play anything, and he would just start singing something, and he would take a little while, and he would find words and put it all together and get it done."

"But it was really that rescue of *Open Fire*, which was so much fun," continues Jim. "Basically the writing on the wall was the record sales. And Warner said, that's it, you're out, we don't want you anymore, you're done. And Ronnie probably had a heart-to-heart talk with Bill Graham, and Bill says, you gotta have a singer. You need to do real songs again. If you really want to get out and play and make some money. For me, it was wonderful. The marriage of that *Open Fire* tech thing with suddenly a soulful singer, and it's like, wow—you couldn't beat it. On a hot night, we were just unstoppable."

"You think in terms of what Gamma did technologically, it just picked up with *Open Fire* and the stuff we built, and that's where I found out about the vocorder," continues Jim, who was most definitely on the same page with Ronnie, ever the rabid explorer of gizmos and what they could do. "Kurzweil was building them and they wanted like $15,000 for one, and Ronnie and I were getting excited about it. Because I think he used one of those talk-boxes on one of the *Jump on It* cuts. It sounds like a vocorder somewhere in there. And I went, you know, Ronnie, look at this. There was an article in some tech mag describing how it works. And I thought, it looks pretty straightforward. It's a series of filters and DCAs, and you just run your guitar through it and you get this combination of sounds. And he looks at it and says, 'How much would that cost to build? And I got back to him in a couple weeks, 'Oh, about $1000 each.' And he said, let's do it. And so after some period of time, it was a little later on, but before Gamma started, I'd built two of them, one for both of us. And that wound up being really a neat toy, for Gamma throughout. Davey always had fun with it, singing with a machine at times."

Rounding out the first lineup of the Gamma band would be Alan Fitzgerald (already back for *Open Fire*), and new to the family, drummer Skip Gillette, who Ronnie knew from his Sawbuck days. "I don't know how he found him," muses Jim. "Just some kid from LA. And it's a mystery; again, I don't know how he made that connection. Just another easy-going guy. A lot of energy."

Explains Skip (who played a chrome Gretch kit with a 24" bass drum), upon his circuitous trip toward being part of Gamma, "Well, actually, it goes back to... do you know who Chuck Ruff is? He was my drum roadie for a long time, in a band called The Westminsters and another band I was in, prog rock. Like when we were 16 and stuff. He set up my drums all the time and we became good friends, and then he started playing drums. We were just best friends, and one thing led to another, and he moved down to San Francisco and joined a band called Sawbuck, with Mojo Collins, and Ronnie was the guitar player. And Ronnie was a janitor at the Fillmore (laughs), and they had a house down there called Thin Blue. And my band Groundshaker went down to San Francisco. We had a house around the corner, but we shared a rehearsal room in the room where Sawbuck rehearsed. They had a room, and Ronnie lived there, Chuck lived there and a lot of people from *Hair*, the musical production, lived there. All kinds of weird people lived there, including Johnny Tease, the famous porn guy."

"Anyway, so we shared a rehearsal room there, and Ronnie lived right outside the rehearsal room, and we always ended up jamming with each other back and forth and this and that. They had a son, Ronnie and his wife. Jill was her name. A nurse or something. But I liked her; I actually liked her. She was really sweet. I used to babysit his son all the time. Now he's some kind of computer genius and shit. Anyway, so Ronnie started playing with Van Morrison and got those things going, and then he went and got with Edgar Winter, and then he called Chuck, when Chuck moved back up here to Reno, and got him the audition with Edgar. Chuck got that gig, and Ronnie left Edgar, and then started his own band, and called me to go to the first audition. I missed it; I couldn't make it. Denny got the gig, and then I started playing with a whole bunch of other people in LA that were really, really, really good but for some reason or another, did not make it. That were better than anybody I ever played with—geniuses. A guy named Tim Dulaine, who was an amazing singer/songwriter. And I also played with a genius named Tim McGovern, who ended up being Martha Davis' boyfriend, and she had a little band called The Motels. He wrote a bunch of songs for them and he started playing with them, and then he got good musicians and they got famous, and when they broke up, she never had another hit, basically."

"That was Straightjacket," continues Skip, on what seems to be his main band previous to Gamma. "If you look up Straightjacket, in Circus magazine, back in 197-something, Chaka Khan, and her boyfriend used to manage this band called Straightjacket, with me and Tim McGovern. And we used to play the Starwood all the time, and Eddie Van Halen was a fan, and he was always hanging around backstage with us, and me and Ed became really, really good friends, way before they got famous and shit. One thing led to another. I was playing with all these guys and playing good and we were recording and shit. I was happy musically. And then Ronnie called me and wanted me to come and audition for the new band he was going to do. He just said he wanted to get away from Montrose. Have a different band without his name in it. But I thought he was going to stay in the same direction he was in with the heavy stuff, like the two albums. Anyway, so Ronnie called me into that group, and the direction he was going in was completely opposite of what I thought. He wanted to sound like Dire Straits or something and I hated that shit."

"And to be honest with you, all of the musicians in Gamma—and I don't tell too many people this, and I don't know if you'll disagree about this—but none of them were anywhere near as good as any of the people that I'd been playing with. None of them were creative. None of them could write songs. All the people I'd been with could write songs every day, beautiful songs, just genius songs flowing like water, Tim McGovern, Tim Dulaine, all these guys. I was lucky all my life to be around people who could just write songs right and left and they were great. I got to Gamma, and it just seemed weird to me that it wasn't a natural part of playing. And so at first I'm going, wow, this is great, but I get to Ronnie and it's this stagnant thing."

Jim Alcivar agrees that the band's first record together, Gamma 1, issued in July of 1979, turned out to be a little on the stiff side. "Yes, well, with Ken Scott producing and mixing... I always had mixed emotions about that one. Dream come true on perfection and quality of sound, but very tedious, because being a perfectionist, you couldn't play anything wrong. The slightest timing thing, 'Oh, no, no, let's do that over again.' And overdubs would take hours and hours, days and days, trying to get everything just so."

"He does that a lot; he's like that," says Skip, on Ken Scott and his finicky ways. "I'd worked with him before—he's really meticulous. I talked Ronnie into using Ken Scott for an engineer, which is another good friend of mine. I don't know if you know who he is. But he worked with Tim Dulaine and some other people with me as well down there. And that was the best thing about that experience. He's good, you know? He's really tight. He's worked with some really good people. He's used to working with really, really good people, and maybe he had to do that with us because we weren't as good. I mean, he's used to working with fucking Billy Cobham, guys that are insane, and Terry Bozzio, the fucking drummer for Missing Persons for goodness sake. Ken did everything. He did all the Supertramp shit, right? The white Beatles album, all the David Bowie stuff, all the Kansas stuff. He goes on and on; he's a genius. He did all the Mahavishnu Orchestra stuff. He did all the Billy Cobham solo albums, and also Missing Persons. He managed them and produced them."

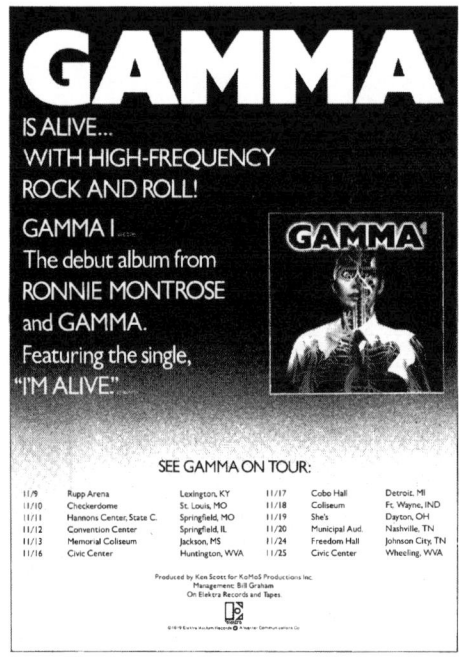

Asked how he might have butted heads with Ronnie, now a producer in his own right, Gillette scoffs, "Ronnie did have a lot of his own opinions which were, you know, whatever they were. I really didn't get along with Ronnie after I got in the band. His musical direction wasn't going anywhere with me. And he wouldn't let me play. He wouldn't let me play! He told me everything to play, he tuned my drums the way I didn't want it, and it was really an awful experience." As for interfacing with the album's challenging electronics, Skip says, "Ronnie and Jim were always into all the technical shit. It was cool. Sure, it was a pain in the ass, but no big deal. It was just kind of like playing with a metronome. No big deal. I do that a lot now."

Gamma 1 would be recorded at Wally Heider and Chateau Recorders, with production duties falling to aforementioned surprise choice Ken Scott. Explained Ronnie in the Gamma 1 bio sent to press, "I understand the way to make guitars work, and particularly sought Ken out for his drum recording technique. He's also got that second nature understanding of the studio, which is not necessarily technical—it's more like knowing how to swim. During the mixing, it was sort of like the student and the master. I really learned a great deal from him on how to work at recording; it was almost like a seminar."

Scott will forever be famed as a Beatles engineer, but the anchor of his vast experience is with all manner of jazz fusion artist through the '70s. Before hooking up with Gamma, he had just come off two records with Dixie Dregs, one with Devo and one with obscure prog band Happy the Man. Post Gamma, he'd work with Jeff Beck on the high profile *There & Back*, and... well, Gamma themselves were a cross between Devo, Jeff Beck and Montrose, weren't they? (with a little Bad Company thrown in). Having said that, Ronnie was interest in Scott primarily for his work with The Beatles, David Bowie and Supertramp.

The album cover art used for Gamma *1* would be created by Mick Haggerty, who would capture perfectly in illustrative form the slight android vibe of the album, which is further enhanced by Ronnie's chosen band name itself, as well as the titling of the album with a superscripted 1. More on Mick later, as he would be back for the second Gamma album, distinguishing himself even further.

Into what matters most, the record opens with a muscular melodic rocker called "Thunder and Lightning," and right away we get the prominence of keyboards, but also both bass and drum performances that evoke thoughts of jazz fusion. Antithetical is Ronnie's block chording, as is the galloping chorus, but then Ronnie gets to solo extensively, and additional ear candy, such as the vocorder, is also utilized. "That's the first song that Davey and I wrote together," noted Ronnie, in the bio. "I had had the music for quite a while, and when Davey came over on the plane and first got to my house, I played him this music and he had written those words on the plane! They just fit together like hand in glove, and I knew something good was going to happen."

"Great song to play live," adds Jim, "but just about everything was. 'I'm Alive,' 'Razor King,' which was an excellent guitar thing, 'No Tears,' 'Ready for Action,' 'Wish I Was... every single one of them was a blast to play."

"'I'm Alive' is just like 'Lucky Man'—a great song, a great story," says Jim on track #2, basically a poppier and more melodic take on the same arrangement and band formula we heard on the album opener. Just one of many songs featuring strange sounds, "I'm Alive" opens with an effect achieved by Ronnie tapping a microphone against his knee and then processing it through a vocorder. Says Ronnie, "'I'm Alive' is a song that Skip came up with, which is a real old Hollies song, and he liked it and thought it would be really good for Gamma, so we tried it and it worked real well."

 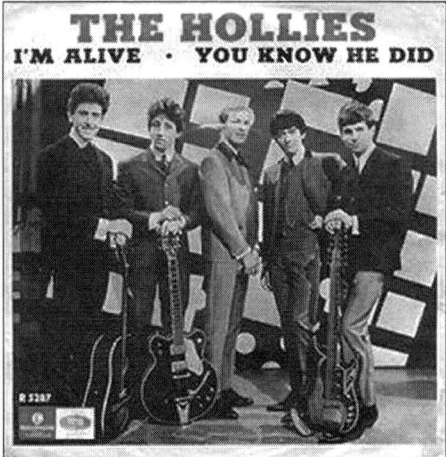

Confirms Skip, "I recommended they do the one hit that they had, 'I'm Alive.' I picked that song out. That was just one of my favourite songs. And we were at Wally Heider recording, and Crosby, Stills and Nash were in there recording too, and I asked Graham Nash—we were playing pool—I said, 'Dude, remember that song you recorded in The Hollies? We want to cover it. Do you know the words?' 'Oh yeah,' and he sat down with us and wrote down all the words and shit. It was cool. It was great."

The Hollies hit #1 in the UK with this Clint Ballard Jr.-penned song back in 1965. Obviously Gamma's take on the song is worlds away, but what is not expected is the difference in chords and melody during the pre-chorus. Lots of keyboards on this one, testimony to Ronnie's seeming contentment not to be the centre of attention this time around, something that arguably stunted the lifespan of Montrose.

"Yes, and he was always pushing for more," notes Jim. "Bottom line, in the mix-down, he could always adjust what he wanted to hear. He always kept the guitars hot, in the mix. And that's kind of what the albums were. It was his band, and he really was this phenomenal player. And, you know, I don't think there ever was really any argument about how strong the guitars were. The keys really just gave him a whole 'nother layer of texture. Because before it was, you know, maybe his rhythm guitar and bass and drums. All of a sudden now you could have strings and synthesizers and all these other colours and wind blowing in the background. Just stuff that you don't always have that option with. It was really the Jack Douglas album that got him further and further into that kind of experimentation. Which I thought was fantastic. Let's try this, what about that?, all these weird ideas. Some of them wouldn't work, some of them did. And that began with his solo album, *Open Fire*. That started with him and me playing with this idea of acoustic instruments with hard electronic synthesizer stuff, and kind marrying these sounds together."

Which brings up a cogent point. As much as Ronnie will be remembered as a guitarist, as a creator without fear, and as the architect of Montrose and Gamma albums, yet another of his unsung talents was indeed as a gearhead, a mad scientist of electronics.

"Almost painfully so," laughs Jim, tempter and enabler of this side of Ronnie. "I'm more the tech guy than the keyboard guy. So I always considered myself an adequate keyboard player, but there are thousands of guys who play a lot better than I do—no question about it. But I had this technological side, where, by the time I met Ronnie, I was building my own mixing boards and starting to make effects gadgets, control systems, and I could do—well, to some degree—almost anything. And what would happen is, we would do one of these albums, and we never thought in terms of, okay, how are we gonna do this live? We just made that record as good as we could. Everything we can think of until, okay, that sounds great, that's what we need. Then we would listen to it later on and go, okay, now how are we gonna do this live? That's where Ronnie, I think, really enjoyed the tech stuff that I got into. Because he was into soldering cords and guitars and pickups and whatnot, but I was into integrated circuits and knob amps, digital systems, and he just jumped all over that one. That answered a lot of problems, like, how do you do switching live, with complex outboard gear and make it look effortless? And it turned out, you just had to sit down and figure out what you needed and dream it all up. And then I would just sit and spend the time designing and building whatever I needed. And then Ronnie got into 'er, and he wanted a foot pedal system, with remote control, this weird gear that you normally don't, or can't do. And it was pretty straightforward. You know, once he got a lot of that action, oh my God, I could make circuit boards, and I built the two vocoders we used throughout the Gamma albums. And it just kind of mushroomed."

And hence there's a sense of the deliberate in Jim's billing on the inner sleeve of the record as bringer of "synthesizers" and not keyboards. A statement is being made there, underscored by an additional quip on the sleeve that warns, "There are guitars and synthesizers on this album." This is likely a bit of a dig by Ronnie at bands who would proudly proclaim in interviews or directly on their album graphics that no synthesizers were used in the making of their latest album.

"I'm Alive," with enough new electronic tricks inside and therefore an eye to the '80s, would score for the band a minor hit single, reaching #60 on the Billboard charts, helping the album to a #131 placement and a 17-week stay on the album charts.

Next is "Razor King," one of three clear and away hard rock highlights on Gamma 1, the others being "Ready for Action" and "Fight to the Finish." The song is distinguished by a pumping bass line from Alan, over which Ronnie drapes a note-dense repeating guitar pattern. Skip picks a cool place to hit a crash on the verses. Synths cut down the middle, while Pattison reels off an aggressive blues vocal over what are blues-framing chord changes, although that element of the song is easy to miss, given the track's modern arrangement.

"'Razor King' is a real interesting song," says Ronnie, in the Elektra bio. "Again, it's my music and Davey's words. It's the story about a guy in Glasgow, whose name was Johnnie Stark. This was in the time of the Catholic-Protestant wars in Scotland. There would be, say, 1000 on each side, you know, marching to do battle with each other and the leaders of each side would wear waistcoats with big straight razors in their breast pockets. The leaders would go and do battle with each other—they were the razor kings. It's the kind of story you can't make up. It was like combat, but eventually hundreds of people on each side would get hurt."

Montrose has got the tale mostly right. As Davey sings from the outset, "There was a man came from my hometown..." offering direct identification, ownership of the lyric, which is confirmed through Pattison's torrid performance. There were in fact massive gang wars between the two sides, who were also partitioned by the Catholics, in the East, being Celtics supporters and the Protestants, in the West, being Rangers supporters. But 1000 a side? Likely not, although hundreds in total have been cited. As well, even though all of this did indeed happen (circa the early 1930s), Johnnie Stark, The Razor King, is the main character in H. Kingsley Long's and Alexander MacArthur's fictionalized account from 1935 called *No Mean City*, which of course was also celebrated with the Nazareth album of the same name, curiously, issued in 1979, same years as Gamma 1.

Skip's point, however venomously put, rings somewhat true, i.e. this idea about the record sounding sterile and essentially not swinging. It's something that can be discerned from "Razor King" which is a prime example of one of these songs we call written heavy but not played heavy.

"I did not like Fitz as a bass player," spits Gillette, continuing to take a razor to the Gamma 1 record and the guys making it. "I played with great bass players that made me sound like I was ten times better than I was. And then I play with Fitz and it was like towing a fucking donkey along. He never made me sound good, and he always was a prick. But when I auditioned, it was different then because they had a different bass player. They used a really good bass player when they auditioned. And then he got Fitz and the band sounded different to me. When I auditioned, it was more like the original band, which is what I liked. That guy was cool. I don't know why they didn't use him (laughs). He was pretty good. And I hated Alcivar as a keyboard player, although he's a nice guy. I liked him; he was cool. Jim is a sweet guy. He never gave me any trouble or anything. He was a nice guy and easy to work with. But I was used to playing with Luis Cabaza, who was Natalie Cole's fucking keyboard player, and you know, he was the piano player for Dulaine (laughs). Come on, I'm listening to this guy who sprinkled fucking shit and it's magic."

"And the singer, I couldn't stand. I hated him. If you listen to Tim Dulaine—go hear a song called 'Colored Candles'—you'll hear a fucking real singer. And Davey comes along with his one fucking range, two-note range and I'm bored shitless. Davey kissed Ronnie's ass. He just wanted a gig. He would go along with anything. And I'm not like that. I'm hard to get along with because I don't kiss anybody's ass. Davey's kind of a hyped-up prick. He thinks he's the fucking shit. I don't like him. I just unfriended him on Facebook, because he fucking thinks he knows it all. He's just one of those guys. I don't like him. I don't like hyped-up people."

"I tell everybody what I think," continues Gillette. "When they all brag and kiss Ronnie's ass... it's funny, all these people go to his tribute and play. Like Ricky Phillips. He never played with Ronnie. He kisses his ass. In fact Ronnie, what I'm remember, what's funny, when we were first recording with Ken Scott there, they didn't like my snare drum sound, so I called Ricky up and asked if I could borrow Tony Brock's snare drum, because I loved it. So all The Babys showed up there except for John Waite, the singer, and brought me the snare drum to record with, and they wanted to come inside. And Ronnie said, 'No, I don't want to have anything to do with anybody called The Babys.' Yeah, but Ricky doesn't remember that one. That's another kiss-ass fuck, if you ask me. He can't play bass worth shit compared to a lot of the bass players I know."

"So the whole experience, to be honest, for me, was horrific," continues Skip. "I don't like the way my drums came out at all. I think they're horrible (laughs). It sounds squashed and flat. Like I say, I wasn't allowed to play or be creative, and it wasn't anything to do with me. To be honest, I hate to be negative, but it was one of the worst musical experiences of my life. And everybody—everybody—is all jacked up about that part of my career. God, it was the worst band I was ever in! I mean, honestly, I don't understand."

As Skip says, he doesn't feel he really had a creative hand in the thing. "Sure, I made up the parts and shit, a lot of the drum parts in 'Thunder and Lightning' or whatever. But I don't know, it's nothing I'm proud of. Nothing is particularly good. Nothing that anybody couldn't do. It didn't end up sounding like Dire Straits. I like some of the guitar, I like some of the synthesizer parts, but it's just too robotic for me. It doesn't flow; it's stiff. And that's the way he wanted it to sound. Like I said, we had big differences the whole time."

Closing side one of the original vinyl is "No Tears," which again presents the band's sophisticated dichotomy between blues and electronic rock. Or rather, a synthesizer smokescreen is thrown up to open the song, and then we are into pretty much a pure uptempo Bad Company ballad. It's a gorgeous song and one of the hidden gems on an album overshadowed by the rockers. Notes Montrose, "'No Tears' is a song that Davey wrote quite a long time ago and it was one of those things that just worked out, the way we arranged it. It was a pretty straight song, and it felt good to all of us. So we did it."

And really, the interesting item down a heavy metal path is this idea that in 1979, there was very little hard rock coming out of America. There was pretty much Gamma, Sammy, Legs Diamond, Blackfoot, Riot and a still rockin' Ted Nugent, with Aerosmith about to combust and Blue Öyster Cult, Kiss, Rick Derringer and Angel already gone pop. Ronnie on the other hand, sat somewhere in-between, although even when poppy, there was an intellectual quality to the music he was proposing. In other words, as varied, keyboardy and melodic as his new band was, it rarely felt pandering to radio. As he himself put it, "We're a vocal-oriented, high-powered band. I'm working with the best vocalist I've ever worked with, one who comes from a background of blues and rock. There's more of the synthesizer element than I've ever had in a band. And all these things coming together are what makes it an especially interesting band."

Over to side two, "Solar Heat" is an exercise in jazz fusion, although closer to a Jeff Beck-type situation. There's not much jazz and all told it's pretty heavy, made modern through panning synths, not that crazy in the playing but more so the arrangement, with the slow reverse fade of the rhythm track, and then, yes, some fierce unison playing between Alan and Ronnie. "Fitz was scared to death to do 'Solar Heat,' that introduction to 'Ready for Action,'" notes Jim. "He had to play that riff with Ronnie, and he lost sleep that night doing it; it was definitely hard to play."

Said Ronnie in the Elektra bio, "It's the kind of thing I like to write. That's kind of a soundtrack for something—for an animated film, say. It really fits well on the album, and it's the kind of thing that could be used as an opening piece. But you can't just open side one, track one of an unknown album with an instrumental piece, but it's the kind of song that can only open side two, so that's what it does on side two. Of course, it also has an ecological message."

Shedding light on where an obscure track like "Solar Heat" could come from, Ronnie told me, "Once again, I've never paid attention to the music industry. I listen to music but I don't listen to current music and I haven't been for a long time. I believe at the Gamma time I was listening to the first Dire Straits record, I was listening to Kraftwerk, I was listening to Tangerine Dream, listening to *The Planets*, Holst, and always listening to big band music, listening to singers, listening to Tony Bennett, Frank Sinatra, Ella Fitzgerald. My father had actually turned me onto Dave Brubeck and that sort of modern jazz thing. It wasn't exactly like if you were a rock guy you'd want to come out and hang in my hotel room (laughs)."

Notes Metallica's Kirk Hammett on Gamma in general and on "Solar Heat" in particular, "For me, Gamma was the guitar-playing that Ronnie Montrose promised (laughs), on the first few Montrose albums. You would hear these great songs on those albums, and you just knew that if he wanted to, he could stretch out and do a long extended solo on any given tune. But on those albums, there aren't any long extended solos; 'Rock Candy' is maybe the longest solo. But think about it, on the Gamma albums there are improvisations all over the place, you know? He plays his ass off in Gamma! I mean, it's the part of Ronnie Montrose that I wanted to hear. So I devoured those albums. I mean remember, when Gamma 1 came out, I learned how to play 'Razor King,' 'I'm Alive.' Oh man, great stuff. And, you know, there's a jazz fusion sort of aspect to those albums as well. First track, side two (sings it), which starts with a keyboard line—'Solar Heat.' That's kind of fusion, and then it goes into 'Ready for Action.' That long run in F sharp? I still play that to this day, when I pick up my guitar to like show off or whatever. Yeah, to this day, I still play that."

"But, I loved Gamma," continues Kirk. "I learned a lot of guitar stuff off of those albums. 'Voyager;' I fucking love that song, and 'Razor King.' And 'Four Horsemen'—how's that for fast and thrashy? I saw them twice. And the second time I saw them, indoors at the Oakland Coliseum, I was amazed at how well Ronnie Montrose played—and he was fucking running all over the place too. Crazy! And I really thought they were great live. Plus I really thought they had an incredible singer with a great voice, Davey Pattison."

Says Ronnie of Gamma *1*'s heaviest rocker, "Ready for Action," "This song is just what the title says— real high energy, real, contemporary. 'Solar Heat' sort of segues into this one." Indeed this is a speedy, heavy metal call to arms, although Ken Scott most definitely applies a close and intimate and even cloistered vibe to it, taking some of the metal out of it, especially during the stealth-like verse. On the solo section, the band break out a bit more, and the energy is detectably higher during the late verse, due to the bass line and Davey's increased urgency of delivery. Still, all told, this is performed and then recorded tight as a drum and lacking in heft.

"This is the other song on the album I didn't write," notes Ronnie, concerning "Wish I Was." "Nick Clainos at my management played it for me, just as a song he liked, and I couldn't believe it. It's a Mickey Newbury song, with beautiful words and real slow— perfectly suited for me to play guitar on and for Davey to sing on. It's a perfect vehicle for both of us."

Newbury, a respected Nashville songwriter and recording artist, first issued the song on his 1978 album *His Eye is on the Sparrow*. "It's well suited to Davey," notes Jim. "This is crazy, but it was the toughest one for me, playing the keys on it. It's just chords; that's all it is—chords, chords, chords, nothing fancy or complicated. But if I wasn't dead on every beat, it was just, 'Uh-oh, gotta do it again.' And that was one that drove me nuts."

Once more, as with "No Tears" and even "Razor King," with the earthy timbre and delivery of Davey Pattison, Gamma sound like a version of Bad Company contemporary with themselves, that band issuing the perky *Desolation Angels* album also in 1979. "Just a blues we were jamming on," dismisses Skip. "Simple stupid blues. Simple song that everybody fucking plays."

Closing the record is "Fight to the Finish," the album's majestic epic, perfectly tuned to the Gamma credo, somewhat heavy but also atmospheric, foreboding, not particularly loud, almost, in a sense, a doomy ballad. Hard to pin, obviously, which is often the mark of a creative stretch of music, as this sculpted aural journey most definitely is.

"That's the one song where I pretty much wrote everything," explains Alcivar. "I used to make these little tapes of song ideas, and that one, I wish I could find the tape. It should be around somewhere, but that's a long story. Other than the chorus; Ronnie needed a chorus, and he put in the changes for that. But everything, all the parts that him and Fitz played, are all stuff I did with the keys. This one little song thing. And that one worked well. We tried to do a few others and the band just couldn't play them. It's complicated. And with 'Fight to the Finish,' I got to wow Ken. I think Ken had a click track on the tapes, just to keep time straight. And I said, 'Okay, we're going to do this little synthesizer introduction thing, and I need... can you get your tech guys to give me an oscilloscope?' And he looks at me, 'What?!' 'Yeah, I need a scope; I need to see the click track, and how it goes through. I've got a little processor that converts that to a pulse signal for the sequencers.' And he was kind of like, okay... And then they hauled the stuff down and got it all set up and it worked like a dream. But it was this whole little actually complicated pattern, that thing that goes through to get into the verses. And we loved that one. But Ken got knocked out, because he wasn't really expecting or understanding the idea of the 6/8 intro in a 4/4 song. Every time he would hear it, he would kind of catch his feet, 'What happened?! The beat changes!' 'No, no, no, it's just 6/8 against 4/4.'"

"'Fight to the Finish' is the strongest song on the album," sums up Ronnie. "This is the song closest to what Gamma is, and is the closest to the direction Gamma will be going in. That's why it's the last song on the record. Gamma continues from there."

Nice sentiment, but not true—Gamma would never sound like this again.

Once Gamma 1 crept its way onto record racks, there wasn't much in the way of press on it or the band in general. Billboard, however, offered their usual straight-laced business assessment of the situation, Mike Hyland writing that, "The main focal point of the band is, in addition to Montrose's guitar work, the keyboard and synthesizer wizardry of Jim Alcivar (a holdover from the Montrose band) and the vocals of Davey Pattison, who at times reminds the listener of Bad Company's Paul Rodgers. Producer Ken Scott, who has recorded such diverse musical acts as Supertramp and the Dixie Dregs, gets a total rock sound out of the band, making Gamma 1 one of the most impressive debut albums to come along in some time. It leaves one primed and ready for Gamma 2."

And do you think good ol' Skip Gillette enjoyed playing live with Gamma? Me neither!

"Live, Ronnie always had me way down in the mix," begins Gillette. "And I was playing as loud as I could all the time, and you could never hear me. It was ridiculous compared to the bands... I should've never joined the band, to be honest with you. And all the guys were pricks, and condescending to me. They treated me like I was a three-year-old. Because they'd all been on the road before. Not because of their fucking talent, you know? But they were pricks. And I didn't like it. I hated it. Like I said, I had no musical creativity and ability in the whole thing. I always wanted to ride with the roadies, which Ronnie refused to let me do. It was weird. He said 'They're in a different class.' I'm like, 'What are you talking about? They're fucking cool' (laughs). I don't want to ride in the fucking plane every night."

"And when we had a really good gig, or I played great, and they would televise it or record it live, if Ronnie made a mistake on it, there was no way anybody could use it. Ronnie just always acted like he was too good. And I could never be as good as Tony Williams. Or Steve Smith. Well, fuck no (laughs). Those guys are geniuses. Tony Williams especially. You know,

Steve Smith is no slouch either, for goodness sake. He's the drum guru of the 2000s. Those are guys... he played with them, right before me, so obviously I was a little intimidated. Especially with Tony Williams."

But you can't deny that the band got a fair shake in terms of getting put in front of big crowds. "Yeah, we opened up for Santana forever, fucking Foreigner. We opened up for everybody—Blue Öyster Cult, ZZ Top. ZZ Top backstage is a circus, as everybody knows. You know, Bill Graham had everybody going through. I liked Bill Graham. He was cool. I liked him as a manager. He was always really sweet to me. I listened to him yell at people—that's the way he got things done. I heard him on the phone screaming at people. I thought fucking A, scare the shit out of those motherfuckers. I learned a lot from Bill. In business and stuff, when people are fucking with you and shit. I used to go up to his office and just listen to him. It was like going to school. He was great. He had a big tepee he would sit in with his phones."

Skip says that from the old days, the band played "I Got the Fire," but "I can't remember what else. Mainly that one. Bill Graham always wanted us to play more and Ronnie didn't want to. I kind of agreed with Bill Graham, because I liked the other songs better. I really didn't like any of the new songs."

Rumour has it Foreigner were not exactly accommodating to the guys here or indeed later, when they had Gamma on 3 for the Foreigner 4 tour. I asked Skip what they were like at this point, which would have had Mick and Lou out supporting *Head Games*. "The lead singer in Foreigner's a big prick. He was a big prick. I came up to tell him how good I thought he was, and he told me to fuck off. Here's one other thing I noticed. During the whole tour we didn't once get a sound check, but we showed up for sound check every day, hung around for two hours until we didn't get one. I noticed that. Mick was always cool. Actually I ran into Mick Jones helping produce Eddie Van Halen, up at 5150, and he remembered. He goes, 'I remember Hershey, Pennsylvania. I remember you.'"

"But musically, it was really frustrating for me because I was getting nothing out of it," continues Skip. "And I found it was a really good lesson for me because I realized I joined the band because I really wanted to get somewhere. And I already had it musically and everything with the bands that were already being recorded by... what's his name, Don Arden was recording us. Sharon's father, he owned Jet Records and shit, and he had us in The Record Plant all the time. And I left that to join Montrose, because I wanted to get somewhere. And I realized that getting somewhere doesn't mean anything. Trying to get in a big band doesn't mean anything if you're not musically satisfied. What's the fucking point? You might as well be pumping gas somewhere."

As for Ronnie's no drugs and no drink policy," Skip says, "That was a really big fucking drag which didn't make any sense to me. Stifled my creativity a lot. I mean, I'm used to playing with Hendrix-type people, you know? And people from Hendrix. And it's part of my natural... rock 'n' roll, you smoke a fucking joint and play. I don't give a fuck; look at Paul McCartney or Willie Nelson. And every time you would get high and start to have fun, he would go, 'Are you weeding it? What are you doing? Get the fuck out of here.' Oh, what a drag. I can't even get high and play music?! Fuck you! And then he turns out to be an alcoholic all fucked-up later on, you know. Fuck him. I hate him. I really do. But the other guys all drank. They didn't do... I was the only one who smoked pot. Everybody else just drank. And they could drink after the shows as much as they wanted, and Ronnie didn't give a shit."

It'll come as no surprise that Skip's days in Gamma were numbered (although one wonders how he lasted as long as he did!).

"Ronnie was like Hitler," says Skip. "He was a prick—and he was cheap. And I was already making ten times more money before I joined his fucking band. And it's kind of a joke to me. It's like, well, fuck you and your fucking stupid 600 bucks a week. And I also thought it was kind of shitty that he had a fucking attitude, and I was presenting him with really good songs some of my friends wrote that were really good songs, and he wouldn't fucking listen to them. Yeah, he was a prick. I presented a lot of bass players to him too, but he didn't want to fucking listen to me about anything like that either. Like I say, it was like being in the army. It really was. Like I got drafted and I expected something else and all of a sudden it was like boot camp. It was a drag. 'Don't play this, don't play that.' It was stifling compared to the creativity that I had been playing with down in LA with really good musicians that could go anywhere at any moment. They all just had a big fucking ego and it was a drag."

Besides his obvious laundry list of complaints, Skip says that in the end—or at least *his* end with this whole regretted mess—it came down to dollars as well.

"All these people that brag about playing with him weren't making any fucking money, I guarantee you. Like when I quit, I had to fight with him. The reason we don't get along and I'm not on any of his fucking shit, was when he fired me, or whatever the fuck he did, he owed me a bunch of money. So I took the fucking flight cases that he had made for me, and he got all pissed-off. I said, 'Fuck you. They cost about as much money... you give me the fucking money you owe me, and then I'll give you your fucking cases.' But he never did, so I kept the cases and told him to go fuck himself. I'm one of the only people that ever stood up to the fucker, you know?"

As for when in the timeline this all happened, Gillette says, "We were off for a long time, and then after we didn't work for a few months, he couldn't pay me for, I don't know, three or four months, after promising to pay me. He just said, 'Well, I've decided I'm going to switch drummers.' 'Well, what about all the fucking money you owe me and shit?' 'Sorry,' you know. And he fucking took off. It was almost like I look back at it that he was trying to get me to quit so he wouldn't have to pay me. Fuck him. I had worked on the second album, like a couple of rehearsals, and it just went to shit, and he decided he was going to change directions. Get a different bass player and drummer like it was going to save his ass. Like we had anything to do with it."

"And I never made a dime off the fucking album. You know why? Because everybody else knew Ronnie was a prick. So when he offered us, 'Hey, do you want points off the album or scale?,' everyone in the band took scale except me. And I think Davey might've taken points too; I'm not sure. But, because they knew Ronnie, they all got paid scale from the union. In scale, when you're in the union, you get paid scale. So those guys, instead of taking points, Fitz and Alcivar and everybody, as far as I know, they took scale, and they got paid by the union, when they did the album. But that's only a few hundred bucks. Maybe $1000, who knows? A couple thousand. And they took that because they thought they never would get any money out of Ronnie. Because they were smart. Because they worked for him before."

"So I never got a dime off the album. Finally I said to Ronnie, 'Hey, dude, when am I gonna start making money off the album? We're doing really good.' And he goes, 'Oh, well, we owe Bill Graham $1 million, from before.' Or somebody told me or something. I can't remember who the fuck told me. The accountant. 'Well, you know, we owe Bill Graham $1 million, and that comes off the top.' And I'm like, what?! So I never made one dime off that album. We recorded that whole album for free, plus they used my picture on the fucking *Best of Gamma* release, on the front, never got a dime off that. I never got a fucking dime from playing with that band, except when I was on the road. $600 a week on the road and $200 a week off the road. It was grief (laughs). Yeah, he was just an asshole all the way around. Really destructive artistically. I really don't understand how he got so famous, to be honest with you. Because all the guitar players I played with besides him were just as good, or way better in my opinion. Honestly, I never could figure it out. But yeah, he was self-destructive. He did that with all his fucking relationships in life."

For a guy starting up in the '60s, and still drumming now in his mid-60s, Skip Gillette's biggest credit is this record he hates so much. Although right after Gamma 1, says Skip, there were a few missed opportunities.

"Right after that I was in a big band, Shandi. I don't know if you know who Mike Chapman is. He produced The Knack and a bunch of people. And he had a company called Dreamland, and this girl named Shandi got the biggest record deal in Hollywood history. And the drummer was a guy named Pat Mastelotto, who is now the drummer for King Crimson. And they couldn't find anybody to take his place, but I got that gig, right after Gamma. So I did that tour, and at that time, Joe Pollard was the first guy that was coming out with the electronic drums, Syndrums. And he provided me with a bunch of them that I loved, and then I used a lot of electronic drums. And when they put Night Ranger together, we were always in touch with each other. They were thinking about having me play with them for a while, but then they decide to just have Kelly play drums. And then he just wanted to sing. Anyway, I probably wouldn't have played with them."

Skip's name is also a footnote in the Quiet Riot story, as the "DuBrow" band transitions into the revived Quiet Riot that would strike six-times platinum with *Metal Health*. "I was playing with them at the time. Another horrible band. Another horrible band. The two bands that people know me from are the two worst bands I've ever been in. They asked me to play on the first album—I said no. I refused to play on it."

"I turned down Ozzy Osbourne three times, in '84 or '85," says Skip in closing. "Yeah, three times in one week (laughs). Sharon was too fucking stoned to realize she was calling me every other day."

CHAPTER 7: Gamma – 2: "Powering it through"

And so we come to celebrate one of the great hard rock albums of the '80s, namely Gamma 2, which found Ronnie Montrose, Jim Alcivar and Davey Pattison putting aside the first album's rhythm section, with ex-Montrose drummer Denny Carmassi re-joining the fold, along with bassist Glenn Letsch, who opens our analysis of an album that is arguably the best of Ronnie's life work, debut from Montrose included.

"Well, you may or may not be familiar with the producer Mitchell Froom. See, I grew up in Connecticut and played in the bar circuit back then. I graduated from college in 1971, and decided to satisfy my thirst for becoming a full-time musician. So I joined a local band and we were playing cover tunes and some originals, and did a little recording around the New England circuit, played ski resorts, nightclubs, that kind of thing. After about six years of that, I decided that I needed to find a way to step up to the bigger pond. And I heard that Los Angeles was the Mecca, the hub of the upper echelon of the music business. So I drove myself out there, with the good wishes of my wife, to get set up there, and she would relocate after I got us set up. So to make a long story short, I get to Los Angeles, and a friend of mine is working at a place called S.I.R., Studio

Instrument Rentals, and I pull right off the freeway and see my pal Guy, and he says, 'Boy, you timed this perfectly. There's a guy here, Mitchell Froom; he's auditioning bass players.' So I walked in, got this tape from Mitchell, went back home, learned the songs, came back three days later and got the gig."

"And Mitchell had just come off the road playing keyboards for Ronnie Montrose on his *Open Fire* tour. So he was really good friends with Ronnie. And part of it, the carrot dangling to me from Mitchell, was that Ronnie Montrose was going to produce our demo. So we drove up north to the Bay Area, to Gary Pihl's house, who is now the guitar player for Boston, and in those days he was the guitarist for Sammy Hagar, and Mitchell Froom's best friend. So he graciously offered his studio for us to do this demo tape at. And for Ronnie to produce. So I came up, we did the song, I flew back to Los Angeles. And the night that I flew back, I got the call from Ronnie and he asked me to join his band Gamma. And we hit it off really well in the recording studio; he thought I would be a perfect fit for his band, and he told me that Denny Carmassi had agreed to join, to come back with him. So I just thought I had died and gone to musical heaven."

Asked how this had sat with Mitchell Froom, Glenn says, "Mitchell had actually told Ronnie that… actually Ronnie did ask Mitchell if it was okay. In fact, Mitchell had told me Ronnie was asking about me. He says, 'I know in your heart you really want to do this. So I'm going to tell Ronnie that it's totally okay for you to do this.' So it was like a big opportunity for me, and he didn't want to stand in my way. Mitchell gave the blessing for Ronnie ask me to join his band, because he thought I would be a perfect fit to play with Denny."

"I don't think there ever really was a falling out with Fitz," reflects Jim Alcivar. "I think it was just, Ronnie made a decision. Even I later got my ass kicked out of Gamma and we stayed good friends after anyway. I didn't really have a problem with that. So I'm sure it was really the same situation with Fitz. Ronnie needed a certain thing to happen, and well, you know, no hard feelings and blah blah blah."

Alan Fitzgerald would move onto considerable fame and fortune as part of Night Ranger, appearing on seven studio albums between 1982 and 1998, including 1983's *Midnight Madness* and 1985's *7 Wishes*, both of which went platinum. Continuing the connection with the Montrose camp, Fitz would revive his relationship with Sammy—he had appeared on 1976's *Nine on a Ten Scale*, 1977's *Sammy Hagar* and the 1978 live album *All Night Long*—by playing off-stage keyboards for Van Halen in the early '90s, as well as on that band's 2004, 2007 and 2012 tours, a role he also played for Bruce Springsteen in 2005.

With respect to the additional switch in drummers, Glenn says, "You'd have to ask Ronnie that. I have no idea. I think when he heard that there was the opportunity to have Denny come back and play with him, I think he must've thought—and I'm just guessing—that it might be a good idea to just do the whole rhythm section, get a whole new rhythm section."

"And once again the Aerosmith connection came out," says Ronnie, who was now going to be working with another Aerosmith producer after having done *Jump on It* with Jack Douglas. "After the first record, our manager said, 'You know, this guy Gary Lyons just finished working with Aerosmith and he'd love to work with you and we can have him.' So we got together and did Gamma 2 which was much more of an Aerosmith rock type of record than Gamma 1, which was Ken Scott/Supertramp synth mix Gamma, more techie. Gary was an absolute maniac; an Englishman and maniac. But I did like working with him because I totally appreciate the English sense of humour, and we just pulled out all the stops and turned everything up and just played. And it was good; I mean it was really good."

"Gary was more like an engineer," says Denny, diplomatically, and really, quite surprisingly, letting on that he's not a fan of the record. "Like an engineer/producer and not a real song guy. We needed to bring in a real song guy, a guy that would really know how to work the songs over and not settle for something, make you really work at it. Not settle for something. I mean, it was a good band, a good combination, even good songs, but they just weren't arranged well and put together right. But it sound really good anyway."

"So we did that," continues Ronnie, "went out and toured, had fun with that, and ended up doing a lot of shows with AC/DC. It's funny, when Denny went with Heart, they played with John Mellencamp, and those guys all came out, because we had just finished Gamma 3, and John's band all came up to him and said, 'Man, you were in Gamma?! We loved that band!'"

"It was incredibly fast, and zero arguing," continues Glenn, on the construction of this classic album. "Actually, here's how it went down. When Ronnie made that call to me, because, he goes, 'Can you fly up to the Bay Area in a couple days, and we'll do preproduction for Gamma 2?' So I flew up, literally came off the airplane, I was picked up, brought to S.I.R. Studios in San Francisco. Denny, Jim Alcivar, Davey and Ronnie were already there set up. I introduced myself to them, plugged my bass into an SVT that they had rented for me, and we just started running down the new tunes. After a couple of hours, we had the album ready. Ready to go. There was one more preproduction meeting with Gary Lyons, who was going to be producing, and then we went across the street a couple of days later to The Automatt and we started tracking. The basic tracks were done in two days, and one song was completely done—there were no overdubs. 'Voyager' was done live in the studio, and it was either the first or the second take. And Ronnie kept his original solo from that take. The album went really fast. It was a breeze, actually. After the basic tracks were done, I left. So I was not there for any more of the recording after that. But a few weeks later, I was in New York for the mastering. My family is back East, so Ronnie and Gary had flown to New York to do the mastering, so I did get to hear that."

As with Denny, Jim also "had mixed emotions about Gary. Half the time he was turning around to Ronnie, 'Ronnie, you need to get an English keyboard player in here.' He was always giving me a hard time. On the other hand, it was because of him that we did 'Voyager,' which I think probably all the guys are telling you, was all done live. It was the only song we ever did live, that any of the bands ever did live. And I love it for that. But with Gary, you can't put a finger on it. Production in the band and the songs are weird, and there's time of year and day of month... it's just this weird, lucky combination where the stars align and things happen right. And you really can't put a finger on that. If it had been Ken Scott, it would've been very different sounding—and I don't know if as good. A lot of things happened to that record that were just nice. It was a little more natural for us, because we just kind of freewheel-played it as it felt. Not a lot of interference, which made it a fun thing to do. Gary was easy. He really didn't fuss around about it. Unlike Ken. And Ken I liked, because with his fastidious control, that had an effect on the sound. Well, that loose, casual guy also has an effect on the sound. Gamma 1 is, I don't want to say sterile, but it's just very different sonically and yet it's almost the same players."

As to whether Gary was serious about this English keyboard player stuff, Jim says, "I'll never know. I have a feeling it was his way of pushing me. And if that's true, that makes him an excellent producer (laughs)."

When I asked Glenn if he recalled any particularly hard nuts to crack on the album, he said, "No, it was just a rock band, live, basically. I would say the arrangements were not terribly complicated. It was just a matter of getting out there and powering it through and giving it a lot of energy, a lot of vibe. I found the arrangements to be not terribly complicated. It was just… we got together and it fit like a glove. It didn't need to be overanalyzed and over-thought."

Gamma 2 begins life as one of the more amusing wrappers of the day, a realist-detailed illustration of a couple of sharks cutting their way through a lawn toward… a woman. And a man?

featuring **Ronnie Montrose**

"That cover was an art department suggestion, I guess, in conjunction with Ronnie," says Letsch. "But I have the original poster of it up on my wall in my studio, and the original has the sharks going through the lawn towards a woman's feet, laying on the chaise lounge, if you recall. Now, there was some issue with a women's organization against violence or something back in those days, and they thought it was a sexist cover. So they air brushed in on the actual album cover, a man's arm, across the woman's legs. As well, there's a cigarette in that guy's hand. Which, Ronnie I remember really objected to, that we were advocating smoking or something. But it was one of those political moves where the record company succumbed to the pressure of the woman's organization. Great cover though. I remember because Playboy magazine gave it cover of the year, and that was kind of cool. I was proud of that."

The distinctive design was cooked up by Mick Haggerty, responsible for Gamma 1 and Gamma 3 as well, plus covers for Supertramp, David Bowie, Blackfoot, Go-Gos, Public Image Ltd., Richard Thompson, Simple Minds, Hot Tuna and myriad others.

Says Mick, "For the addition of the man's hand we have the Rolling Stones to thank, and their depiction of a woman chained to a billboard on Sunset to promote their album *Black and Blue*. The predictable furor of women's groups and their threats of boycotts, while music to Jagger's ears, scared the less than brave hearts at Elektra who originally insisted that there be a man *and* a woman both lying on the chaise, which would have looked incredibly stupid. Last minute negotiations persuaded them to agree to the hand and to Ronnie's dismay, I added the cigarette to at least give it a little post-coital edge. I'm glad that the animal rights folks were not protesting that week or

I might have had to change the sharks into moles. Working for Ronnie was an artist's dream. For all three Gamma covers the phone would ring and Ronnie would just give me dates. Then a few weeks later I would present him with my best shot, he loved them all, and just pushed them through Elektra. Remember, this was years before marketing departments had any say in imagery and we were free to invent visuals that attempted to be challenging and incongruous and to not just pander to market stereotypes. I'm proud of all of these packages."

Once into the sizzling grooves of the record itself, Gamma 2, issued August of 1980, kicks off with "Mean Streak," a panoramic hard rocker that put the band's many weapons on display immediately. Denny gets to hit hard like his hero John Bonham, Davey Pattison sings soulfully like a Scottish Lou Gramm, Ronnie fires up a criss-crossing riff with gorgeous licks in betwixt, Jim waxes and wanes on synthesizer, and Glenn plays around the complex cathedral of sounds like a Motown great.

"Davey is, in my book, one of the greatest blue-eyed soul singers in the world," notes Glenn, who later played with Pattison in the context of Robin Trower's band. "He's amazing. And aside from having this incredibly soulful voice, he's one of the most down-to-earth people in the world. He's the kind of guy that when you meet him, you feel like you've known him your whole life. So we've been close friends for well over 30 years. He's just awesome."

"Davey is a wonderful, wonderful singer," seconds Robin Trower. "He's great to work with because he's such an easygoing guy. He just tries to give me what I'm looking for and most of the time does. He's a wonderful natural musician."

As far as Letsch's obvious bass skills (his day job is writing bass instruction books for Hal Leonard Publishing) are concerned, "I would have to say that my roots are probably in the British invasion, back in the Beatles days, McCartney, and then immediately after them, Led Zeppelin and The Who. And from that point I started going back to my childhood days and looking at Little Richard and who played for Elvis, Bill Black and those people, and right about that time, the British invasion, when the car radio had all the great Motown stuff coming through. Everybody was wondering, who the heck is this great bass player on all[1] these songs? This guy's unbelievable, and that guy was James Jamerson, of course. So I got into that very heavily. And also at that time I got heavily into James Brown, started analyzing all that. So I would have to say that my roots are in black funk, R&B and English hard rock."

Alcivar gets one of his two co-credits for "Mean Streak" (the other being album closer "Mayday"), Letsch positing that, "I think Jim was writing motifs with synthesizer that became signature routines, or part of the songs. You know, Ronnie loved the keyboards, and together, Jim and him were like pioneers, getting those Prophet 5 sounds to mesh with hard rock guitar. It was just a beautiful thing. And Jim was such an electronics genius, if you will. His set-up looked like Keith Emerson's on stage. He was like the mad wizard, with all the patch cords and everything. With all these oscillators and what have you. Jim was his own pioneer too. Brilliant guy. Just to back up about Ronnie's gear, I believe it was with Gamma 2, and it could've been Gamma 1, he switched to solid-state amplifiers. I don't recall the name of the company—possibly Laney—but that changed his sound. That took a little of the edge off and I think he thought it matched the keyboards. But he was always tweaking gear and changing pedals. It's funny, because rehearsals at S.I.R. would be mostly Ronnie and Jim with soldering guns, working with the foot pedals and us reading Mad magazine waiting to start rehearsal. The band played great and so we only needed to run the songs through once anyway. It was more of a formality than anything, because that was a great band."

Next up on the album is a heart-raced speed rocker called "Four Horsemen." At least it starts that way, with the band turning in a Rainbow-style rave, thenceforth relaxing into a gorgeous groove and an even smarter arrangement. This is a high point of the Gamma catalogue, with changes and switchbacks that are legion.

Says Letsch of the album as a whole, in a statement that could apply specifically to this textured track, "Oh yeah, I thought we were ahead of our time. I think we were one of the first bands to fuse a hard rock energy with the modern sensibility of synthesizers. So I thought it was cutting edge cool. Plus, live, we were a powerhouse. It was really, really cool."

"I don't think there was anything that was influencing our sound," muses Pattison. "It was what it was, and me, being straight off the boat from Scotland, certainly had an influence on the lyrics, because I was writing songs about Glasgow and Scotland. 'Razor King' comes to mind, which was about gangs in the '20s in Glasgow. So there was certainly that influence in it. I don't think there was much difference between the first two albums, although I think Gamma 2 was the best album we did—just my opinion. It's an extension, really, of the first one, where we were just getting to know each other, certainly as songwriters together, Ronnie and I. And Gamma 2, of course we got Denny Carmassi on drums, and that made a whole difference as well."

As regards original bass player Alan Fitzgerald, Davey quips, "He's one of those talented guys—I hate guys like that (laughs). I haven't seen him in a long time; Fitz was a good guy. But yeah, he ended up the keyboard player for Night Ranger. They were all great people. Glenn Letsch, to this day, we're great friends still, but I don't see much from Denny. But it's funny, we don't live very far away from each other. I don't really keep in contact with them too much, tell you the truth."

Of course as we've discussed, Ronnie had a reputation as being a hard guy to work with, a sentiment with which Davey somewhat concurs. "Well, with me, I guess it was a different thing. I speak to Ronnie all the time. Ronnie in the old days could be difficult, let's put it that way. He knows it; it's not something I can't talk about. He could be difficult from day to day, but now we've all gotten a lot older. Well, with me, he always let me do what I do. He doesn't direct me in any way. 'Here's the song, there's a microphone, the machine's running, sing away.' And he's always been like that with me. So, you know, it's fun. But it was his thing. I never experienced much problem with him, although he has a reputation for being a little naughty at times. But I never saw it. It's actually difficult to explain. Hmm, I guess it was the nature of the business basically, more than anything else. It was his record deal, so he's under the gun, so he's got to deliver, and I guess there's the stress of that. I mean, who is he going to complain to? We're right on the road and the record company is giving him shit for this, that and the next thing—he's going to take it out on the band. Because there's nobody else to take it out on. It's a difficult business and it's even worse now. In actual fact, it's easier now, because everybody is in the same boat (laughs)."

Back to the record, "Dirty City" follows, with a gritty realism out of the Phil Mogg handbook (and back-up vocals from Ten Wheel Drive's Genya Ravan). This one's a bit of an AOR rocker, with a slippery chorus (note the siren sounds) and a whole pile of nice synthesizer textures.

"I've always liked 'Dirty City,'" note Glenn. "It always had that pounding vibe, like an old Frankie Miller tune or something—who we all loved. It was about Glasgow, so it was reminiscent of those guys from that era." Ronnie turns in a tough heavy metal guitar solo, but as usual, it's well-reasoned, earthy, traditional. Says Glenn of Ronnie, "He's just an incredibly melodic hard rock guitar player. One of the best. And when he is on, on stage, he is as good as anybody. And he's usually on. I just saw him play out here in my town, where I live; he was playing for a corporate event. So he called and invited me down, with his latest version of Montrose. And you know, Ronnie is 60, and he was amazing. It was as good as ever."

With respect to Alcivar, Glenn adds, "He was just a big pussycat, so easy to get along with. Just really helpful for me, I remember, when I joined the band. I didn't know a lot of things. I didn't know the protocol when I joined. And he just sort of helped me along. He was cool. Just an easy guy to hang with. Ronnie and Jim, you know, they were always at rehearsal with a soldering gun, opening… in those days it was these big patch cables. It looked like Mr. Wizard on stage. It was like stuff you see in a museum now, but it was a technological breakthrough at that point. Those guys were always fiddling with oscillators. In fact (laughs), most of the time there wasn't any rehearsal. We would come up for rehearsal, and Ronnie would have his pedal board open and he would be soldering all the joints, and then him and Jim would be taking synthesizers apart and putting in new oscillators and generators, and it would be quarter to five, and, 'Oh, we better run the set down.' And we would run the set down, and everybody knew what to play. Boom boom boom, pack it up and go on tour. Not over-rehearsing. Everybody was a great player. So you just had to know the parts and know the arrangements and let it fly. But I mean, even the name Gamma, I think it had to do with Ronnie's fascination with technology and gamma rays and all that. He was always a 'Sharper Image' kind of guy, reading about space exploration and that sort of thing."

Glenn downplays suggestions, most pertinently by Hagar, that Ronnie had a fragile ego, that he lacked confidence and he made up for it by overly taking charge. "Boy, you know I don't know anybody in the music business that doesn't have some sort of delicateness to their ego, that they don't like criticism. Without trying to be politically correct, Ronnie has been a great friend of mine for 30 something years. He's always been just awesome with me, so I've never had any issues. I'm able to speak frankly about a mix for a song and he takes it pretty well."

Closing side one was "Voyager," a hard blues that evokes images of Montrose circa *Paper Money*, or even Robin Trower, as mentioned, a man and a band that has claimed half of Gamma from time to time. "I think 'Voyager' is my favourite track on that," notes Letsch, "although I like 'Mean Streak' as well. I thought 'Voyager' had the most spontaneity, because it was one take, and we just went for it, and there's a lot of interplay, I guess conversation, between the bass and drums. I always liked when we did that."

"To me, 'Voyager' was the classic Gamma song," seconds Pattison. "It was the biggest hit we ever had and it got more airplay than anything, to my knowledge. I also liked 'Four Horsemen.' 'Skin and Bone' was a good song; there's a lot of good stuff. To me, Gamma was somewhat ahead of its time. I mean, you hear the early Metallica stuff. That sounds like Gamma to me, you know? And they're Bay Area guys too, so that's got to tell you something. Lyrically, again 'Voyager' comes to mind as a favourite, as well as 'Four Horsemen,' 'Mean Streak' and 'Dirty City.' I wrote the lyrics for that and am pretty proud of that one."

Notes guitarist Tal Morris, who played with Ronnie in the '90s, "I was a huge fan of 'Voyager,' obviously, one of the greatest tracks of all time. And we were working, and I just had to bring it up—that solo. And he told me that solo was one take, and he said it was this magic moment of... he felt like as he was playing it, that nothing could go wrong. And he was basically surfing. It was like he was riding something, that it was playing itself, that the cadence of it and how it resolves and feels and everything was just a magic moment. And he recognized that. He wasn't taking responsibility for it. He wasn't like, 'Yeah, this diminished fifth, and then I moved into, you know, obviously, a long single note because the moment called for it.' Nothing like that. He knew that it was a confluence of elements and he was riding it, and recognizing what to do and let go—he was letting go and letting it play itself, basically. Another thing, when he talked about Davey, he was totally enamoured with Davey's voice. And he had said openly that he had finally found the sound that worked with his guitar and the way that he played. Because Davey has this lyrical aspect and was bluesy and had sinewy aspects to his voice and the range he sang in—it all fit and so he talked fondly of that."

O'er to side two, and Gamma turn in one of the greatest versions of Thunderclap Newman's 'Something in the Air' ever crafted and documented. Again, the Trower-powered pipes of Pattison meld serendipitously with the all-encompassing sound Ronnie was able to get out of his guitar.

There's a reason, explains Glenn, for the mesmerizing soupiness of the axe tones on Gamma 2.

"A technological thing I remember, Ronnie had a hexaphonic pickup, for the making of that record. And a hexaphonic pickup is a six-pickup pickup. So each string has its own pickup. So each string goes to its own amplifier, and then he would spread those six amplifiers out in a semicircle, and he had six microphones on it. So his guitar took up six tracks. So his guitar basically took a stereo spread from say, nine o'clock for your low E string, to three o'clock for your high E string. And the others proportionally in-between. So the guitar sounded really wide and huge."

With respect to his choice of guitars at this point, after saying that in Montrose he played the Les Paul and a little bit of Strat, Ronnie told Andy Secher he was now back to the Strat: "I played the Strat a little bit with Montrose, especially on the early albums. But I became more and more dependent on the Les Paul because it was easier to keep in tune and it gave off a cleaner sound. With the Strat, because its neck is thinner, you have a tendency to play faster and a bit sloppier. Speed has never been a priority for me. The Strat I'm using now has really been customized. I've got a workshop in my basement at home, and I took my Strat and dug a trough in the back of the guitar. That allows me to slide the pickups up and down, which gives you an incredible variation in tone. You can make it sound like you're playing with either the lead or rhythm pickups that way, which really gives an extra dimension to your playing."

"Well, we needed a single," furthers Letsch, on the interesting cover choice of "Something in the Air" for the album. "The record company wanted a single, and I guess they didn't figure that any of the other material were obvious singles. And Ronnie wanted to do something that had some political-ness to it, that buzz, an undercurrent of rebellion and so forth, that happened in the late '60s to early '70s, with the Vietnam War and everything. He wanted to make a bit of a statement."

When I asked Pattison who picked "Something in the Air" to cover, he said, "Well, I didn't. Maybe Ronnie picked it. But also maybe Bill Graham picked it. He was famous for picking songs that had been famous before and re-doing them. 'I'm Alive' for that matter, was an old Hollies song, and we did that, and that was a hit song. So I guess… Bill was very shrewd when it came to stuff like that. I would imagine that came from somebody at Bill Graham's office. 'Something in the Air' was Thunderclap Newman. Even now you've got to keep the label happy. You gotta give them something that they think they can make their money back with."

Ah yes, Bill Graham. The legendary Fillmore promoter was none other than Gamma's manager, reprising the role he played at least peripherally for Montrose, which resulted in the band garnering some very impressive live billings, most notably AC/DC (touring *Back in Black*) and at the end, Foreigner.

"I was very fond of him," reflects Davey. "He was always very, very nice to me. The music business lost a true pioneer when they lost Bill Graham, because since then, certainly in the Bay Area, the music scene has gone to shit. Nobody can get on the radio anymore—you know this. It doesn't matter who you are. They don't care about music; they care about advertising."

When I suggested to Glenn that Davey thought Bill might have had a hand in picking "Something in the Air," he ventures, "Yeah, he probably did. I was the new guy on the block for the making of that record. I was pretty much, 'Sure, you wanna do this? Great!' At that point I didn't feel it was quite my place, 'Well, why are you doing that song?' I just joined the band a week before (laughs), and I was a bit glazed over about the whole thing. But Bill was the best. He was the ultimate manager; he could just get it done. Whatever he needed to do. He got us on the best tours, the best everything. I mean, we got the Foreigner *4* tour in Europe. We had the AC/DC in America. All those Day on the Green's that they did at the Oakland stadium every summer—we always got on that. He was incredible. He could make it happen. And I always remember about him, every gig that we did in the San Francisco area, we'd walk in the dressing room and there would be a bottle of Dom Perignon on ice with a little card that said, 'Cheers, Bill.' Just a little classy thing like that…"

But Bill could also be a bully. "Oh yeah, oh yeah. Two times that I can recall. One was, we would go into the office to get mail or sign some papers or something like that. It was one of those warehouse things where each room was kind of partitioned. So there was no ceiling separating his office from the other areas of the office. So you could hear him bellow on the phone, to like some promoter somewhere, and man, when he let go, it was frightening. That voice, it got deep—it was a deep baritone and he would just let it ring. And he had a poster up on the wall: 'Yea, though I walk through the valley of death, I will fear no evil, for I am the meanest son of a bitch in the valley.' But he would hang up the phone, and he would come out and say hello and he would be a pussycat. He could just turn it on or off. And I've got one more quick thing about that, because when we'd play the Bay Area, like the Cow Palace, often we would be the opening act. And he was renowned for the shows starting absolutely on time. If the concert was listed as eight o'clock, the show started at eight o'clock. And he would come up to the dressing room, and if it was like 7:55, he would just open the door and go, 'If you guys aren't down on stage in two minutes, you're not going on.' So you went down and you were ready. And it worked."

Glenn doesn't recall ever seeing Bill pull some muscle on behalf of Gamma, but, he says, "I'm sure he did. I was never around to see it. I don't know what favours he pulled to get the tours we did, but he got it done. The first tour, which predates me, they did a Foreigner tour and they did a Styx tour. And then for Gamma 2, we did AC/DC, and then did a bunch of Santana through the Southwest, where they were huge, so those were arena gigs (Ronnie: "We did a lot of tours with Santana and I remember going out and jamming with Carlos, which was a lot of fun"). And then we went over into the UK tour, Scotland and England, and then we did Europe on that tour, and then we came back and we did our own large club tour, if you will, Park West in Chicago kind of thing. In Europe, we headlined, and I've no idea who the back-up bands were. We showed up in the middle of whoever was playing, get there a half hour or 40 minutes before we went on. And then straight into Gamma 3, because in those days, you toured for eight months and then you recorded so the next album was out in the stores and you were ready to go again."

After "Something in the Air," it was back into the swaggering modern hard rock. "Cat on a Leash" is a cogent and potent cross between Aerosmith and Rainbow, if that gulf is at all bridge-able. I suppose that would put one at top-flight Led Zeppelin, maybe circa *Physical Graffiti*, on which this proud track could hold its own, no problem.

"Skin and Bone" is equally impressive, again, in possession of a languid heat. Carmassi gets to throw in boulder-tossed fills like Cozy Powell, and Pattison is free to wail the blues. "Oh, Little Richard comes to mind," says Pattison, asked about his vocal heroes. "I saw Little Richard when I was like ten years old, and I had no idea what the man was doing, but I said to myself, 'I wanna do that. Whatever he's doing, I wanna do that.' He's a huge influence. Ray Charles, John Lee Hooker, Muddy Waters, the blues guys. I was brought up on the blues."

"For the solo on 'Skin and Bone,'" recalls Alcivar, "I went home with the tape of the rough tracks and I worked that thing out note-for-note exactly. And spent hours and hours and hours playing it. Because I was going to walk in, I'm gonna play that damn thing and I'm not to get any static from anybody or grumbling about it. I go in there and sit down—and in fact Davey was there and he got to see it—one pass through, did it. And he looked at me going, um, and Gary, I think he just says, 'Um, can we do that again?' And I said sure. 'Drop it an octave.' 'Oh, okay.' I do the same thing again, at an octave lower, and it's very subtle—you can really even hardly hear it—but this subtle little low end bass would swell up on the sustain notes, which is a neat effect. And so he was always working for us. So I think Gary... that was just his method of pushing."

"I would have to say 'Skin and Bone' reminds me of Humble Pie," adds Letsch. "That was my favourite rock band of the English era. Marriott was the ultimate stage powerhouse, and Greg Ridley was my personal hero, and my role model. You know, when he stood on stage and wrestled that bass, I just looked at that and went, 'That's what it's all about right there.' He was pivotal in my growth as a player."

Both "Cat on a Leash" and "Skin and Bone" sport lyrics by one Jerry Stahl. "Jerry was a connection of Mitchell's," says Glenn. "Jerry went on to big writing for various television shows (note: *Alf*, *thirtysomething*, *Twin Peaks*, *CSI*). He turned out to be quite a big deal in sitcom writing and so forth. He was pretty good with words." Furthers Davey, "I think he's a bit of an actor, actually, and Ronnie met him in LA, and was influenced by him."

"More in the writing business," adds Glenn, asked if Jerry was a rock 'n' roll guy. "He would be writing articles for Playboy magazine and that sort of thing. He and Mitchell grew up together, if I recall correctly, out in

Petaluma. Yeah, Jerry became embedded in the Hollywood community as a writer for TV and movies, so he was good with a pen.

Davey's lyrics were more kind of soul lyrics. And of Jerry, Mitchell used to use this word, 'outside.' You know, 'Jerry's lyrics are just outside.' If you look at the lyrics to 'Skin and Bone,' it's actually the story of a heroin addict (laughs). And actually Davey felt uncomfortable singing that. He said, 'This isn't us.' But it was an edgy-sounding song, so it fit. But I would agree Jerry's lyrics were more outside, modern day beatnik, if you will. The next generation of beatnik. I think he related to that outcast thing, or not part of the inner circle, if you will."

"A lot of lyrics are that Jerry Stahl guy," says Jim, "that Davey was at odds with here and there, because some of it was a little unnatural to him. He never showed up. It was literally, Ronnie would just get sheets of lyrics. 'Here's some lyrics, here's some lyrics.' But 'Voyager,' that's a Davey song. I don't know how he felt, but it always struck me that Davey got a little less credit than he should have. He was so instrumental in the melodies and lyrics."

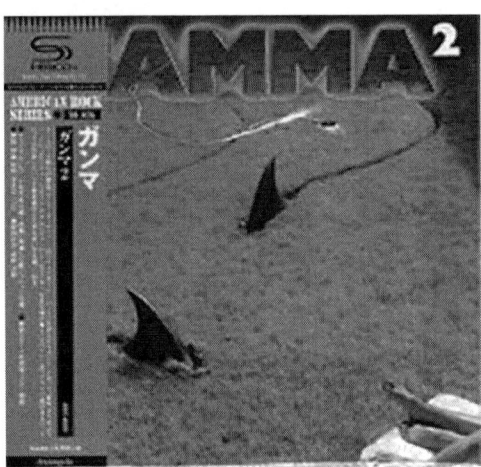

Gamma 2 closes with a big jammy rave-up called "Mayday," fully the sixth seriously heavy rocker on this album of eight tracks, with both "Something in the Air" and "Voyager" being quite guitar-drenched to boot. Once more, everybody plays up a storm, Letsch hammering on a high one-note run for the chorus, and an insistent thump for the verse. But it is Denny who gets to go crazy once again, his dry Bonham-esque sound becoming a true signature of the record.

A lot of that is down to production, which, again, for this album fell to a co-job between Ronnie and the infamous Gary Lyons. Known as one of the legendary wild men of the business (especially in his UFO days), Lyons hit the big time with the first Foreigner album. Yet working with Gamma, according with Glenn, he was quiet as a church mouse. "There was no wild man. I hate to sound boring, but you know, there was no wild man thing that I saw. I believe he had his wife with him and they stayed at the Best Western, and we went out to dinner a couple of times. All I know is that he just worked. I'd have to say I never saw a drug or anything, ever, in the studio with him, or those guys."

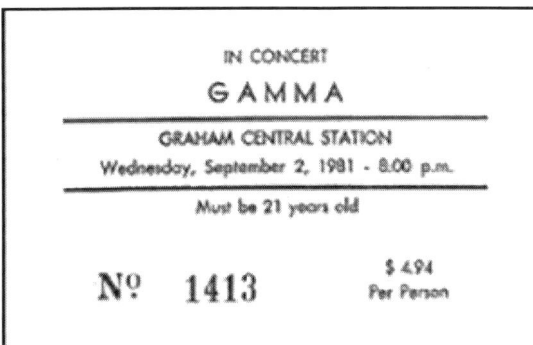

Adds Davey, "I got on well with him, although I wasn't thrilled with the production on it. But you know, I'm a singer, so I'm a bit fussy when it comes to that. No, Gary was fine with me. It would've been better, I think, if the band had produced it. But of course you've got a major label deal, so the label is pulling the strings. But I don't have a whole lot of problem with Gary. I'm not a technical guy. Just give me a microphone and I don't care which one. Just let me sing the song. I'm faster now actually, but for the Gamma stuff I would do normally two or three takes, and then punch in the ones that we liked and punch out the ones that we didn't. And we'd redo those. But pretty much one or two takes."

"Mayday" was credited to Ronnie and Jim, although Alcivar told me, "And neither of us are lyricists (laughs). It's strange. If it was Jerry, I think he would've had to have credit on it. It's probably Davey." Asked about the heaviness of the song, and in fact the album in general, Alcivar adds, "That would just come down to the mix—it really would. Ken was more... he's an old Beatles engineer. So he's got an entirely different mindset on what things should sound like and their relationships. And 2, I believe Gary and Ronnie mixed together on that one. And I don't know, after you've dealt with it a couple weeks straight, your ears are exhausted. After a while you don't know what you're hearing anymore."

"The first Gamma record was done in LA," continues Pattison, contrasting both situations. "And for me, I was thrilled to bits. Because my whole life, I had grown up in Scotland desperate to go and make records in Los Angeles. That was my Nirvana. And I got there and I hated the place (laughs). I didn't like LA at all. I didn't like the nonsense and the bullshit that goes on. The second one was done in San Francisco, and I guess it was a question of culture for me. It took me a long time to figure out what was going on in America. In fact, it took me years to figure out, okay, I know what's happening here. I was struggling under culture shock when I first got here. Because it's completely different from the way I lived at that time. But it was exciting and I was meeting a lot of people. Bill Graham was managing Bob Dylan and Van Morrison and I was meeting these people. You can imagine what it's like for a young guy coming off the boat and all of a sudden sitting in Bill Graham's office with Bob Dylan. I was used to playing bars and pubs and stuff over there."

As mentioned, touring for Gamma 2 found the band hooked-up with none other than AC/DC, blowing up big with *Back in Black*, their first album of the Brian Johnson era. Johnson, like Pattison, hailed from up north in the UK, Newcastle area, not quite Scotland, and also like Davey, he was a relative unknown stuck into a band from away.

"That was my first big tour," recalls Glenn. "Yeah, those guys were awesome. You often hear that headlining bands having an elitist vibe. I didn't get that at all. Those guys were the coolest. We would meet them down the hotel bar after the gig. I tried to buy Angus a drink, '7 Up, please.' And we would sit for two or three hours and they would do their pub thing, where they would sit and tell jokes and just howl, and we would all go upstairs to bed. They were a great band. Very cool. I don't think Angus was ever a drinker, personally. I saw no evidence of it. I mean, I was actually surprised when he didn't even want a beer after the gig. Nothing. And it's like well, the guy expends so much energy. This guy has his thing dialed-in. He knows what he needs to do to stay sharp."

"Fabulous," seconds Davey. "That's the most fun tour I've ever done. I mean, saying that, the two brothers are Scottish, you know (laughs). So I always got on good with those guys, and Brian and I became friends. He's from Newcastle, which is right on the border. They're very earthy people, no bullshit, no rock stars, just nice, nice people. I just enjoyed the hell out of that tour."

"I know we did some Foreigner stuff," recalls Jim. "No connection with them whatsoever. It was strange. When you came into town, the band, Foreigner, stayed at one hotel, and the crew stayed at a different hotel. So they kept very separated from everybody. So we didn't ever really meet or see them. The only thing I really remember about them was the sound system was fabulous. I heard everything, and Davey would have the same reaction, probably. I could hear myself coming out of the overhead monitors, coming back louder than my rig on stage right behind me. It was stunning how good it sounded on that stage. But yeah, I don't have a feeling one way or another about them, other than it sounded great."

Asked about the set list, Letsch says, "I think we opened with 'Ready for Action' from Gamma 1. I know we did 'Mean Streak,' 'Four Horsemen,' 'Dirty City,' 'Voyager.' Occasionally we did 'Something in the Air.' That just felt too commercial for us. 'Cat on a Leash,' I don't think we did that too much. We always did 'Skin and Bone' and I know we always ended the set with 'Mayday.' And then we would come back and do 'I Got the Fire' for the encore. That was it for Montrose. Ronnie wanted to distance himself from Montrose a little bit, and solidify the identity of Gamma."

"Ronnie was a fireball on stage," notes Letsch, both Glenn and Davey agreeing that the band was more than capable live. "He made sure that there was a follow spot on him, and of course on Davey. That was the big interaction, because it was Gamma featuring Ronnie Montrose—that's how it was billed. Literally, in print it was often like that. And I think that was Graham's thing. Because a lot of people didn't know who or what Gamma was. It wasn't called Montrose, so people had to know that it was the son of Montrose (laughs)."

At this point Jim Alcivar leaves the story, and with his father Bill working on his memoirs in his 90s, I asked Jim if we'd ever see something like that out of him. "I don't know (laughs); I've spent the last 30 years as an aerospace engineer. So it gets pretty dull. I live in a little town called Fountain Hills; it's in the northeast corner of Phoenix, Arizona."

Asked when exactly he left music, he says, "Oh dear, I've never really left. I'm sitting here looking at... I've got the largest modular synth now that I've ever owned in my life. A keyboard here and a rack of stuff here. Never technically left. Just really decided not to make a living at it anymore, because that took all the joy out of it. I always contended that the best thing that ever happened to me was getting booted out of Gamma."

And the story there? "Well it was just that my time was up. Mitch and I worked together on *Open Fire*; another keyboard player, excellent musician and producer guy. And him and Ronnie started chitchatting and going back and forth, and it finally came to that point after five years with Ronnie. I think that might even be a record, one person straight throughout the whole time. And so it was just time. He says, 'Okay, I'm gonna take Gamma out and it's going to be Mitchell playing keys now.' And I went, okay. And honestly, at the rate I was going, with the booze and the partying, I probably wouldn't be alive—good possibility. And things took a dramatic turn in the band. All the tech stuff that I loved kicked in. And I'm now a half partner in this aerospace company that I'm trying to get out of. I want to retire. I want to do something else. Because I don't need the money anymore. And man, I've got a room full of musical gear. And now I know how to build it—from scratch (laughs)."

Ronnie Montrose and Davey Pattison contemplating fame and fortune with Gamma. © Ted Roarke

Gamma playing Maryland, September 24, 1980; left to right, Jim Alcivar, Ronnie Montrose, Davey Pattison and Glenn Letsch, with Denny Carmassi not shown. © Rudy Childs

Record label promo glossy sent out with Gamma 2; pretty much the hottest-burning Gamma lineup. © Elektra Records

Artsy record company promo photo used with Gamma 3; note Ronnie's signature piercing gaze, and the presence of the mysterious Mitchell Froom, second from left. © Elektra Records

Ronnie and Davey, touring a "3.5" version of Gamma, captured live at One Step Beyond, Santa Clara CA, October 10, 1992. © Paul Vincze

Ronnie during the prime Gamma years, updating his hairdo for the '80s. © Ted Roarke

Gamma '92, featuring drummer Michele Graybeal, soon to become Ronnie's wife. © Paul Vincze

Ronnie, on the *Music from Here* tour, looking neat and tidy in one of his famed crisp white shirts. © John Wardlaw

Ronnie showing the effects of age and illness, but still bending those notes. © Jim Summaria

Ronnie and John "Wedge" Wardlaw, during the sessions for the Anti-M album, *Positively Negative*. © John Wardlaw

CHAPTER 8: Gamma – 3: "Jack said, 'I don't hear a lot of guitar.'"

Gamma: greatly unsung, hugely under-rated, but with a big black mark upon them that metal aficionados will never excuse. That would be the poppy, new wavey and very electronic Gamma 3 album, which found Ronnie hooking up with old buddy Mitchell Froom, who synthesizes all over the thing, much to the horror of those who soaked in the resplendent hard rock magic of Gamma 1 and Gamma 2.

"Well, Gamma 3 was bringing in Mitchell Froom and just a more articulated sense of keyboards and sequencing and structuring," explains Montrose, ever the fearless frontiersman of rock. "And we brought in a friend of Mitchell's named Jerry Stahl, who actually, there was a movie about him with Ben Stiller called *Permanent Midnight*. And Jerry was just a great lyricist. Pretty stepped-out lyrics, but that's basically what that was all about. Gamma 3 was just trying to get huge sounds with guitar and synth and obscure vocals, and still trying to do… still trying to cater to record companies. Ill-placed whims about having a single and whatever. So we came out with a couple of songs. We redid the Hollies' 'I'm Alive' on the first Gamma record, and then on Gamma 3 we did a song called 'Stranger,' which was a pretty decent kind of a single song. But once again, there's no real formula unless you're going into the total generic pop stuff, which I've never done."

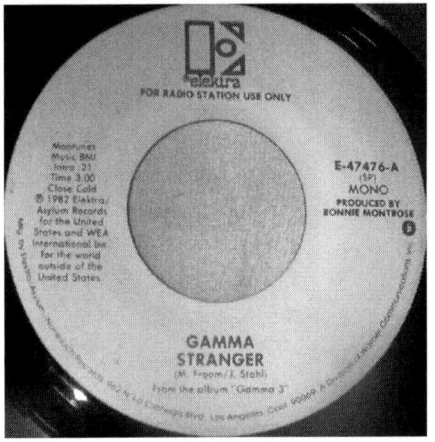

"Mitchell had worked with Jerry," adds Glenn, "and Jerry had already written some lyrics for the Gamma 2 record, so there was already this sort of writing relationship. So Mitchell was the person that set Ronnie up with this lyricist, Jim Stahl. From Ronnie's perspective—and I can only imagine what he was thinking—there seemed to be this natural progression into using Stahl's lyrics. Jerry and Mitchell had a bunch of writing, Mitch did the music and it was sort of a logical progression from there. Because I know Ronnie doesn't like to repeat himself often; he liked to forge into new territories. In fact that was one of the records they did together, coincidentally, *Territory*. And so the sounds changed considerably, because Mitchell wrote on keyboards. So there became a natural progression to delve into Mitchell being the songwriter for Gamma 3. And he started to have a good relationship with Ronnie, and there was less of Davey's involvement, which would've been more of that gritty thing. It became a keyboard record, and Ronnie's guitar playing, which is still great, became supportive to the keyboards. And that's, from my perspective, the explanation of why it's such a dramatic departure."

Still, it was a bit of a shock to see Jim Alcivar gone… "Well, I think it went back to the connection with Mitchell Froom," says Letsch. "Mitchell had always kept in close contact with Ronnie. He had Ronnie produce his thing, and then there was the band that I was in, and then after I joined, there was more contact with Mitchell. And I know that Ronnie was looking for people to write songs with. And Mitchell offered to help him write songs, so they wrote, and it just felt like, for Gamma 3, a logical thing to consider Mitchell joining the band. So Mitchell let me join Ronnie's band, and then less than a year later, he joined us (laughs)."

Gamma 3, issued February of 1982, features yet a third Mick Haggerty cover image, and again, it's a perfect match to the music enclosed. His visual for Gamma 1 was cold, dark and futuristic, and for Gamma 2, he reflected the great classic rock era of Hipgnosis, along with the organic quality of the album in pleasing colours. This time, we get three sparse shapes on a white background, pristine, cold, geometric, like the music and the wrap of Genesis' 1983 self-titled, as it were.

Opening the record is "What's Gone is Gone," and we're off to a perky start, Denny and Glenn turning in a behaved and well-meaning but brisk rhythm track, over which Mitchell carries the day, with Ronnie left to colourize barely detected.

"'What's Gone is Gone' would probably be my favourite," says Glenn. "We worked that one out live, and we played it with Foreigner on tour in Europe, right before the album came out, so we were testing the waters with that song. And I think we started the show with it, as a matter fact. I thought that was great, and I'd say 'Stranger' and 'Modern Girl,' which we also did live, were my favourites from the second side. And so the album came out great; it just sort of evolved a bit. I was actually a little surprised hearing the final mixes. I remember, Jack Blades commenting, because he had heard the final mixes, and he goes, 'I'm not hearing a lot of guitar.' And I went to Ronnie and said, 'You know, Jack said, "I don't hear a lot of guitar."' Ronnie really didn't like that at all (laughs). He just kind of went, 'Hmm.' I don't know if he even realized that subliminally it became more keyboard-dominant. It's definitely having Mitchell there that changed the songwriting direction into more electronica, if you will, and less straight guitar, a little less balls. Davey brought the ballsy side of it. Davey wasn't too pleased. He thought the formula was working with what we had."

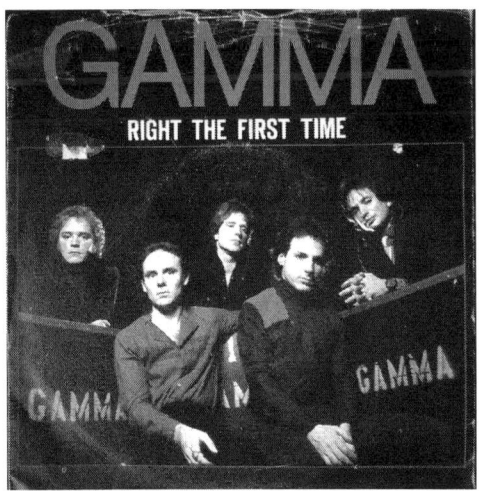

"Right the First Time" is next, and again, keys are prominent, but more incongruous is the flood of pop melody on the radio-friendly chorus. Ronnie does offer a few power chords, but mostly he's just plucking out a muted performance of the song's innocuous central riff. The song was issued as a single, backed with "No Way Out" in Canada, Germany and the US and with "Condition Yellow" in other parts of Europe.

"Moving Violation" opens a little more progressive, like something we'd hear from Rush on *Grace Under Pressure* or *Power Windows*, that is until the verse kicks in, and we're presented with a swaggering stack of power chords that wouldn't have been out of place one record back. The futuristic art rock returns for the chorus and for the break, over which Ronnie solos very much like the Alex Lifeson we know from the '80s.

Notes Glenn on this track, "I couldn't find a place to really find a great pocket and make it feel good. It was already kind of preordained by the keyboard, and the bass was more supportive, just there to kind of back that line up. That was the only negative." Asked if any of these songs were compositions that Mitchell had in his back pocket for a number of years, Glenn adds, "He did not. Because I was in a band with him. I guess we were called The Freeze, and we would've changed the name to Yellowjacket, or vice versa. So I was involved in all of those songs he sculpted, and none of that stuff that went on Gamma 3 existed before they started collaborating together."

Denny gets to step out a bit on "Moving Violation," adding a bit of a complex tribal beat, to the point where he actually garners a songwriting credit, one of two for him on the album. Glenn gets none, while every other track is credited to Ronnie, Mitchell and Jerry.

"I actually didn't consciously alter what I would naturally play," explains Denny, concerning his performance on the record. "As a drummer you can only interpret the music that you are presented. But I remember we were very curious about this electronic music that we were hearing from Europe, bands like Ultravox and Alan Parsons Project. It was the beginning of the '80s, and Ronnie was being heavily influenced by electronic music. He was a big fan of Kraftwerk. And I could see that the electronic thing was the direction he was going. It was always in that band, right? We were stretching, searching for a new sound. We had Mitchell in the band and we were trying to peek behind the curtains and rearrange the furniture a bit. I thought it was really an exciting time. I didn't use an electronic kit because they really didn't exist back then. They were just starting to come out in Europe when we went over on the Foreigner tour. I tried to contact Simmons when we got to London, but they were a fledgling company back then. But, when I went back to London with Heart a couple of months later, I was able to make contact with them and I was able to secure one of the first Simmons electronic drum kits to come into this country. I used them on the Heart *Passionworks* album."

"That whole Simmons thing is kind of an interesting offshoot, "continues Denny. "It was something new and interesting. We were all kind of dabbling in that. But Ronnie was way into it. I certainly wasn't against it. You kind of drift around as a musician and you are influenced by different things at different times. So when I got in Heart, I got a set and I used them for a while, and but it was just kind of a fad thing and I went back to a regular drum set."

And as for Davey's reaction to not writing his own lyrics for the album, I take it he was not happy.

"Yeah, Davey is just kind of not happy about anything," laughs Denny. "Well, Ronnie was always changing. When you look back on it, you can see it. Hindsight is always 20/20. When you're in it, you just don't realize what is going on. Ronnie was always changing and he always had this thing about singers. I don't think he ever got along with any of them that I played with. That I know. There was always conflict. He had a hard time with sharing the spotlight, or being gracious about it. So yeah, Davey was not... they wrote some pretty good songs on that first Gamma record. I wasn't part of that record, but they did some great songs on there. The ingredients were there. But you bring in a guy like Mutt Lange or even a Ron Nevison or somebody like that, and things could've been a lot different."

"Mobile Devotion" opens with a flood of synths, after which the band lays on us some neo-prog and even a verse that verges on metal. But really, as the track progresses, it becomes a platform for keyboard and guitar soloing. Halfway through, there's a stark about-face, and we're into a half time trudge with acoustic guitar and distant keys. Again, the vibe of the band in many places on Gamma 3 is evocative of post-*Abacab*

Genesis, along with shades of modern Yes and once more, Rush from sort of *Signals* through *Hold Your Fire*.

With "Stranger" we're back to a more conventional hard pop song, something that potentially could be a hit in the then-burgeoning MTV age. It is obvious with this tasteful uptown solo, that Ronnie had made the transition to the new decade, and that he could have made a huge name for himself as a session player. His work on highly catchy instrumental "Condition Yellow" reinforces that fact, and further brings up the thought that Ronnie and Mitchell could have been a crack team in the movie soundtrack world.

"I almost feel that Mitchell Froom *is* Gamma," laughs keyboardist John Warlaw, who had Ronnie play on one of his records in the '90s. "I love his keyboard work. I think for being how early that was in the '80s... that was the first Gamma album I heard. I had somehow missed 1 and 2. A friend called me up and said, 'You've got to turn on KCYD. They're playing an entire album, featuring Montrose, called Gamma. You gotta check it out.' And I caught the second half. And I started hearing the cover song 'Stranger,' which has the Morse code synthesizer. And that goes into 'Condition Yellow.' And other than mostly solos, 'Condition Yellow' is just a really cool techno, electronica song. And I think Ronnie's soloing, in the middle and the end, just makes the song. But Mitchell Froom was really a strong direction that I think Ronnie really want to embrace, and he met up with Mitchell and I think they just took off in that direction together."

"I love the fact that Ronnie took the band and kind of returned to that Montrose sound, but without being Montrose," continues John. "He wanted to embrace keyboards. So there was his original band Montrose, which is really all about rock 'n' roll, and then after doing his solo album, *Open Fire*, which definitely embraced instrumentals, being one of the first of its kind, he brought some of that to Gamma. So he brought both the idea of instrumental music and keyboards into hard rock. And again, what I loved about Gamma 3 was that he completely embraced keyboards, even though he is the man in the band with the guitar. He took a backseat to the keyboards and just added his influence of guitar solos and rhythm in the background, and let other people take the lead."

With "Modern Girl," the band strike a nice balance between modern synth sounds and acoustic guitar, which is central to the song's verse. Hooks aplenty and gorgeous production distinguish this one as arguably best choice for a single, potential squandered. What's more, Ronnie, practically a new guitarist on Gamma 3, sounds like David Gilmour in rock mode, or again, Alex Lifeson, who is rarely imitated.

"No Way Out" is probably the record's toughest no-nonsense rocker, brisk, muscular, guitary, with Mitchell still providing a number of sounds, but taking a back seat to Ronnie's riffs and squealing solos. Gamma 3 ends with "Third Degree," essentially menacing arena-rocking progressive music with this arrangement, but forceful enough that its frame would hold a heavy metal song. And let's emphasize that as we make our way to the end, we should remind ourselves again at how sophisticated it is that atop these futuro-art rock battles between Ronnie and Mitchell, that we get an old school post-British blues boom singer from Scotland, even if he didn't get to write his own lyrics.

Allmusic's Whitney Z. Gomes calls Gamma, "a band with proven chops to spare, trying to be cutting edge without cutting loose," summing up the record as, "some kind of fluff-prog (sometimes akin to *Grace Under Pressure*). Of course the production and drums are totally '80s, while still avoiding the shrillness that taints so many pieces from this period. No traces of new romantic chilliness or bare-bones heaviness hide here, but the nebulous in-between yields some killer cuts. This record doesn't meander as aimlessly as many art projects, but it doesn't send the hooks as fast and furious as perfect pop either. Each song has classy elements, making up for when the overall alchemy doesn't quite work."

Wrote Jeb Wright of Classic Rock Revisited, reviewing a reissue of the album, "By the time of their third CD release, Gamma 3 in 1982, the band had begun to move away from the guitar-oriented music found on their first two releases. Much of this was due to a new member in the band, keyboardist Mitchell Froom, who co-wrote most of the album. Froom went on to become a very famous music producer, but as this release proves, he was also a talented songwriter. His influence took Gamma from being a total guitar band to being a band where the instruments blended together, with more emphasis on the entire song and not just a distorted six-string axe. At times, this methodology worked well, as heard on the opening track 'What's Gone is Gone.' This was music that was aligned perfectly with the sounds of the day. It was Montrose-meets-Alan Parsons and for the most part, it worked. Ronnie Montrose is still a major part of the album, and his playing was more than proficient. By working so closely on the arrangements with Froom, Ronnie took things to a new place, some fans believing it to be a better place, while others missed the raw edge the band left behind."

In summation, Ronnie has to chuckle at how Gamma 3 had his fans all tied up in knots.

featuring **Ronnie Montrose**

"Yeah, for sure. Well, again, with Gamma 3 this was in a sense me going, I don't want to end up doing this again. So I went to Gamma 3, where I worked on it myself and started going back to more tech, had Mitchell in playing keyboards and had Jerry do more lyrics, which Davey never had an affinity for. It was where I wanted to be at the time. And the funny thing about those first three Gamma records is that there is a complete 'split the camp' thing going on. People either love the first one, the second one or the third one. I don't know a lot of people who like all three. I get people that go, 'Man, Gamma 2 ruled! What happened?!' And then I get people who say, 'Wow Gamma 3, you finally came to your senses—it's beautiful.' I can tell by getting a sense of your tastes that you like more of the heavy rock. So I would bet that Gamma 3 doesn't resonate with you so much. And then there are other people who were on the other side of the fence from you who say, 'That old rock stuff is just too pedestrian (in an English accent). What the fuck is the Four Horsemen?!' But there you go again, you want a repeat of Gamma 2, you want somebody to do the same project again, to complete the process for you. And that's not what it's about. You follow your music, man."

"Yeah, he does like to do that," reiterates Glenn of Ronnie. "From what I gather from discussions with him, he's always searching for something new around the corner. It's a creative quest. So that's why I think his albums go in different directions from album to album. I respect that."

Presented with the idea that Ronnie had a love-hate relationship with hard rock, Glenn figures, "Boy, once again, that's a psychological question for Ronnie. I don't think he ever had a love-hate about hard rock, but I do think he also wanted to be considered more than just that. As well as I do too. I mean, I got pigeonholed as a hard rock bass player. It's like, I can play all styles. I love playing songs in jazz and rhythm and blues. When I came back to play with Ronnie, after Gamma, a couple years later, he asked me to be on his new Montrose tour, and I played on the *Mean* album. And I had about a five-minute solo on tour, and people were coming up to me and going, 'Wow, you've gotten a lot better!' And it's like, what are you talking about? I was always able to do these things. I just never had the opportunity. You get typecast. And my guess is that Ronnie didn't want to be typecast as just a hard rock guitarist. I don't want to be typecast as just a hard rock bass player."

And style of music aside, on Gamma 3, what falls out of the above discussion is that Ronnie had found and eagerly utilized another music-writer, because, let's face it, his track record shows that he was not a prolific writer himself, given the covers on the records and the lack of Montrose or Gamma rarities. What's more, Ronnie had found a wordsmith seemingly brimming with ideas, whereas, as he intimates, maybe it was hard getting enough productivity out of Davey. Glenn himself was a frustrated writer in Gamma. "Yeah, I was. But at that point, it was a closed shop. Gamma 1 and Gamma 2 was Davey and Ronnie. And Gamma 3 was Ronnie and Mitchell. And with lyrics by Jerry. So it was a closed shop in that regard. But yes, I would've liked to have had more input in that."

"I never liked Gamma 3 very much," sums up Pattison. "It was a complete departure from what we were doing. The first two Gamma records, I enjoyed a lot, and I wrote some stuff on them, as you probably already know. But I think what it was was, he brought in a keyboard player, Mitchell, who was very much influenced by modern keyboard sounds of the '80s and stuff. I guess it was just basically a search for a hit record (laughs). But it wasn't my cup of tea. I didn't enjoy that. It was a little bit off the wall, for me. I'm a straight-ahead kind of guy, you know what I mean? I like straight-ahead music, and that was a little (sigh)… I don't know, going by the fans that I've talked to over the years, Gamma 3 is their least favourite album. So I didn't particularly enjoy that experience."

As discussed, Gamma got another plum gig, this time with Foreigner, for a little record of theirs called 4, currently sitting at six times platinum in the states. Says Glenn, "Gamma 3 was… we went right to Europe. Actually, before it was released in America, we went to Europe and did the Foreigner 4 tour for six weeks. Foreigner was the biggest band in the world at the time and the crowds were great. And then, I guess at the end of that tour, Ronnie decided to call it quits with the band, and actually focus on a duet with him and Mitchell doing instrumentals. You know, combining the keyboards and the guitar. So unfortunately, we didn't get a chance to promote Gamma 3 in America. Ronnie moved on to his next venture. We were actually a little surprised. I guess Ronnie prided himself on changing directions and working new creative paths. That's when Ronnie made one of those shifts to a new direction, if you will. That's when that Mitchell Froom and Ronnie Montrose synthesizer and Linn drum machines and guitar album happened. So he just totally wanted this new thing. I guess he thought he was cutting edge with that. It didn't last very long."

In fact, Ronnie shockingly called it quits right in the middle of the tour, returning to America and beginning the duo band with Mitchell described by Glenn. Denny had gotten a call at three in the morning while the band was in Europe, and on the other line, Ronnie was telling him he was going home, and not to worry, everything will be all right, which of course, it never was again… except, actually and oddly, for Denny, who wound up with a long, productive and rewarding career with Heart. Gamma had ended with the proverbial whimper, although the door shut with a bang.

"Ronnie and Mick Jones didn't quite see eye-to-eye," says Denny, which must had added an extra layer of discontent to the situation, even if the gist of what happened was really all Ronnie and his pattern of self-sabotage. "So there was a lot of tension. There was a lot of, what you call it, show business one-upmanship. You don't get to use all the lights, you don't get to use all the PA. You're playing too long. We're going to pull the plug on you. There was a lot of that very childish stuff going on. I actually did play with Foreigner—I did their 30th anniversary tour, about ten, 15 years ago."

"Mick Jones and I, to this day, are friends," muses Pattison, about the band's last grasp toward the brass ring. "Yeah, they were cool guys. I used to get compared to Lou Gramm all the time, which pissed me off, when I first came out here. But I think Gamma had run its course at that point. Well, Denny went to Heart—he left the band and went to Heart, for obvious reasons. And I think that took the wind out of everybody's sails. I think we were all kind of tired at that point."

Many fans and insiders believe Gamma could have, and should have, been superstars. I asked Davey if he thought that the band's label, Elektra, should shoulder some of the blame.

"Oh, there's no question in my mind. I mean, I remember a conversation. Robin Trower and I were taken to dinner by executives of Atlantic Records in LA. And the topic of conversation was, if Jimi Hendrix was alive today, could he have a record deal? And they were saying no. You know, I hate record company people. They don't know about music. They know about money. And they just didn't pump enough money into it. Gamma in my opinion, could have been huge. Certainly with the first two records. They just didn't... it's all about getting stuff out there. You know, Bill Graham did his bit, because we were touring the world with huge bands. Playing arenas. It's the record company that didn't support it."

And as Ronnie told John Wardlaw, "Gamma disbanded because during the Gamma 3 recording there was such an attempt to manufacture a 'hit single' that it was again seeming to me like the music business was again becoming to me, upper case 'BUSINESS' and lower case 'music,' and the 'music' was even in parentheses! I am very aware now that music is a business, but there is also a way to go about making music that is true to yourself as opposed to just going through the motions and making things that would just be commercially successful. I think that Gamma sort of got to that point through management and label and the whole deal and it didn't feel right so I stopped it. Period."

CHAPTER 9: Montrose – *Mean:* "I was just continuing on the path, my brother."

Hitting a new personal level of blowing things up, higher than *Paper Money*, higher than losing Sammy, higher than an instrumental album, higher than the synthesized shock of Gamma 3, as alluded to, Ronnie came home from his promising second life and toured as an instrumental duo with his new creative muse Mitchell Froom.

Notes engineer Roger Wiersema, who came on around this time and was on board as engineer and live soundman 'til the end, "Correct. I was doing the Mitchell Froom/Ronnie Montrose duo stuff, which was with Ronnie on guitar and Mitchell and the machines. After Gamma had broken up, Ronnie and Mitchell were doing their own thing. Mitchell was the keyboardist guru and synth guru and sequencer guru, and he programmed the bank of Oberheims and Moogs and then he played keyboard solos, and Ronnie played guitar to the whole thing. But the bass and drums, Froom programmed on sequencers, so they could go out, just Ronnie and Mitchell, and do the duo show. It was all just Ronnie and Mitchell and it was a fun time. Jogging my memory back, they played some Gamma, they played some Montrose, they did some *Open Fire* stuff—I mean, 'Town Without Pity' was certainly in that set—so, yeah, good times."

Parallel to the themes of career sabotage and fearless searching for art, the duo allowed Ronnie to explore further and with even less distraction (like, say, one of them accursed lead singers!), the sonic possibilities of technology.

"He spent every cent he made on gear," laughs Roger. "He was definitely a gear junkie, and he would modify every piece of gear that he ever got. Most of the gear he got, he would strip all the silkscreening off of it so it would just be blank. So if anybody ever found a piece of gear, they would have no idea what to do with it, and where the ins are and where the outs are or where the controls are—nothing. He would make it just like custom-bought (laughs). Even if it was just a stock box off the shelf, he would take it and customize it and make it Ronnie's, make it his own."

And hence, again, evocations of Jeff Beck, which would manifest more as the years rolled on, through a spate of instrumental solo albums. "He listened to Jeff Beck, and he and Narada Michael Walden were good friends, from that Jeff Beck era. But Ronnie had his own style that was very different than Jeff Beck's. There is some influence there, and Ronnie was familiar with Jeff Beck, and certainly Jeff Beck is another gearhead (laughs). Ronnie played because he loved to play. If he wasn't playing, he would be out fishing or cooking (laughs). He loved to fish and he loved to cook."

"I mean, he didn't give a shit what anybody thought," continues Roger. "He's just going to go off and do his own thing if he feels like it. It was a lot of the demise of Montrose as well as the demise of Gamma. I mean, the story with Gamma was, they were on tour in Europe, in London, I think, and the next show was in Paris. And the band got on a plane to Paris and Ronnie got on a plane to New York. That was the end of it. That's the story I heard. I can't confirm that because I wasn't around at that time, but that's the story I heard."

Next up for Ronnie was *Territory*, issued on Passport in 1986. The record featured a smattering of vocals, with Ronnie himself singing George Harrison's 1966 Beatles song "Love You to." Ronnie worked with a dozen people on the record, including Mitchell, who was one of four keyboardists on the project. "*Territory* was a hodgepodge album at best," said Ronnie, speaking with future collaborator John Wardlaw. "It was a bunch of demos I had put together. I had just produced Jeff Berlin's *Champion* album, which was on the Passport Jazz label and a person, whose name I forget, at the label asked if I had anything that could be put together for a record. I had some demos I had done with Mitchell Froom that were on there and demos I'd done for other things. It was basically a thrown together album. That is one of my least favourite records, yet I get a lot of people who tell me they really like it!"

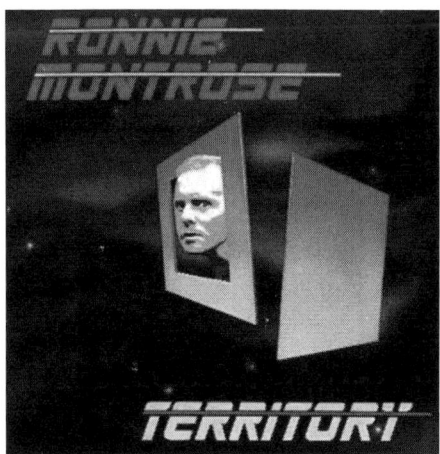
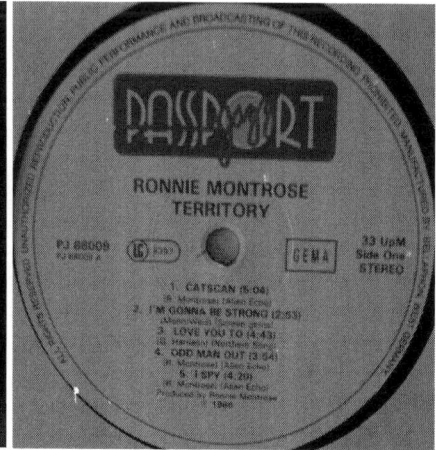

The following year, however, Ronnie was back with *Mean*, a full-on commercial rock album with vocals, under band name Montrose. And if anything can be said to be an outlier in terms of creative integrity—specifically lack thereof—in Ronnie's tumultuous canon, it would be the gritty Hollyrock party metal of this crunchy curio.

Except... you gotta hand it to Ronnie, even if the record was straight-between-the-eyes obvious, the business of the band at this point was novel to say the least. *Mean* essentially got toured *before*—and only before—the album hit the stores, and by a version of Montrose featuring a different singer and different drummer.

Explains Glenn Letch, "I was in that version of Montrose. After Gamma and everything, we still stayed in touch, we were still very close. And Ronnie wanted to go out as Montrose, and so his manager called me and said, 'Ronnie doesn't want anybody else on bass—he wants Glenn; we've got a singer, and do you know a drummer?' And I'd been playing club dates with a drummer named Steve Bellino, and so he went out on tour with us. The opening act was an act called Buster Brown, out of Louisville, Kentucky. And we did all the states, and James Kottak and Johnny Edwards were in that band. We hit it off with those guys—they were really wonderful people. Johnny is an awesome person, and James is too, but Johnny I've stayed in touch with. So when it came time, we put all the songs together as demos, and then I guess Ronnie wasn't that satisfied with the singer we were using and Johnny could hit the high notes no problem. And Johnny and James were best friends at the time. Ronnie flew them out, and I stayed in the band, and we tracked the whole thing in two days."

"We had a little bar band around the southeast, and we played the chitlin circuit," adds Edwards, vocalist on *Mean*. "You know what that is? (laughs).

And we got quite popular. We were called Buster Brown, and we were one of those bands that would go to a club... we had a great big old PA system and lighting system, a truck and roadies and everything. So a lot of times, if the national act is coming through, then they would hire us to provide the PA and the lights, and then we would open the show. And then the national act would play and everybody was happy. And so Ronnie came through. He was doing a tour through that part of the country, and this was back in, gosh, probably '84? And so they signed us up to do this, for about a two-week stretch there. So we would do all these one-nighters. It was brutal. We would do that every gig. We would get there early and set up the PA, do a sound check, and then we would play and then he would play and then we would tear everything down and load it in the truck and drive all night to the next place and do it all over again. That went on for a couple of weeks. And we got to know Ronnie through that."

"I cut my teeth on that first Montrose album, like a lot of guys," muses Johnny, asked to assess the gravitas of the Montrose name. "Boy, it's hard to know how you get the lightning in the bottle. It's hard to put your finger on that. But it seems like it's just that chemistry that comes about. It was America's version of Led Zeppelin, really, the way I see it. It was original; there was nothing like it at that time. Who was playing music like that? Nobody. So it was completely original, and the production on it was just perfect. All the guitar sounds... nobody was getting guitar sounds like that. So Ted Templeman, gee whiz, gotta hand it to the guy. First Van Halen album was supposed to be re-creation of the first Montrose album. So it's hard to say how they captured it, but they sure did. The songs are great, all the grooves and drumming are perfect, the performances are just right, Sammy Hagar, golly, what a great singer."

"And so I think Ronnie deserves a lot of credit for establishing what American blues rock is supposed to sound like," continues Edwards. "To me, he's one of the seminal artists in that category—that's the way I think of him. As a guitarist, I don't think his proficiency is there like a Van Halen or whatever, Steve Vai, Yngwie Malmsteen. It's not like that at all. It's more rhythms and riffs and songs that you can really sink your teeth into. It's just that whole approach that spawned a million other bands, including probably 20 of the ones I've been in (laughs). That came out of that whole thing. And even the Gamma records, yeah, I wore those things out. Davey Pattison—my goodness."

"And so I was just really thrilled that Ronnie was a down-to-earth, approachable person, very easy to talk to. And a lot of fun, great sense of humour. I think he gained some respect for us, how hard we worked. We had some little self-produced albums and things that we put out there, and we played some of that for him, over the course of this little tour that we did. So then everything kind of wrapped up, and we were ready to go on and do some more recordings and things. So, our manager suggested, hey, why don't we get Ronnie to come and produce a demo tape for us? Maybe that will get us a little more attention; he knows what he's doing in the studio. And so we paid him to come out to Nashville. We recorded a demo tape down there in the studio, like four songs, and he came in, did that, and we spent two or three days on it."

"And then about, oh gosh, maybe six months later, he called up and said he wanted to record a new album. And he offered... he asked if the drummer, James Kottak, and me, would come out and do the album with him out in a Menlo Park, out in the Bay Area. So yeah, we got excited about that, and we did the whole thing. Most of the songs were already written. He gave us some opportunity to contribute, but the time was so short—we spent two weeks out there and recorded the whole thing. And then he sent it out to Enigma Records and they put it out. So there was not a lot of time spent on it. It would've been nice to have had more time, but Ronnie was financing everything himself at that time. So there wasn't a whole lot of budget to work with, and that's why everything is compressed within that timeframe. But he was just a prince as far as I'm concerned. I couldn't imagine a better mentor. We loved his music, all the years, every album that he ever did. It was a wonderful experience all the way around."

Confirming the inverted timeline, Edwards reiterates that, "It was all written before we got there. He kind of did it backwards. Most of the time, you get together, write a lot of songs, make a record and then tour, right? So it was the opposite of that. He kind of put a band together, went out and toured, and the songs were already written when James and I were hired to come in. And yeah, I don't know why he felt like he needed to change players. It was the singer in the band and the drummer. I don't know, it's just something about the energy and the motivation that James and I had, that I think Ronnie was interested in. Some fresh players without any baggage. But I think Ronnie wrote everything, including lyrics. I don't remember any issues like that. But it was so quick that I didn't even bother to drill into exactly who was getting all... Of course there was one cover song on there, 'Game of Love.' And the rest of it, I think Ronnie wrote. I think he had ownership of all the songs, and that's why it felt like he was in control of it so he didn't have to worry about who was recording it."

The drummer on *Mean*, James Kottak (Kingdom Come, Scorpions), turned out to be the biggest rock star of the entire Montrose family, save for Sammy Hagar of course, and maybe Denny Carmassi, given his chart-smashing years with Heart.

"Yeah, yeah, he and I are from Louisville," says Edwards. "We grew up separately. We didn't know each other much, and he's a few years younger than I am, and was playing in some other bar bands. We went through a few drummers, until finally we were writing songs and recording songs. We were one of the few bands out here doing that. And James was really motivated to write songs. I asked him if he wanted to join us, and he's, 'Oh, yeah, yeah, yeah.' He was a real spark plug that way and a great drummer. Once he joined, our base of support really expanded. Because he's not only a great drummer, he's a great promoter, and really motivated the whole thing forward. So we had a very successful regional band."

Although up into 2016, Kottak was off to rehab, relinquishing the drum stool behind Scorpions to Mikkey Dee of Motörhead fame. "He's always been a mess that way," says Johnny. "You know, he and I went through some other thing. He wanted to move out to LA. We broke up Buster Brown. He moved to Los Angeles, I moved out to the Bay Area and got with this other band out there. And James and I regrouped about two years later and we formed another band called Wild Horses and we had a record deal with Atlantic. And that was all set to go when I got hired by Foreigner. So I kind of backed out of that, and James never forgive me for that (laughs). He was so pissed-off that I backed out of this project. And I have some regrets about it too. So we got the deal with Atlantic, and I backed out to join Foreigner, and they hired another singer and another guitar player, did the album and put it out. They played a few shows, but I just don't think they could get any traction. And then after that, James went through a few things, and then he got with Scorpions. But he's always struggled with that. It's one of the things that helped me decide that maybe I should take the offer with Foreigner. Because James was always problematic that way. And I just can't take too much of that. I've seen it so much over the years. I just try to avoid it at all cost."

As for the other half of the rhythm section on *Mean*, namely Glenn Letsch, Edwards recalls, "We spent maybe a month together total, doing different things, and I just thought he was great. His sense of humour... it's amazing that I remember any of that stuff (laughs). He was always just making people laugh like crazy. Love the guy, fantastic bass player; he's one of those guys that could pick up anything and just play it right away without any monkey business or, 'Let me try that again. I didn't quite get it the first time.' He was always bam—right there."

As Ronnie himself explained it to me, "The motivation to make the *Mean* album was that I had just finished *Territory* and I had done it all. I had these things I wanted to do, like the instrumental *Open Fire* on Warner Bros., and really enjoyed them. Certainly they didn't enjoy the financial success and notoriety of the early albums, but when you make music and you work at making music, sometimes you just have to suck it up and do what you want to do. But I had done *Territory*, and I had started some songs for the *Mean* album, and what ended up happening was somebody said to me, 'Hey, I think Enigma would like your new album.' So I talked to them and then we did *Mean*."

"At that time, having gone around the country playing instrumental music, I had run into this band called Buster Brown, and Buster Brown was this band from Louisville, Kentucky, with Johnny Edwards, who went on to play with Foreigner, and the drummer was James Kottak who was with Kingdom Come and then the Scorpions. So I had brought them out from their existing band, and I used Glenn Letsch on bass and I said, 'I just want to make some rock music.' I just want to play some tunes and I really like Johnny's voice and James is a hot drummer and Glenn is a good player. I just wanted to do a rock record. And I'd written some of those songs before and we put those together in less than a month and we just slammed it down in the studio and I had a great time doing it. I was just continuing on the path, my brother. It seemed like the right thing to do at the time."

As alluded to, the *Mean* album is a swaggering hard rock album perfect for the heady hair metal times, issued in a time and place ruled by the multi-platinum likes of Mötley Crüe, Quiet Riot, Ratt, Poison, Cinderella and Whitesnake, soon to be joined by Guns N' Roses, Skid Row, Warrant and Mr. Big.

"Boy, not much," demurred Ronnie, when I asked him what was different tonally about the *Mean* album, for him. "I'm always exploring equipment, techniques, guitars, sounds, pickups. Where ever I was at at the time, I worked from that level. I started playing a Strat instead of a Les Paul and using the whammy bar for straight vibrato. That's something that I didn't used to do."

In the notes we did for *The Very Best of*, Ronnie said of the artfully arranged yet still rough "M for Machine," "I wrote this one when I was up for consideration to compose the score for the first *Robocop* film. I didn't have enough orchestrating skills at that time to land the job, but after reading the advance script, I came up with this song. It was originally called 'Murphy's Law' (as Robocop's alter ego was named Murphy). The line, 'm for Murphy' in the chorus was changed to 'm for mercy,' and the title became 'M for Machine,' which sounded more high-tech."

Concerning slightly southern-rocking album closer "Stand," Ronnie said, "I've been told by folks who've heard this song that it 'really reached them.' That tells me I achieved the desired effect." As for rude rocker "Ready Willing and Able," his only comment was, "When you listen to this one, think James Dean in the chicken car race scene in *Rebel Without a Cause*. Got it? That's it."

Elsewhere, opener "Don't Damage the Rock" is kick-ass barroom metal at a brisk pace. Second track "Game of Love" should have been a hit, given its warm chords, drinkable chorus, and loud and proud no-nonsense electric delivery here. "Hard Headed Woman" is just b-grade trash metal like Kiss with their eye off the ball, as is "Man of the Hour," although there's a snarling biker rock vibe to this one. "Flesh and Blood" is more of the same stiff, leaden Kiss rock, albeit with a modicum of Bad Co./southern flair, represented by the boys from Louisville, or at least Edwards, who can phrase at times like Paul Rodgers.

All told, the record sounds like a demo, or at least a really raw and electric, down-in-the-gutter form of "dirty" hair metal, which, actually, really started to catch fire with Guns N' Roses and Skid Row, plus other "authentic" acts like Salty Dog and Badlands.

Muses Johnny, "Now that I can look back and I've had some more experiences with songwriting and production and everything, I would've liked to have had more time to spend developing the songs a little more and developing the band. It seemed like it was kind of a do-it-yourself thing, and the timeframe was short and the budget was low. Ronnie financed it all himself, paid to fly us out there and everything, gave us some money for doing it. He actually sent the record off to Ted Templeman to see what Ted thought of it, and if he could get some interest there. And Ted did respond. He was like, 'Yeah, sounds awesome; sounds like it just needs to be finished' (laughs). And that's kind of the way I feel about it. Some of it could've turned into something better if we would've had more time."

Production credit went to Ronnie, but along for the project was Ronnie's ever faithful right-hand man Roger Wiersema, credited as engineer, the team working at the Music Annex in Menlo Park. Notes Johnny, "We were working in a 24-track studio, not a top-notch studio, but a decent place. It had a good sounding room and a control room and a pretty good console. So, I mean, it's more than one person can do, to really direct the project, and also be at the controls and do all the handling. I mean, this was on two-inch analog tape reels. So just managing the machine, and bouncing tracks around and all the editing and splicing of things... all that stuff requires to have a field engineer punching in and out, tracking everything and organizing everything. It requires a skilled engineer. And Ronnie had worked with Roger on other projects, so they really made a good team."

"But Ronnie was actively involved in, okay, let's patch in this gear on this track, use this kind of compression or microphone. Roger would be hands on, moving mics around trying different things, more the physical nature of it. And Ronnie would be coming up with ideas. He would plug things in and out too—he was a wire nut, just like me (laughs) and a lot of people. He loved his electronics. He gave me this record player that is still one of my prized possessions. This thing is so cool. It's made by Sony, right? And you hang it on the wall, and it's about a foot tall and about four inches wide, and it has a slot you can hang it on the wall, and there's this slot where you slide the vinyl LP record down. It goes around, and it's like you're looking at a clock or something. There's a stylus in there that plays the vinyl record, and then you could plug headphones into it. It was like a Walkman for vinyl (laughs)."

Addressing the rough and raw nature of the album, Johnny figures, "Ronnie had experienced fame in a rock band. I felt this way about Ronnie's trajectory. You know, that early Montrose stuff is so flipping awesome. And it's just hard rock, just straight American blues-based hard rock. And then he just kept getting more and more into complicated things, more instrumental stuff, and his guitar sound changed. I remember he got so upset one time. We were doing a show during that tour that we did, and somebody came up to him from the audience in the middle of the set and got his attention and said, 'Hey, could you take some of that chorus out of your guitar?' (laughs). He's just like, oh my goodness. I couldn't believe, you know, having to contend with this. But it was kind of true. I mean, he had changed his guitar sound over the years. He was using more effects and more chorus and more complicated things. And I think he had been advised, you know, recently prior to this album, to start getting back to his roots. And I think that's why he was trying to do a more stripped-down, straight-out, bam bam kind of record."

"Ronnie was wanting to do more of a rock record," agrees Roger, "and pull together some players to do more of a rock record. I remember at the time, Ronnie told me, 'We're doing a rock record, but don't tell anybody' (laughs). Because he wanted to keep it on the hush-hush until it actually got released. He kept it on the QT, pretty much. Got together with the drummer, and the bass player, and they worked up some tunes. Ronnie was doing his own thing, and I was sort of Ronnie's hands on the board, trying to make his ideas turn into the twisty, slide-y things."

"Ronnie didn't elaborate a whole lot where those lyrics came from," continues Johnny, "and what he had in mind. To me, you can listen to the songs and kind of figure it out. I know that he had a lot of things going on, but he never let us that far in. Obviously there were some demons there. But I never got that close. He was always so respectful and generous to me and James. But he was always on it. He was really well organized, making lists and things. I still use his methods when I organize projects. A lot of that I learned from him. He was really on the case. He kept everything bam, bam, bam."

Of note, besides the one cover, two tracks are not assigned to Ronnie alone. "Flesh and Blood" and "Pass It On"—shades of "I Got the Fire" to this one—find Ronnie sharing songwriting credits with both James and Johnny.

"You would be surprised if you weren't surprised," laughs Letsch, on getting such a commercial and easily digestible album out of Ronnie at this juncture in his increasingly arcane career trajectory. "Let me put it that way. It wasn't that he was impulsive, but he always wanted to go in a new direction. And I think also, ultimately, the Montrose band was his marquee moment, if you will. And it was always the popular thing to take out on tour. And to me, there's nothing cooler than a trio and a singer. To me, that's the quintessential rock band. And we got to do it with that, or before that album, I should say. So I thought that was cool—I loved that tour. But I thought the sonics of the album didn't come out as well as I thought they would. And even Ronnie said, in retrospect, he wished we'd remixed the record. And I said, 'We can always re-track the whole darn thing. It only would take us a day.' We didn't get around to doing that. But I thought the songs were great. That was a powerful band. The songs were a lot of fun, and particularly what I enjoyed, as I say, live, we did it as a trio. It was a trio and a singer. And the bass I guess would be more important—I have to be the rhythm guitar player and the bass player when he takes a solo (laughs). So it gave me a little more opportunity to cut loose."

But to clarify, there was no tour of the *Mean* album after it became a physical entity on store shelves, hideous front cover notwithstanding. As Ronnie told John Wardlaw, "I knew we were not going to be able to do a band but I just asked them if they wanted to do a project. Had I known that Buster Brown wouldn't have stayed together, I'd have suggested we go out and tour a little bit with that band, because it was a tight, fun band to be in. But at that point I was under the assumption I was just borrowing John and James from Buster Brown and they were going to get a big deal and go out and do that, so I enjoyed it. A bunch of silly rock songs but I enjoyed it."

"I ended up going to Nashville to produce a demo for them because I loved the band," Ronnie told me, reflecting further on the fizzling of this short-lived lineup. "And they tried to get the deal out of that and that didn't work for them and the band ultimately broke up and disbanded and went their separate ways. So they were involved in other things and we didn't tour. That's one of the things that always kind of irked me about the music business. You know, I'm not biting the hand that feeds me, I've stayed alive fortunately being able to make somewhat of a living playing music for 30 years now. But the whole machinery of make the record, tour, promote, it never really worked well for me. I know it's a necessary evil but it's not something I've embraced over the years."

In closing, Edwards reiterates that, "The whole situation was so weird. First, Ronnie did the whole tour and we were just an opening band, providing the production. Buster Brown was doing all the production and opening the show. And then Ronnie would play with his other singer. I can't remember the guy's name, but a really talented guy. After all that was over, about six months later, we went out and did that album. But this Buster Brown thing kind of had a life of its own too. We had an enormous following and a lot of grassroots and work and people really thought we were going to make it big. So we were really attached to that, with all our friends and everything. And I think Ronnie kind of sensed that we were quite committed to that, and it was going to be next to impossible to relocate myself and James out to the West Coast, just to maybe play some gigs here and there with Montrose. It just wasn't enough to put that kind of commitment into it. And so no, we never did a single gig."

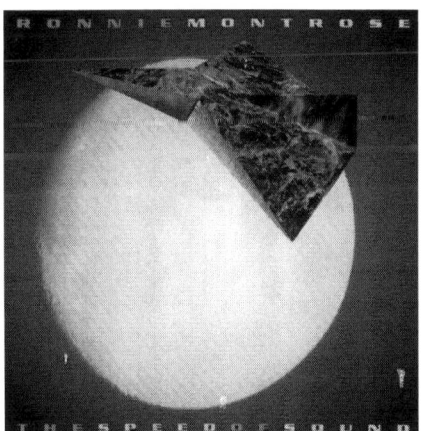

Stacked with potential, "Montrose" was summarily dispense with, leaving Ronnie free to re-enter a fated underground, through the release of another instrumental album, 1988's *The Speed of Sound*. Ronnie told John Wardlaw that, "*The Speed of Sound* is my favourite instrumental album I have done so far. I did *Speed of Sound* with the well wishes of Bill Hein and with his encouragement which was great because he really didn't want anything other than a good instrumental guitar album. We had done the *Mean* album and the problem with the album was that the record company didn't have the ability to follow up on the promotion and air play that was gained when we covered Wayne Fontana and the Mind Benders' 'Game of Love.' So at that point, you know, Bill Hein, kind of as an extension of good will said, 'Listen, just go make me a definitive guitar album.' I had a budget for it, the timing was right and I got one of my favourite drummers around, Johnny Badanjek who played with the original Mitch Ryder and the Detroit Wheels on all of those wonderful hits they did. I had actually played with Johnny a couple of times before. He played on Edgar Winter's 'Free Ride' also. The basic band was the trio of me, Johnny Bee and Glenn Letsch. I just had such a great time! It was a really fun album. I was pleased with the work that I did on it and the inspiration was really there for me."

Various cameos took place in the mid-'80s as well, including a lead guitar slot on "(She is a) Telepath" from Paul Kantner's *Planet Earth Rock and Roll Orchestra* album and a guest slot on a 1987 Neville Brothers track called "Whatever it Takes." Analogous, he also performed with the Berkeley Symphony on a piece written for guitar; the symphony had previously performed Ronnie's "My Little Mystery." Ronnie also turned in a fine production job on *Breaking the Silence*, the first album for well-regarded Bay Area thrash metal act Heathen, Montrose also producing Wrath's *Nothing to Fear* that same year, namely 1987.

Ronnie also produced *Champion*, a 1985 album credited to Jeff Berlin & Vox Humana. As Ronnie told me, "I like Rush; they're just such an enigma. I produced a record for bass player Jeff Berlin and Neil came in and just played his ass off on Jeff's record. I had Steve Smith and Neil Peart in the same room, same time. And I was a Neil fan. I liked him; he was a good guy. He did a couple of good songs on there, where he and Steve just went at it, soloing at each other and it was really nice. Interesting record. Closing track "Champion (of the World)" is drummed by Neil alone, and features lyrics and backing vocals by Montrose. Ronnie's got his buddy Roger Wiersema along as engineer, but Montrose indeed gets blanket production credit across this complicated album.

Toward the end of the decade, Ronnie guested on the *Guitar Speak* compilation and performed on two tracks for b-grade hair metal act Heist. As well, in 1985, Ronnie joined for a few months promising Seattle act Rail. The band had just lost their guitarist Rick Knotts, and Ronnie was itching to work. A tour ensued, billed variously as Rail Featuring Ronnie

Montrose and Ronnie & Rail, over the course of which the band would play Rail songs as well as "Rock Candy, "Matriarch," "Rock the Nation" and "Something in the Air."

Ronnie also collaborated with John Wardlaw on his Anti-M project, appearing on four tracks on 1995's *Positively Negative*, as well as contributing to a reunion of the original Montrose for "Leaving the Warmth of the Womb" on Sammy Hagar's solo comeback album *Marching to Mars*, from 1997. As Ronnie told Wardlaw about the experience, "It was only after getting together with the four of us in the studio, hanging out and jamming with each other for the first time in about 20 years, that I rediscovered and realized how awesome a trio that was."

Nine years later, when I asked Sammy if he'd like to continue working with Ronnie, he said, "I would, but Ronnie is kind of on his own trip. The Montrose reunion thing, we've done it a few times, and I've taken him out with me the way I've done it with Michael Anthony. We did the same kind of thing with Montrose, where they come out at the end of my show and we do a 30-, 40-minute set with Denny, Bill and Ronnie, and it was great. It's just that Ronnie, musically, has changed a lot. He's kind of got more into a jazzy, fusion place, and that's without vocals, and it's not really user-friendly for a singer. So I'm not really user-friendly in jumping into his thing. And when he has the Montrose reunion, he has another singer now, a guy who does a great job for him. And I'm not a very retro guy, as you can tell by my new record. *Livin' it Up* pretty much says Sammy's really not that retro. I'm really not that interested in going back into the studio and doing a Van Halen record, unless we all grew together. To me it's all about people you have around and musicians that grow with you, either in the same direction, or in a direction that coexists very well with yours, together. You know, Ronnie and I have grown in different directions. He's a great guy and still a great player and all that, and I did a song on his new record for him."

Ronnie also worked with guitar virtuoso Marc Bonilla and appeared on "Eye of the Storm" from Edgar Winter's 1996 album *The Real Deal*. Ronnie's *Mr. Bones* album from 1996 was the soundtrack to a Sega video game of that name, after which Ronnie moved to LA for a brief period.

As for the dearth of another Montrose album, Ronnie said, "I wasn't interested. I literally just wasn't interested. The only time that there was any consideration of doing a reunion album as it were, and I don't like that word, was to have the original band get back together. I worked really hard at doing the 25th anniversary of the first Montrose album and I contacted Ted Templeman and talked to Denny, Bill, Sam, everyone, and I really thought that would be a great thing to do, Montrose sort of 25 years later. But the problem was that Sam was so contractually bound to all the things he was doing. And it's not that he was in this situation where he could just do anything he wants and follow that whim and that muse because there are so many other people around that need to be involved on that kind of level. I don't really have an interest now. It comes and goes away. If it's there and it happens, fine, but I don't have any interest even in pursuing it. And if it ever happens, it will only happen because everybody says let's do this, it feels right. And I don't think it would never happen again."

And there would be additional solo albums from Ronnie, flying under the radar of all but the most committed of guitar aficionados, namely *The Diva Station*, for Enigma in 1990 (on which Davey Pattison sings two tracks), *Mutatis Mutandis* (I.R.S. '92), *Music from Here* (Fearless Urge '94), *Roll Over and Play Live* (RoMoCo '99) and *Bearings* (RoMoCo '99).

There was even a version of Gamma that kicked around in the early '90s, with Davey, Ronnie, bassist Marcus Miller, keyboardist Chuck Terpo and on drums, Michele Graybeal, who was to become Ronnie's wife on November 8, 1997.

Telling Wardlaw about his new studio and new life, Ronnie explained, "It's taken me a year to build and get together. After I finished with the *Mr. Bones* thing, I relocated to Southern California, partly because I wanted to and partly because of Michele's work. She works at Warner Bros. Animation. But it has been a long process because I'm kind of a renaissance person. I not only like working in the studio but I'm a hands-on, kind of build the patch bay, solder the connectors, wire it up guy. I really enjoy that part of it as much as making the studio work. So it's taken a long time to assemble and put together but it has been rewarding and will be a reliable working full-service studio for me and my projects. I could not have afforded to do the projects I've done without it."

Asked about today's technology, Ronne figured that, "Really, it's all about tone and feel for me these days, and I've worked that out to accurately get those things across to satisfy me. I happen to arrive there technically different than someone else may." Digital versus analogue? "Listen to the new Steely Dan CD and tell me it's 'cold.' It's digital, and one of the best albums I've heard in a long time. I have problems with the basic 'retro-snobbery' mentality sometimes. I like both mediums and don't have a problem with either, as long as the content is delivered with passion."

"*Mr. Bones* was a tedious, long, exhausting experience for me," continued Ronnie. "When I first went in there I was told by the producer, 'We want you to do the soundtrack for this game—it's a *guitar*-driven game' Perfect! I actually ended up acting in it, I did a bit part, played a blind, hermit guitar player. I not only composed, but I did all the motion capture moves that were then morphed on *Bones*, so it's my moves when he plays! I was told it was going to take six months and it ended up taking two years! It

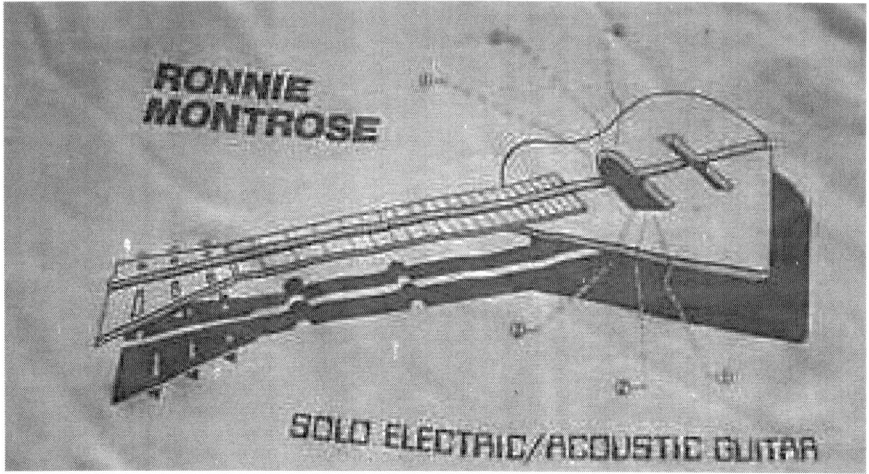

was very... just a tedious process of having your music sampled and cut and pasted in such a way. On the *Mr. Bones* soundtrack CD, none of the same constraints were there. I was able to call in Myron Dove and Billy Johnson from Santana and a keyboardist named Joe Heinemann. I played them demos and we'd just make music and it was such a release and such a joy after two years of tedious work with the game part. Just to go in and play music with world class players! Wow! No midi! I also composed and underscored lots of cinematic pieces which I really enjoyed because I felt I came through even though it was a serious challenge for me."

CHAPTER 10: Gamma – 4: "What Davey likes to call it is 'Gamma grown up.'"

If there's a slight but substantial relationship between Gamma 3 and what would become Gamma 4, we should also discuss the fact that there was, as keyboardist Chuck Terpo puts it, a "Gamma 3.5," a live act only that sits perfectly between 3's ahead-of-the-curve 1982 release and 4's low-key, indie issuance in 2000, coupled with a UK Dream Catcher launch the following year.

"It was '92, to '93—for about a year," recalls Chuck, now a top piano tuner, but with a rich history before Gamma and even after Gamma, as part of other bewildering Ronnie incarnations. "I remember we broke up in '93. Basically, Davey and Ronnie splitting. And I had been playing with Davey probably two or three years. At that time, Ronnie approached Davey with putting Gamma back together, and contacting the original members, but they were all doing different things, or just not interested in doing it. So there was Michele Graybeal playing drums, who was Ronnie's girlfriend and eventual wife, and Marcus Miller playing bass. There's a famous jazz player, Marcus Miller, but it's not him. Just the same name. But he's South Bay, California; I want to say Saratoga, Los Altos, San Francisco. And myself and Ronnie and Davey."

"Ronnie, Michele and myself all loved to fish and camp, and the three of us went fishing and camping a lot," continues Chuck. "They eventually married, and they were still married when I had lost contact with him. And that had to be, I would say five years later or so? Somewhere along there, although I might be off a year or two. But see, I played with him after Gamma broke up. I went back to playing with Davey. We formed a new band, and then Ronnie called me and asked me if I would like to do some Montrose shows. And I said sure. And so that had to be '93 and '94. And he was doing different things then. And then I went out with him and Michele. I think the bass player's name was Craig (ed. Craig McFarland). And so we played shows, and then he played some shows with Pat McCormack, and then Tal Morris; I think Tal was just about one six-week thing. And then I did some more shows with him. So off and on, I would say I was with Ronnie three years."

"He was such a hell of a guitar player, and he was so meticulous," reflects Terpo, asked about his lasting impressions, given what was soon to happen. "And I would say that that goes for both anybody knowledgeable that saw him play as well as musicians that played with him. He wanted everything right. It started with him. I mean, Ronnie had his—excuse me—shit wired tight (laughs), and he wanted you to have your shit wired tight. And that would go all the way down. I first got brought into the band because when he approached Davey about him doing this, they had all the pieces except the keyboard player. Davey and I were real tight, and Davey said, 'You know, we used Chuck. I've been working with him two years. Love working with him.' So it was really Davey who got me the opportunity."

"And then of course, you've got to be able to play his stuff—and I did; I learned it, I did all my homework. And then we rehearsed pretty hard when we rehearsed. But before we would go on the road, one of the things is, we would have an evening or a night that all we did is go through our equipment and make sure everything was perfect. I mean, right down to... you don't want to hear any noise, any dust in a volume pedal. Every cable. Every cable. There's a lot of cables (laughs). I remember checking every cable in my whole keyboard rig, and I had a big rig, and making sure that the connection was good, and that we sprayed it with this spray you use on electronics to clean them and make sure there's no dust, before we would go off and do shows. Not before every show, because you would do that when we had a line of shows. And that was all at Ronnie's insistence."

"And he was the one leading the way in helping you, if you needed help with anything. It had to be right. We would solder and we would re-solder something and it had to pass inspection (laughs). You could say it was overkill in a way, but not really. It's just professional; he was a real professional. I know other people that worked with him at different times that said, 'Oh, he's tough to work with,' but I never had a problem with him. I enjoyed working with him and I think we got along well. I knew how to handle Ronnie, you might say. I'm not saying that in a negative way, or trying to have the upper hand, but I knew he always meant well, even when he sounded brash. But he was just such a melodic player. His tones, everything that he chose was just excellent. And when I did something, I remember we were in the studio, and he had me write this middle part for a song, and when I did it, well, okay, I like this or I like that, but we've got to do this and we've got to change that. Okay, all right, whatever you want. And then sometimes, I remember the one time we played it one time, and he would just go 'Done.' Done. You know, that's it—done (laughs)."

And of course Chuck was working with material from these three disparate Gamma albums from a decade earlier, with the favourites being... "'Fight to the Finish.' There were some great things that they did originally that I loved. 'Razor King,' of course. I liked a lot of the dynamics in that. Besides a lot of unusual chord structuring, there were a lot of dynamics where you would go from really powerful ballsy tones to just super-quiet. And I really enjoyed playing a lot of that. And I hated that we broke up when we did. We had four new songs and had recorded those four songs, and still not a lot of people know about those four songs."

More on that later—that material would indeed emerge on Gamma 4— but I asked Chuck to detail a little more deeply the state of "Gamma" at this juncture.

"Absolutely we were called Gamma, and before we did shows, they did publicity and all that, saying Ronnie and Davey Pattison together again for the first time in however many years will be performing these shows. And then they would go do autograph signings at record places, and they released *The Best of Gamma*—they did release that at that time, when we were together. I forgot about that. And then most everywhere we went was sold-out; they weren't big venues, but most of them were just jammed. Ronnie and Michele were pretty new. I think they'd been together at least a year, and not over two. Somewhere in there. And then they got married while we were together again later, because it was a very small wedding, and Davey and I were the only two guys in the band there. And so on the road, Ronnie and Michele pretty much stayed together. And Davey smoked, and back then I smoked, so the smokers kind of had their rooms, and Ronnie and Michele didn't smoke. So it was fine. There was no uncomfortableness or anything like that. We were having fun, you know? And Davey even, in the beginning, Davey is like, I need the money. And this will make good money. And Davey and I were happy because we were getting paid fine, and they were making even more. And so they got along fine. But really, Davey started getting tired of it there towards the end, and we needed to get back to what were all about. You know, I love soulfulness too, but I always loved rock. I love high energy, adrenaline rock."

"We never went off the West Coast," answers Chuck, asked about the extent of the band's touring. "Never, and how many, I don't know. I'm going to guess 20, 25 dates. At first it was only places kind of around here, from Santa Barbara to Sacramento and San Francisco, San Jose. And then later, Tahoe, Oregon and Washington, a raceway up in Washington, a big outdoor thing."

"I don't think there was a Gamma after Gamma 3.5, or whatever you want to call it," continues Terpo, who is fully aware there was a Gamma 4 album. "There really wasn't. Until now, where Davey has got all guys that never played with him or Ronnie, and they're doing what is called Gamma+, where they do Gamma songs and then a couple of the Trower hits, 'Bridge of Sighs' and a couple other. But there was no Gamma after that. And Ronnie and Michele did Montrose or Ronnie Montrose Band, and Pat McCormack did some. Ronnie did some acoustic things; he liked that a lot. But there was no Gamma. Ronnie had Montrose or Ronnie Montrose, and then him and Michele split up, and before they had split, they'd moved down south, and that's kind of where I lost contact. I was doing other bands and other things. I knew he was in Sacramento when they were split-up. And I did talk to him on the phone one time around then. I guess at that point, well, soon after that, is when he met Leighsa."

In between there was Chuck's own stint in The Ronnie Montrose Band, which helps confuse his timeline concerning Ronnie and Michele. "It was all instrumental, and I remember we did 'Town Without Pity,' the old Gene Pitney song. We didn't do 'Bad Motor Scooter' and some of the things that people were wanting. We were doing what Ronnie wanted. And no Gamma. I think we started in San Diego and worked our way up the coast to Seattle and then back to San Francisco. Ronnie had said, 'You know, Chuck, I can't pay you what we got in Gamma. You'll see, Montrose is not going to pack the places, or most of them, like we did in Gamma.'"

Chuck intimates that Davey never felt right doing the sort of material Gamma had on their three albums, calling it, "'Crap! Crap, mate!,' he used to say. I don't know what he told you, but, 'Wank wank widdly widdly.' He's soulful and he will describe himself as soulful. And I know one of the things he found out about right when we met, there's a girl Cynthia Shiloh that worked for Michael Narada Walden who introduced us. She knew Davey, and Davey was looking for a keyboard player. And I used to play with Bobby Womack way back, and Mary Wells; Motown, in the '70s. And when she told Davey that, he went, 'Bobby Womack?! One of my all-time favourites.' So Davey really related a lot more to that. In Davey's band we did some rock stuff, but it was definitely more soulful and bluesy—it wasn't your butt-kicking Gamma rock 'n' roll. But I thought he sang Gamma great. I mean, just like Robin Trower. Geez, some of the stuff he sang with Trower... and they're different styles. But he sang all of the Gamma stuff just so good; he really did. 'Voyager' and just all of them. But I guess deep down in your heart, everybody is different, to what turns you on. If you're going to get to sing or play your ultimate style, what is it? And that was not Davey's."

No question, Davey's voice is what makes Gamma complex, plus it's absurd to think of a Gamma without him. Even Ronnie is more replaceable in Gamma, which gives legitimacy to the Gamma Davey has had going after Ronnie's death. I mean, he is that towering vocalist, and the prime lyricist, and the front man. In my books, all that is more important 90% of the time than any guitarist, even if that guitarist is the writer of the music. But Davey's voice had a greater obvious fit to the music of Robin Trower. But given that he was essentially celebrating the earlier hits of Trower, that couldn't have been particularly creatively self-actualizing either.

"No, you're right," agrees Chuck. "Because he would tell me how Trower would say, 'This is what you do,' and it was all about Trower. And Davey used to say, when you talk about music, it's all about the song—it's not about the guitar. And it's really not about the vocal. It's about the song. And to Trower, it's always about the guitar. But he got paid well. So…"

And this seemed to be a problem ingrained in Ronnie from the start as well—with a twist. With Ronnie, there seemed to be a healthier natural appreciation for the song over the guitar. But unfortunately, with Ronnie, if it wasn't always about the guitar, it was certainly about the guitarist— him. Ergo, as has been stated, he always had problems with lead singers, eventually butting heads with Van Morrison, Sammy Hagar, Bob James and Davey as well.

"Well, I think it was about the guitarist, you're right; I think it was. With both of them, yeah. When you're that good, you kind of have that ego. Davey and I were really close for a long time, and he would talk about 'the damned guitars' and 'Damn guitarists—it's all about them. You know, 'Widdly widdly wank wank.' And he sang with two great ones, no doubt. But I don't think he had the creativity with Trower that he had with Gamma, because with Gamma, he wrote a lot of that stuff."

I asked Chuck to elaborate on this other side of Ronnie, the outdoorsman, pressing him if he actually had all the gear and everything. "Yeah, pretty much. Well, I have more than he had, but I grew up in the South, and I did love to fish and camp, and I had a boat when we met, and that was good for fishing and camping. And we would go places and do boating, camping. We would load everything in the boat. The only way you get to the campsite is by boat, and we'd stay for a few days and fish. He was still a modest and mediocre fisherman, but he got onto those things real quick. He just needed somebody to show him. And he had done a lot of different kinds of fishing. I've done a lot more different kinds, from just catfish and bass and to moving out here and start fishing the bay for sturgeon and striped bass and halibut. And he hadn't done that before. Never been sturgeon fishing before. I took them sturgeon fishing, him and Michele. Bay fishing. I remember Michele saying, 'I think he was happiest at those times.' Which, you know, a lot of people would think is unusual. You don't picture a rock star, or rock legend, whatever you want to say, being happiest when he's out in nature, fishing, you know?"

As for Ronnie talking rock 'n' roll out in the wilds, Chuck figures, "He didn't talk that much about it, which means to me that he was a little bitter about it. He wasn't bitter enough to be sitting and cussing people out, but since he didn't talk a lot about it, I didn't bring it up. Most of his road stories and stuff would be something funny or crazy that happened on the road, to the band or the crew. It really wouldn't be about the record companies. And I'd talk about sometimes with Bobby Womack on the road, where we'd all jump in the limousine with like nine of us and travel all over the country in that thing, and it would smell so bad, I made me a place in the back compartment. Things like that that we would laugh about. But not really, oh, so-and-so really fucked me over. Still, I think he had a bad taste in his mouth about some things."

"But yeah, Ronnie and I and Michele got along really good. Much better than they did with Davey. But a lot of that had to do with fishing and camping and cooking too. I love to cook; Ronnie loved to cook and he was a very good cook. And we would get together and especially go fishing and catch fish and cook a big dinner and sometimes we would just get together and do barbecues. And he wasn't doing that with anybody else in the band."

Also obscuring the timeline a bit for Chuck is what the name of the damn band was, that he was in with Ronnie. "I think he just called it Montrose. You know, honestly, I can't remember whether it was booked as Montrose or Ronnie Montrose. But that would've been '93, '94. It was after Gamma, and there was a little space in there, and then I played shows with him. And then Tal Morris, if Tal remembers when he played with him. I played some before, and some after Tal. And I did not want it to break up. I admit there were certain people, without saying the name, there were certain ones that weren't going to let it go on. And if this person is through, that's it. That's the end of that. Because it's not going to stay unless those two, Ronnie and Davey, stay together. Other than that, forget it. And Davey did his thing. I played with him, and Ronnie asked me to go out and do some shows, and actually Davey got mad at me for doing some. 'Oh, you're playing with Ronnie now?' And I said, 'Well, what do you mean? You make it sound like I've joined Ronnie forever, or for...' 'Well, you're playing with him.' I said, 'Well, he asked me if I wanted to play some shows, and yeah, it's fun, and I get paid.' It was only for, whatever it was, a month. And I said, 'There'll be some more later on. Just like you. Let me know; I'd love to do it.' So, you know, I played with both of them. I actually played a lot more with Davey. I played a lot with Davey, for over ten years."

But Chuck remembers Gamma "3.5" with fondness. "Yes, and Roger Wiersema will talk about that too. Roger love that stuff. Roger told me at the thing we did for Ronnie's passing, he said he thought that our Gamma band was the best Gamma. He said, 'When you played the Stone on New Year's Eve, that band was so hot and so tight.' He said, 'I thought that was the best of all the Gamma performances I had seen.' Now that's... Roger is not really the kind of guy to just say that to make you feel good. He definitely was a guy who will say things to make you feel good, but he wouldn't say it if he didn't mean it. He was one of Ronnie's best friends for many years. He was—and is—an excellent, excellent sound engineer, and spent a whole lot of time with Ronnie. I'm sure he watched him change and go through the whole thing, into the severe alcoholism."

Notes Roger of his involvement, "I would do the odd tour dates, but if he went out for a month or two, I wouldn't do the tours. So I would do the showcases and the local dates, because I had a live sound background. The live shows were pretty much the studio band coming together and doing the stuff live. I mean, he would work on the live show, there would be a couple rehearsals, and then they would go do the showcase. Rehearsals weren't a whole lot. I mean, there were three or four hours, and they would be done. He always had great players, so they knew what to do."

As Chuck alludes to, there was a 16-track compilation called *The Best of Gamma* giving the band at least a modicum of a presence, and this was followed by the semi-bootleg *Concert Classics* CD put out by Ranch Life/Renaissance Records in 1998 (also out as *Alive in America* with a different cover). Says Ronnie of the rough tape of the band in 1979, "These guys simply took a board mix of a radio broadcast Gamma did from a club in Denver, and claimed to have 'mixed and mastered' it. They were so 'astute' that they even mislabelled my instrumental version of 'Town Without Pity' and called it 'Open Fire,' without giving the writer credit. We threatened a serious lawsuit, and let it go with a promise from them to cease and desist. Unfortunately, copies keep showing up. Very frustrating, indeed. Hopefully, the ones that are around now will be the only ones."

Aside from the dodgy business of the release, Ronnie has artistic cause to be upset as well. The mix is crazy heavy on keyboards and synthesizers, with bass guitar getting distracting articulation as well. More distant is Davey and drums, followed by Ronnie and his versatile, thought-provoking guitar work. Track-wise, the package presents all of Gamma 1 live save for "Solar Heat," along with the bafflingly over-rated "Town Without Pity," and renditions of "(So You Wanna Be a) Rock & Roll Star" and "I Got the Fire." An interesting curio, and valued given the dearth of live Gamma material out there, nonetheless the set is more of an amusing Jim Alcivar showcase than anything.

And so pan forward an additional seven years past Gamma 3.5, and there was indeed an album called Gamma 4. "Yeah, I enjoyed that," says Pattison. "That was a fun album to do. Although it's not as rock. I guess, again, we got a little bit older and a little bit more mellow in our old age, and that came across. I like those songs. Those songs are closer to my own solo records than the early Gamma stuff."

Indeed, the previous year, Pattison had issued his first solo album, *Mississippi Nights*, noting at the time that, "I had a bunch of songs, and the only way to find out if they were any good was to go into the studio and record them with a band. I am for the most part, happy with it. The minute I am *totally* happy with any album it will be the last one I make. I've been fairly busy recently. Soon as I finished vocals on Gamma 4, I sang four songs on my friend Pete Sears' forthcoming album, and I did a bit on a 'musical' album based on the life of Leonardo da Vinci."

Into the middle part of the decade, Davey would do a second solo album, *Picture This*, and two covers records with Michael Schenker as part of the Schenker Pattison Summit before returning to records and live work with Robin Trower.

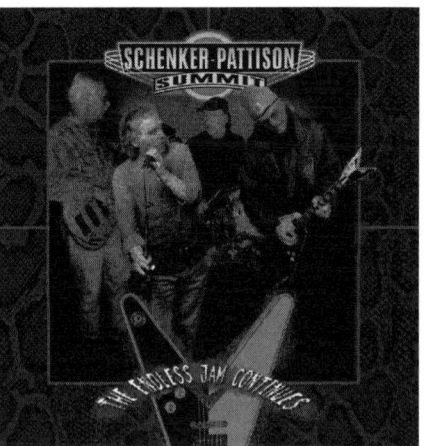

"What is beautiful about this record is that we got into the studio, and it was just like we had not even not been around," chuckles Ronnie, speaking just before Gamma 4's release date. "Especially me and Davey and Denny and Glenn. I mean, our new keyboard player, Ed, works on my projects, a very gifted musician. But the four of us, it was like immediately back into the routine. I don't know if you've been following what Denny's been doing, but he's played with Heart and Coverdale Page, and he's like me, in his fifties, and man, he has not missed a beat. He's better than he ever was—it's unbelievable. What Davey likes to call it is 'Gamma grown up.' But it's really strong. It's just all the music I'd been writing for the last year and it's all come together. I'm really happy with it. If I can mix it the way I want it to sound, I'm going to be a very proud man of this project."

"At this point, at this writing, it's going to be on my website," said Ronnie, concerning distribution. "The problem is, is that I technically do better on my website than I do if I give it to a label. The only way that I could do better with it on a label is that if they loved it so much that they'd really go and make it a priority."

"This is why I'm an enigma. I can get really heavy but then I can go the opposite," shrugs Ronnie, turning back to his always-shifting musical identity. "Have you heard my album, *Bearings*? Nothing but acoustic music. I've never stayed in one game. That's the deal. And to be lumped into a thing... like Ted Nugent—the thing he do, he do real good but I can't do that. But Teddy, Teddy, Teddy, you can't just go out and do 'Wang Dang Sweet Poontang' and 'Dog Eat Dog' day after day. You paint yourself into a corner. And I dare say it's the same with AC/DC. When you're in a corner like that, then everybody knows what you do and that's what it is. But you are right, Motörhead is great, Lemmy is Lemmy, he'll always be Lemmy, I agree with you on that. Some people are just icons and you want them to play their hits. On that spectrum, I went to see Kraftwerk and I went nuts. They did nothing new, just all my favourites, the look, the sound, 'The Man-Machine,' 'Autobahn'... it's an interesting thing. The same with Tony Bennett: you want to hear him sing 'I Left My Heart in San Francisco.' You want to hear singers do what they've done."

As background to the Gamma 4 situation, Ronnie told John Wardlaw, "Actually, I was scheduled to produce a band in Italy, and wrote a couple of songs for them. I played one of the songs on the phone for Davey and asked if he'd like to do a guest performance on the project. He agreed and told me he loved the song. The project fell through, and as I had more music and it felt right, I called Denny, Glenn and of course Davey and suggested that it was time to do a new Gamma project. Everyone was into it and we brought in my friend Ed Roth to handle keyboards. I wrote most of the basic structure for the music, as well as lots of lyrics. Davey and I really tightened everything up at his place before we went in, and I also encouraged everyone to play loose and add their own personalities to the mix. It really was 'all about the hanging out' as much as the music! We had to stop laughing about old times enough to record. One of the funniest things was that after not hanging out for 20 years, it felt like it could have been two weeks. We slipped right back into the groove."

"The opening song is called 'Darkness into Light,'" says Ronnie. "There are songs on here that are more brutal than anything that has been on any of the Gamma records, just more electric guitar, bass, drums, keyboards—I mean just brutal, intense guitar—and there are some things that are completely the opposite, some love songs on there."

"Darkness into Light" is indeed the record's heaviest track, as well as its stand-out, given its stark and highly memorable structure, placing a raging full band heavy metal riff against a quiet bass guitar-dominated lope come verse time (says the record's bassist, Glenn Letsch, "That's clearly my favourite song on the album. I think it came together as fast as he presented it to us"). It's hard to have more dynamics in a song than this, but it's nice to use that word, for that's what Gamma had been about from the start. Davey's vocals are moody and bluesy over a dark and contemplative set of chords which again, hearken back to the drama set by songs like "Fight to the Finish."

Denny gets to be heard loud and clear as well, Carmassi saying that, "For me, Gamma 4 was a chance to play with Ronnie again. I always loved playing with him. There are certain people you 'get off' playing with. I've played with many guitar players over the years, some with big reputations, and Ronnie stands out as one of the best. Ronnie found me playing in a little club in Northern California. I'll always have a sense of gratitude towards him. If I can help out in any way, I'll be there. It's worth it just for the laughs. Seeing Glenn and Davey was a gas too. Too bad Mitchell wasn't able to make it. I don't remember much record company interference. Ronnie probably had to deal with that more than any of us. But that's the beauty of an internet record—you can do whatever you want. The record was a lot of fun to make. Hopefully that fun got caught on tape."

Clearly this is the most fun song in terms of what a bass player would enjoy. Still, as Glenn says, "None of the bass parts were particularly, intentionally, too tricky. It was just trying to glue the song together, if you will, and trying not to be too obtrusive. Make the songs meld together, at least for our style."

But then "Love Will Find You" is one of those love songs Ronnie mentioned as contrast, and certainly we now have a disconnect with the Gamma of the first three records, this one being pure R&B, as is cover "Resurrection Shuffle," only this one is upbeat party music with honky tonk piano and horns, arranged by Marc Bonilla, featuring Jim Gammon on trumpet and Edgar Winter on sax.

"Yeah, Ronnie really wanted to do that song," laughs Glenn. "And let's do it. The fun thing about that lineup was it all came together really fast. There was another new keyboard player that played on that, which was Ed Roth, and he was a real quick study. Ronnie would play him an idea and he would play it right back. 'Learn the riff.' 'I just learned it' (laughs). So it was fast. Everything was always fast with Gamma in the studio. One or two takes. Denny, of course, is my favourite drummer anyway, whether I got to play with him or not. But such a pro; I mean, take one would be the right one, usually. That's how we did 'Voyager.' That song was one try, one take only, for everything. The guitar solo, everything. That was a live track in the studio. That one stands the test of time."

Concerning the styles here jarring to and against the Gamma legacy, Glenn explains that, "So many years had gone by at that point, and I think it was really an opportunity to just get the old guard back together again in the studio, and let's do one more for the Gipper, so to speak. But that would be Ronnie's... well, here's the interesting thing. A lot of the songs were co-written by Davey and Ronnie. But you have to remember too, that there's 20 something years that had gone by. So directions and styles had evolved and branched out quite a bit from probably the rawness of the old Gamma stuff."

Denny recognized that the songs were quite un-Gamma-like as well, and that Ronnie was gonna do what Ronnie was gonna do. "Yeah, Gamma 4 was kind of a fluke thing. That's kind of, you know, the whole story. You couldn't lean on Ronnie. He was a hard nut to crack. There was nobody that he would really listen to. I mean, he had some good bands and he had good producers that would try... Ronnie was a difficult guy, man. That's the whole story."

Denny, of course, plays on the whole record, but it was recorded at the studio of another top-shelf drummer, namely Troy Lucketta of Tesla fame, who is credited as the recorder of the basic tracks. Notes long-time engineer and soundman Roger Wiersema, "I did a little bit on Gamma 4, but not a whole lot. I was off building studios by that point. Ronnie just sort of put the old band back together, and tried to pick up where they left off. So, they recorded it in Castle Valley, and I think it came out a great record. Didn't sell a whole lot. I thought it was done in the same vein as the first three Gamma records, so… Sort of the Montrose band with keyboards, and a little bit more poppy. And certainly Davey adds that whole sense to it as well. I certainly wasn't around for any of the writing. I was just there for engineering and at that point I wasn't engineering a lot of Gamma 4; I was just around for the sessions. But Davey is a great guy. He's a phenomenal singer, and Ronnie always thought, this is my favourite singer (laughs). He said that many times. And Denny, oh, Carmassi is the best. We loved Denny; he's phenomenal."

"Oh No You Don't!" doesn't fit the plot either, being an uptempo boogie rocker, again with horns, more aligned with the southern feel of "Resurrection Shuffle." This one is one of fully four contentious tracks cooked up by Gamma 3.5 in the early '90s, as is "Bad Reputation," which feels more like Gamma, at least in the writing, if not the soft billowy arrangement.

"Careful what I say here, because I don't want to say anything that makes enemies from anybody," begins Chuck Terpo from that incarnation. " But some of the songs were rearranged with stuff taken out, and then released later by Davey and Ronnie. Not by the band, but by Davey and Ronnie together, when they had been the ones that couldn't get along (laughs). So, you know, these two, plus 'Last Man on Earth' was one and 'Prayers' was one. But everybody that I know that has heard the original versions that I have, and a few people have, they just say, why in the world would they change that?! Because these are just not that great. Well, it was what they wanted to do. And then we didn't... you know, Michele and somebody else had writing royalties in there, and then once they took our parts out, they didn't have writing royalties anymore. Michele and myself. These are things that happen in music."

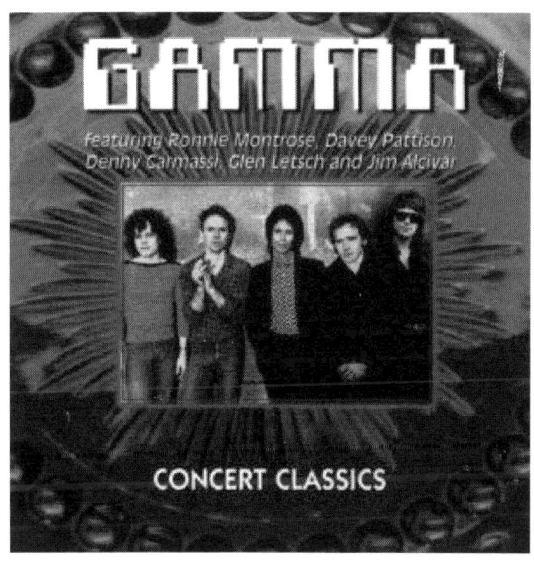

"So yes, these songs we had were 'Last Man on Earth' and 'Prayers,' which is about the homeless plight, and 'Oh No You Don't!' and 'Bad Reputation.' 'Oh No You Don't!' was a butt-kicker; it was butt-kicking rock 'n' roll. We played those four in our show, and they all went over real good. 'Oh No You Don't!' was really good (sings it). I mean, it was butt-kicking and precise and a real guitar song, just a real ballsy chord pattern with Deep Purple-ish kind of stuff underneath. And then 'Bad Reputation' was kind of in the middle and it had more keyboard work in it and was more medium tempo. See, we recorded those in '92. I still have my writer's contract in my safe, and I still have the original CD. And so what happened is, you know, Ronnie and Davey wanted to try to pick up some money around then, and so, okay, we're going to go back in the studio and change a few things and they took the credit and that's what happened. And so that was nine years earlier (laughs). I did at some point end up talking to Leighsa about those four songs and thinking, hey, these can be released too. It's the same songs, but earlier versions."

"Last Man on Earth" is a slow blues, and so again, yet another rootsy, traditional rock 'n' roller here, and none of the "future-forward" vibe of Gamma 1 and Gamma 3, nor much of the metal of Gamma 2.

"The Only One" is a worthy acoustic ballad along the lines of "Wish I Was," with Davey singing it tenderly and with soul. But then with "Out of These Hands" it's back to R&B Gamma, although this time with a certain amount of loud, distorted guitar—Nazareth-meets-Hammond. This one sports a Montrose/Hutchins credit." That's one of Ronnie's friends," says Glenn of the new name. "He is a luthier, painter/acoustic guitarist. Just a real creative guy. And he became a really close friend of Ronnie. And so I guess they collaborated on that. Actually, CJ Hutchins painted one of my basses for me. I started my own line of basses for a little while called Pipemaster, and he painted a few of them for me. A real talented guy."

I asked Glenn if Ronnie was playing a different guitar this time around, versus early Gamma. "He was continually changing guitars. People would make guitars for him, and he liked a particular neck. He liked a thick neck and a really wide neck. And I can relate to that, because I've got big fingers. So, you know, easier to press the strings down. I don't recall whether Ronnie's fingers were big, but they were incredibly dextrous. Not just because he could play guitar. But he could've been a surgeon or something. He had this real precision. To watch him solder something was like... we had a joke, we used to say he's like a Nazi surgeon. The precision, the delicate attention to detail. And the joke in the band was, 'Never let Glenn Letsch near a soldering gun.' Because there would be solder everywhere except where it's supposed to be. Methodical, he was. And he could do these little tricks with his fingers, you know, the way that magicians could twirl dimes and quarters between their fingers. He could do all that; he was just a natural."

"Prayers" is perhaps the record's second of three strongest tracks—along with "Darkness into Light" and "The Low Road"—this one being a touching song about family and childhood naïveté and the plight of the homeless. Strings, a gorgeous acoustic part from Ronnie, intimate singing from Davey with an accompanying female vocal from Michele... this one is a classic, again not anything to do with what we think of Gamma, but a superlative track all the same.

Gamma 4 closes with "The Low Road," a Zeppelin-esque epic o'er which Davey pines for Scotland.

"I enjoyed that song a lot," notes Glenn. "That one has Davey's Scottish lyric. And it's interesting that you call it Zeppelin-esque, because I suggested to Denny, do like maybe a 'Ramble On' kind of thing, where the drummer is actually just slapping a beat on his chest, with a microphone on it. And I remember Denny doing that, and I said, yeah, maybe we should do that. We didn't end up doing it, but that definitely came to mind on that. I thought it was a really cool song. But those percussion ideas were just batted around, and sometimes they happen, sometimes they don't happen. It's all part of the process."

"There are many things I miss about Scotland," says Davey. "I miss my family and friends on a day-to-day basis, I miss the caustic, irreverent sense of humour. I was like a fish out of water when I came here 20 years ago—total culture shock! I will never forget the look on Glenn Letsch's face the first time he saw Edinburgh Castle when Gamma toured Europe. I think the sense of history just took him so much by surprise. A fond memory. I truly believe that America has done more for this planet in 200-odd years than the rest of the world put together. As a Brit however, I have some serious problems with the situation with guns in this country. Where I come from, there are no guns. You can count on one hand the people who are killed with handguns in the UK. For me it's really quite simple—no guns, no senseless deaths. I sincerely hope this comment does not offend anyone reading this."

CHAPTER 11: Dying of Nothing – "That Saturday Ronnie changed his mind and it was over."

Aside from a smattering of soloing cameos on small releases and a bit of production, Ronnie was completely under the radar in the 2000s... until his death on March 3, 2012 was announced. Ronnie had been battling prostate cancer but it was generally believed he had beaten it. Shortly thereafter it became known that he had taken his own life, Ronnie shooting himself in the head. The toxicology report had his blood alcohol level at .31%, enough to kill or at least hospitalize most people and about four times higher than the most lax of legal limits. Some studies call .2% the lethal limit. For a male of Ronnie's height and weight, .31% would represent in the neighbourhood of 13 to 15 drinks.

As his obituary read in Canada's National Post (syndicated from the New York Times), "Ronnie Montrose, an influential guitarist whose band, Montrose, was a mainstay of hard rock in the 1970s and the launching pad for the singer, Sammy Hagar, died Saturday at his home in Brisbane, California. He was 64." Published too quick to know the details, the obituary then states that, "The cause was complications of prostate cancer, said his agent, Jim Douglas." The two column obituary, with picture, ends with, "Montrose is survived by his wife, Leighsa; two brothers, Rick and Mike; a son, Jessie; a daughter, Kira Ratliff; and five grandchildren." Sure to cause the proverbially "spinning in one's grave," the large headline for the otherwise satisfyingly substantial piece reads: "Sammy Hagar got his start in guitarist's band."

Night Ranger guitarist and good friend of Ronnie's Jeff Watson has some thoughts about why Ronnie might have taken his own life. But first I got him to provide a bit of background on his and Montrose's relationship, which is illustrative of Ronnie's extensive behind the scenes stewardship of local musicians.

"Sure, well, I had a band called the Jeff Watson Band, and I had been working with Sammy Hagar. I met Ronnie through Sammy and Fitz, who I started Ranger with. But I met Sammy by calling him from a music store and telling him his guitar player sucks. And I got a hold of his producer, Carter, at Capitol Records. Carter goes, 'Kid, you've got some balls. Here's Sammy's number—you tell him.' So I called Sammy and he goes, 'Fuck, Watson, you got some balls. I don't need a guitarist, but if I ever do down the road…' I get this call down at the music store, 'Watson, it's Hagar. My guitar player died. Come on down.' So I went down, drove my '71 Pinto down to his old house in Mill Valley here where I live now and we just ran some stuff. I was pretty wet behind the ears still. It probably worked out for the best. We're still friends to this day, but I don't think it was the perfect fit. I wasn't ready to jump onto big huge coliseum stages."

"But we did try a few things, and I met Fitz doing that. And because I had the music store, I was manager there, he wanted to get some gear, so I started getting Sammy and him some gear at great deals. Fitz started hearing my demos I was making at local studios, up in Sacramento. My family's from the Bay Area, but my dad was in the state Senate. So I had to grow up near the state capitol for the early part of my life. So he heard them and he heard my guitar-playing, as did Pat Travers and Pat Thrall. And Fitz goes, 'Whoa, something's gonna happen with this; I want to be in on this. I want to produce you.' So Fitz produced my first stuff and I was on the air, on the radio all the time. Then I was getting ready to do the next batch of songs, and Fitz was going out with Sammy's band. Because he played keys with Sammy, and he played bass with Montrose and Gamma, right? So Fitz goes, 'Hey, you know, Ronnie heard your stuff; he wants to take over production. Because I've got to go on the road.'"

"So Ronnie jumped in, which was fantastic, and produced the next batch of stuff, which got on the air up there. I never had a product in the store.

I wasn't as smart then as I might be now (laughs). So I was playing these shows, I was on the radio in hot rotation, and I didn't have any product to sell in the stores. Not the best business model. But anyway... But the songs still exist and it was pretty fun. And then Sammy got me on a couple of big shows opening for him, and then Ronnie put me on a huge Ted Nugent show in my hometown at the time. And that was cool, and Ronnie came up and hung out for that. And then Fitz said, 'Hey, I want to start a band, and you've got to be the guitar player.' So I basically packed up and said, okay, fine, and moved down here to Mill Valley, moved into the band house where Fitz was living, along with the guys from Ranger and Sammy's drummer. I mean, it's very incestuous band stuff."

"I recorded at all those places Montrose recorded at," continues Watson. "Wally Heider was the first recording studio down in the Bay Area that I worked at. That's where Fitz took me to record my Watson Band stuff. So I worked the same room. In fact, a really funny thing, Fitz had purchased from Ronnie... Ronnie needed some dough, and sold Fitz his 1959 Fender Bandmaster amplifier, with three 10-inch speakers in it, in a road case that says Montrose on it. That's the amp he used on the first three albums. And I bought it for 500 bucks, and I've been offered $20,000 for it. But I don't have it because I sold it for $750 to pay rent back in the '79, '80. Of all things, right? That amp was amazing. That's the amp I used on all my early stuff. I would love to have that back now."

"Anyway, long story short, Ronnie was certainly a mentor of mine. He really drove me to really work on my craft. He would call me very late at night, from shows all over the world, when we were first getting together. I would see the phone ring, and I would be sleeping, and I'd go, I know that's Ronnie. It'd be like, 'Jeff, it's Ronnie.' 'Oh, hi Ronnie.' 'Jeff, what are you doing?' 'I was sleeping, you bitch.' 'I've got something to tell you, man. You gotta work on this. You gotta work on the lyrics to that song. 'And he was just always, always pushing me. He totally took me under his wing. I was just a kid, but he heard me play, and he knew I had what it takes, in his opinion. So that was very encouraging. He was very instructive to me, as an artist. And I'll never forget that."

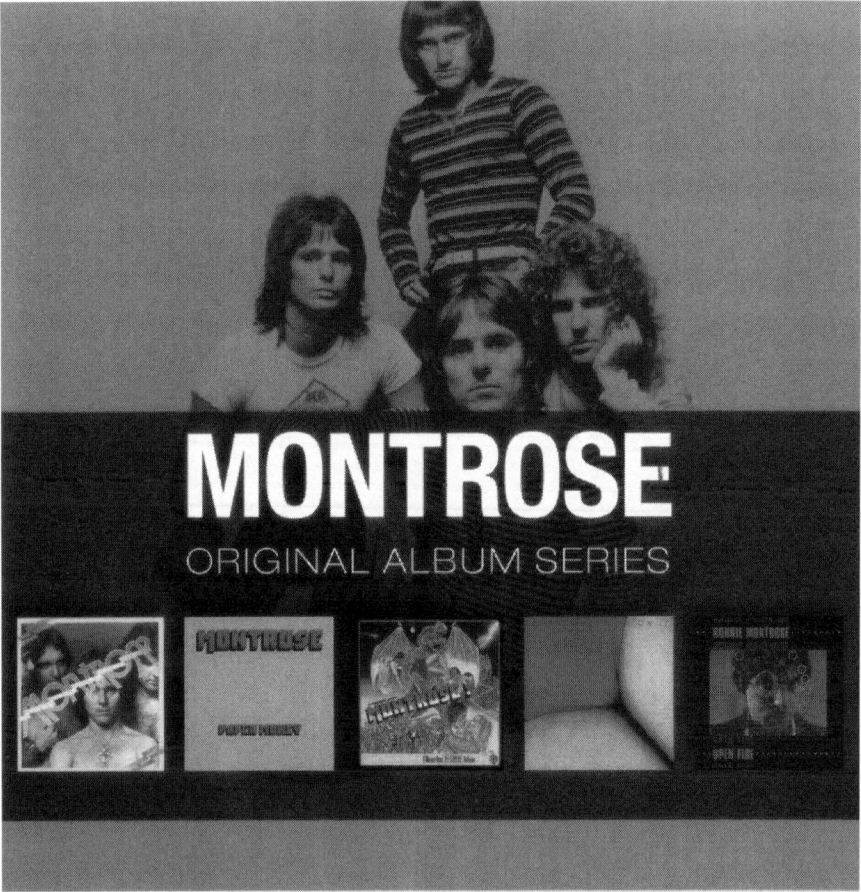

"There was no hope in his heart," reflects Watson, as we get around to the uncomfortable topic at hand. "At all. Ronnie had no hope in his heart. For his career, his health, his life in general. You know, he had Leighsa, his wife; he had that, and I'm not sure why that didn't give him enough strength to persevere. Touring was tough too. Because they were doing 40 shows in 45 days, in a van, and maybe sharing driving too. But it was brutal. And playing clubs... it was just loserville compared to what Ronnie was used to. I think that had to be an element in Ronnie's ultimate demise. But we were shocked. When he took his life, it was just... we did a benefit concert, and we were all just going, 'What happened?' And I don't know too much about the details of it, and I probably could find out, but I don't want to, you know?"

"I think he realized the train had left the station," continues Jeff. "And he had been on the train, he stepped off the train, and he couldn't climb back on the train. I think that's how he would've visualized it. Everything was piling up on him at the same time. It had to be so overwhelming. Every door he opened, he walked into a wall, kind of thing. And there were no more doors for him to escape from himself. But I think every door and window opened to a wall. And I think that was just... he was trapped in himself a bit. It was real sad."

"I was shocked," agrees Chuck Terpo. "Tal called me and said, you know, 'Ronnie is dead.' And first thing I thought, because I knew he had had cancer before, I said, 'Oh shit, the cancer's come back.' But that was not it. And then I found out, in a day I guess, that he committed suicide. He shot himself. I was stunned. And then I still thought, well, the cancer must've come back. You know, because I lost two very close friends in the last seven, eight years myself to cancer, and one of them especially, one was down the last few months, and I wouldn't have been surprised if he just took an overdose. Get it over with. Because he was dead man walking and had no chance of coming out. And I could see that if I were in that position, it would be much more understandable. It's like assisted suicide, if you're terminal. I thought, that must've been it."

"But then it was none of that. Well, what the hell?! That's for Randy, Steve and Dan, who knew him best at the end. But, you know, they said he was just drinking like crazy. When I played with him, in '92, we all drank, but Ronnie sure didn't have any drinking problem. That had to develop later. We would always have a little shot of Courvoisier before we went on, and I'd say sometimes, 'I'm having one more.' 'Chuck, no, just one.' And when we camped, he would drink beer, but rarely hard liquor. But just according to the other guys, in his last year or two, he would drink a bottle a day. And I guess he had already gone to rehab a couple of times. I mean, that's my hearsay from them, because they just said he had really gotten a bad alcohol problem and he just could not beat it. And at that point, I guess, he texted Leighsa, or called and left a message, and he was gonna do this, and he did it."

"But it shocked the hell out of me, no doubt. It really, really shocked me, and then again, after the shock goes away, I realized that Ronnie did everything his way—on his terms. And that was his terms. This was something where, maybe, he did not want to be remembered as an alcoholic, and all washed-up. Great guitar player who wasn't great anymore. You know, he gained a lot of weight, and I'm not saying it makes it right. I'm just saying I understood a little better. He's not been the first one of my close friends that has committed suicide. If only I had known. I'd have been to his house in a minute. But we don't know that, when someone does it. It's just done. So I was very shocked and very saddened. I still think about him all the time, quite a lot, and I just wished that it hadn't gotten to that. I just wished it hadn't gotten to that. I know a couple people there, in the band, I think especially Randy really tried to help him, with his alcohol problem. And he just couldn't whip it, or just wouldn't keep trying or whatever. I don't know."

"Every day. Every day," answers Roger Wiersema, a tough interview, but unexpectedly opening up on this tough topic, when I asked him if he is still trying process what went wrong. "I mean, Ronnie and I were as close as anything. He was best man at my wedding, I was best man at three of his weddings. He was my daughter's godfather. And we were working on... he was doing the live DVD from the Uptown, which he just recorded a couple months earlier, and we were just going into the studio to mix that. I'd gotten back into engineering again, and I was actually going to engineer the album. I did engineer all the Uptown live recordings, and was going to mix it with Ronnie. And we met on Thursday to talk about what we needed to get fixed on it, and then Saturday it was over. Very strange. In fact, when we were in the studio on Thursday, he had talked to Sam, and Sam was putting together the summer tour of the 30 years of Sammy or whatever the tour was going to be. He was going to open with Montrose, and then go into the Sammy and the Wabos and then do the Van Halen stuff and then do the Chickenfoot stuff. It was that whole thing. And we were talking to Sam, and Ronnie was excited about working with Sammy a little bit more. And they sort of mended all the bridges and life was going to go on. But that Saturday Ronnie changed his mind and it was over."

"I never saw any of it," says Roger, looking for clues. "He and I always had a great relationship. He could call me any time of the day or night, and he never said anything about how depressed he was or what was going on in his life that would affect anything—nothing."

Shuddering over Keith Emerson's decision to end it all in 2016, given that he had physically lost the ability to play, I asked if Ronnie's reported problems with his hands might have had anything to do with it. "Yeah, I mean, a little bit. But it never affected his attitude or his shows, and he never told me, 'I can't do this anymore. And I'm not going to do it anymore.' He was upbeat, and I mean, the Uptown shows were some great shows. We had some great performances recorded, and he was back in the game."

As for his weight gain... "Oh, it had gone up and down a little bit. He was an aging rock star, and he could do anything he wanted. But he was working on getting more in shape, because he was excited about going out with Sam, and certainly Sam is in pretty good shape, and he wanted to be able to keep up with him. But until really the last six or eight months, he didn't even talk about Sammy. The only time he talked about Sammy was a photographer that got hit by a car in front of a show, who photographed a lot of the early Montrose shows, and Sam wanted to do a benefit for him. He just didn't talk... didn't talk a whole lot about Sammy. This is four or six months before he passed away. His dog had died just before the Uptown shows. That would've been like a couple of months earlier. And he was very attached to his dog, Lola, and that certainly had him a little depressed, with Lola passing away, but I never thought it would lead to him committing suicide. Never saw that part of it. No, just... he was my best friend and I still miss him every day."

Notes long-estranged Montrose singer Bob James, "He'd got the cancer, he got over it, he actually apologized to all the people that he did wrong. The only details that I know is he became sorry for everything he had screwed up, and done to people in his life, and unfortunately, his wife had to find him like that. It's unfortunate. Seriously, I feel sorry for his wife and I feel sorry for his kids, that he ended his life like that. He was married a few times, but I think this gal that he was living with seemed to be pretty nice." But Bob was no longer close, after his departure in 1977. "I talked to him a couple of times. I pretty much told him my thoughts, like I've told you. And I'm not sure that he was super-interested in what I was saying. But I think he got my story."

Long-time bassist and close friend with Ronnie at the end, Dan MacNay says there were many factors, but going out and playing at a club level was not one of them.

"Not at all, no, no, no. This is the weirdest part, Martin. This is the weirdest part. I was with him. I was running around and playing in the band and all that stuff with him the last couple of years. And I'll tell you what, man. To be honest, he was happier then than when I first started playing with him. I started playing with him like maybe five years before he died; that was my first gig with the guy. And then it spread and just turned into me playing with him all the time. But basically, he was happier in the end than he was when I first started playing with him. I know that sounds weird—I know it sounds really weird—but he was... he actually had a thing figured out with

Guitar Player magazine. He was doing this whole charity thing, where they bought a bunch of guitars and he would sign them every night and raffle them off, and he'd make tons of money for all these charities, every night. That was something that came out of his head. Genius. And Michael Molina from Guitar Player magazine, said, 'Yeah, we'll buy the guitars.' So we were always dragging around stacks of guitar all the time with us, and he would play on 'Bad Motor Scooter' and then he'd sign it on stage and then give it away at the merch table at the end to the raffle winner."

"I know that he was up drinking whiskey for two days," continues McNay, asked what he thought triggered Ronnie's tragic decision. "I know that he was sleep-deprived. I know that… you know, there's personal things that I know that I don't know that I feel comfortable talking about. I mean, honestly, just… but I will say this. Just consider his age, consider that he was one of the most… like he had a wicked sense of humour, but he was one of the most dirtiest motherfuckers I ever knew. I used to love hearing his road stories, with women. You know what I mean? All the debauchery and shit that they did. I mean, honestly, I was like, dude, you are my hero (laughs). You are truly my hero. What he would like do to like supermodels and shit back in the day was fucking amazing. But consider his age, consider that he basically was honest with himself… you know, at 64, man, you think about things just keeping up, you know what I mean? That being his hands and whatever else, right? And he's married to Leighsa, who is his fourth wife or something, and she's like 40-something, you know? So I think… I don't know, man. All that stacked up, two days of drinking whiskey and sleep-deprivation. Sleep-deprivation is a bad one. And an honest mind. I mean, what could happen, right?"

Asked about how long the drinking had been bad, Dan figures, "I wouldn't call it steady, but I would say that it did ramp up before that. I mean, but it was quick. It wasn't like it was drawn-out over a bunch of months. It was like maybe a couple months before that, that it just started kind of ramping up." As for thoughts that the cancer was coming back, "You know, maybe he thought that. It's hard to say. Maybe he thought that. I would hear him complain about his body, and his hands from time to time. He'd go out one night and have a tough time on the guitar, and then the next night, maybe not so much. And then the next night it would be like that, and then the next night, not so much. So he was definitely battling with his hands and his body, and when you're travelling around you don't get that much sleep. I'm still doing it with the Great White guys currently, and I never get any sleep. But Ronnie had amazing hands. He had these abnormally large crazy weird hands. You watched him play a chord on his guitar… he'd play what you call the big boy A chord, and he would actually wrap his thumb around and hold these notes. And he's got like these crazy chords going *and* his thumb wrapped around the neck. It's not typical—he had crazy hands."

"So I think everything factored. I mean, he lost his dog. He had his bulldog that helped him through his cancer and everything. And that was like definitely his best friend. I know it's sort of a stereotype, but that dog was his best friend. He had lost his dog. And his new wife Leighsa, her mom moved in with them. And I remember saying, 'Well, is that going to be okay, dude?' And he's like, 'I'll never have to do another dish again.' 'Yeah, but you've got two... you've got your chick and your chick's mom up in there.' And it's not the biggest place in the world. It was a nice place, but it was very humble. And I don't know, man. There were a lot of things that changed right before that happened that had contributed. I would never discount the fact that he had a deep love for his dog. I would never discount the fact that his dog passed away, that he was thinking... that that started him on a path."

"I don't know," shrugs Denny Carmassi. "The Ronnie that I knew was totally different than the Ronnie that was there at the end. Ronnie, you know, he was a different guy. He was smoking, he was drinking, he was doing this, doing that and the other thing, and back in Montrose he totally did nothing; he was totally straight. And that's kind of the Ronnie I knew. I've no idea. Obviously his mental state wasn't good. Whatever was going on there was not good." As for the theory that having to play the clubs again made him despondent, Denny can only say, "I'm sure it did. That's not any fun. That's just... that's not good."

"I played with Ronnie on one of his last gigs," reflects another class Bay Area drummer, Leonard Haze, of Y&T fame. "I played in his band for a couple of shows, which was just stunning. I liked Ronnie a lot. And I'd known him a long time, yeah. Sam, I've known a long time too. But just that whole thing with Ronnie, he was just... that was a hurtful one. My grandma used to say, about getting older, the hardest thing is seeing your friends die. And she said, 'When you get older, God seems to take things away. When you're young, he gives it to you. When you're old, it starts to get taken away.' And I didn't understand that until I started getting older. Now I understand what she was saying, you know? It makes sense now."

"You could never stand in another man's shoes," notes Ricky Phillips (The Babys, Coverdale Page, Styx), who was involved with the Ronnie Montrose tribute concert, which we'll address later. "I always think that when those things do happen, whoever the person was—could be anybody, Ronnie or whatever person—if he could have just made it through that week or that day, then all might've been just fine. But you never know. And I hate to even speculate, because I don't want to pretend to know Ronnie inside and out. We were great friends, close friends, and I cherished his friendship, and I still do. But when people go to that place, what has taken them there, it might be years of getting there, and I imagine it was that way with Ronnie. The one thing that is in the back of a lot of our minds is, we know that the cancer was in remission. He had told me once on the phone that he would never go through that again, what it took, like that two years it took to get through that stage of the pain and agony that he was in. And I'm not so sure that he may have gotten news that it had come back. I know that that happens quite often. And if that's the case, maybe still, whatever the moment was that made him take the turn it did, I have no idea. But nevertheless he left an incredible legacy and he left a lot of friends who adore him."

"I got an email from someone who said, 'Have you seen the news about Ronnie?'" remembers John Wardlaw. "And then of course I heard that he had died. It didn't come out for a few days that it was suicide. And while I was shocked, I had heard that he had stuff going on with depression, even though I've emailed with Michele Graybeal since and she says she had never heard anything about depression with Ronnie and she was married to him. And in my own mind, I kind of said, he just went through that whole dramatic thing of fighting cancer and beat it. And I almost wonder if he came out of it, got back on the road, and then suddenly realized like there wasn't a big enough challenge. You know, you reach that goal, and then suddenly rather than embracing that he could be out there playing again, I think he just might have thought he fought a battle and won, and there wasn't anything big enough left to defeat. But I certainly can't evaluate what went through his mind. He was married, and from talking to his wife, Leighsa, it sounded like things were good with them. So yeah, it's pretty shocking. I was devastated. He and I had been talking about him playing on the next Anti-M album. Which, amazingly enough, still isn't finished."

"I'm going to say within a month or two, he and I had several emails together," continues John. "We actually did make an agreement at that point. I did temporarily take down my site, because he said, 'Hey, I'm putting up the full-blown Ronnie Montrose.com.' And he didn't mind if I had a few pages up. But he said, 'As long as you scale it back.' So I scaled it back on his request. Because he had actually almost everything up on his site I had anyway. But at the same time, it wasn't in animosity or anything towards me. And he and I were talking about recording together. He even said, 'Call me soon; we'll talk about it.' So it was all positive. But beyond that, then like two months went by and then that's when I heard. So yeah, not a word from the way he sounded to me. That anything was going bad."

"I know that before he went into cancer treatment, and then after the cancer, he was working on an album called *10 x 10, Ronnie Montrose & Friends*. And I have heard that that is still in the works of being attempted to be released, but it was not 100% completed. So my understanding is we still might see some Ronnie Montrose music we haven't all heard. The concert for Ronnie Montrose was wonderful, being able to see all those people coming out to pay tribute. I was actually really surprised when I got an invitation to go to that from his wife. Because I was like, well, I know he and I knew each other, but you don't really know where your name falls in someone's list of things. And she was all, 'Oh no, Ronnie talked about you a lot.' And that made me feel really good, to know that I wasn't just some guy who built a website and he played on my album. It was nice to know we really were friends. Because that's kind of hard. When someone is someone like him, and then hey, I'm a musician, he enjoyed my stuff, he mostly enjoyed my sense of humour, we had a good time talking and we got together three or four times. But you still don't know."

"To be perfectly honest, it doesn't make sense to me, based on the time I spent with him and what I know of him," reflects Tal Morris. "Ronnie was probably one of the most intelligent people I've ever met. As a result, he could be hiding a lot of things that I never knew. And possibly, you know, as much as I saw him engaged in a variety of things at a level I could only dream about, he could've been tortured on equal points. But I just don't buy it. Like seriously, the guy was an electronics genius. He was an inventor. He had a way of applying himself at any given moment to almost anything. He had a support network with a wife that was completely devoted to him. Any indulgence that he might want to get into. It just doesn't make any sense to me. As someone told me, he was an alcoholic, and alcohol does strange things to your decision-making power. And if you're caught into a cycle and you can't stop drinking, that can create its own reason for wanting to end your life that has nothing to do with your circumstance, your business or anything else. You're trapped, and you don't want to go into rehab. There's the public outcry and the embarrassment and what that means. Who knows? That could've been its own reason."

As for the grind of touring perhaps getting him down, Morris says, "That seems feasible. Doing this might have lost its lustre. This is conjecture now, but maybe he didn't see an end to the treadmill, and it depressed him to the point where he would end his life because he didn't see a possibility of things changing. And to do that created its own negative power."

"Crown Royal was his drink," continues Tal, who adds that during his time with Ronnie, the mid-'90s, it wasn't an issue. "It wasn't debilitating at all. He definitely had a rhythm that was set with the workflow and sound checks, and there were no missed opportunities. Always on time, and his clothes were always washed and folded, and he was the world's greatest T-shirt folder. I mean, the dude was so intense. We'd go to a gas station and he would give you a seminar on how to wipe the windshield properly. He was so intense. And on stage his T-shirts were perfect. They had no creases; there were never wrinkles. And he wore a T-shirt on every gig. And one day, and I'm like, 'Dude, how do you get your T-shirts like that?' And aha!, he showed me, and he's packing a suitcase—he's not even hanging the stuff. And he's showing me how to fold a T-shirt so that it doesn't have any creases when you put it on (laughs). Everything he did was a big deal. Like, okay, kid, you're on the road—here's how you do laundry. Here's how you do a sound check, here's how you deal with acoustics in a room. Okay, you're overpowering your room right now. You have too much bass. You have not enough bass here. Interesting."

And all that knowledge is now wasted by what might be classified as a bad decision, one that might have passed given any series of small, mundane interferences, yet one that perhaps couldn't have been made without a number of factors lining up. A waste. A waste as far as the rock world is concerned, just given what was in his head.

"Yeah, you could say that," muses Tal, "only because it's not documented. I mean, literally, if somebody, or him, was involved in legitimizing the information, he would be saying such things. But there wasn't someone there to archive. There wasn't someone to help him funnel his... We have no idea what he knew when he passed away, with regards to his intellectual knowledge of electronics. I mean, literally, it's incalculable. There's no way to know. Because he wasn't the type of person who pursued it. He wanted someone to... I think he wanted somebody to notice it, and to come into his circle, and say, 'Let me help you with that, Mr. Montrose. Let me... oh, we need to document that.' 'Okay, let's do that.' But he wasn't the type of guy going, 'I need to find somebody to help me document this or that. Let's talk about room acoustics, and here's what I know.' He was not that kind of guy. It just wasn't part of his tapestry."

"The number one story he told me that'll I'll never forget—and it was hysterical—had to do with this idea... because he was a macrobiotic vegetarian at one point. I mean, hardcore scientific research, health-oriented, 'I'm going to live forever,' 'you guys are poisoning yourself' point of view. Just incredibly intense. Because that's what he did. He got intense about anything. So here's the story that he told me. This is second-hand from him, based on a tour he did with Lynyrd Skynyrd. So he's touring with Lynyrd Skynyrd, and at the time, he's a macrobiotic vegetarian. He's carrying his food in a vacuum-sealed or O ring-sealed briefcase. And he's hanging out backstage at a festival or something with Lynyrd Skynyrd. And they're all eating southern food and doing what they do, and Ronnie's off in the corner with his very specific vegetarian food and doing his thing, and they find it very funny. And they make fun of him, and it turns out it's this thing on the road that's a back and forth. And one of the guys, I don't know who it was, but someone in Skynyrd went up to him and put his hand on Ronnie and said, 'You know what? When we're old and grey, and we're sitting in the rocking chairs, and things are falling apart, I'm just going to get to walk up to you and say, "There's Ronnie Montrose, dying of nothing."' It was this kind of esoteric, philosophical point of view, that, you know, here's Lynyrd Skynyrd enjoying their lives, and everyone's gonna die. So do you want to die of nothing or do you want to die of fun, basically (laughs). 'There goes Ronnie Montrose, dying of nothing.'"

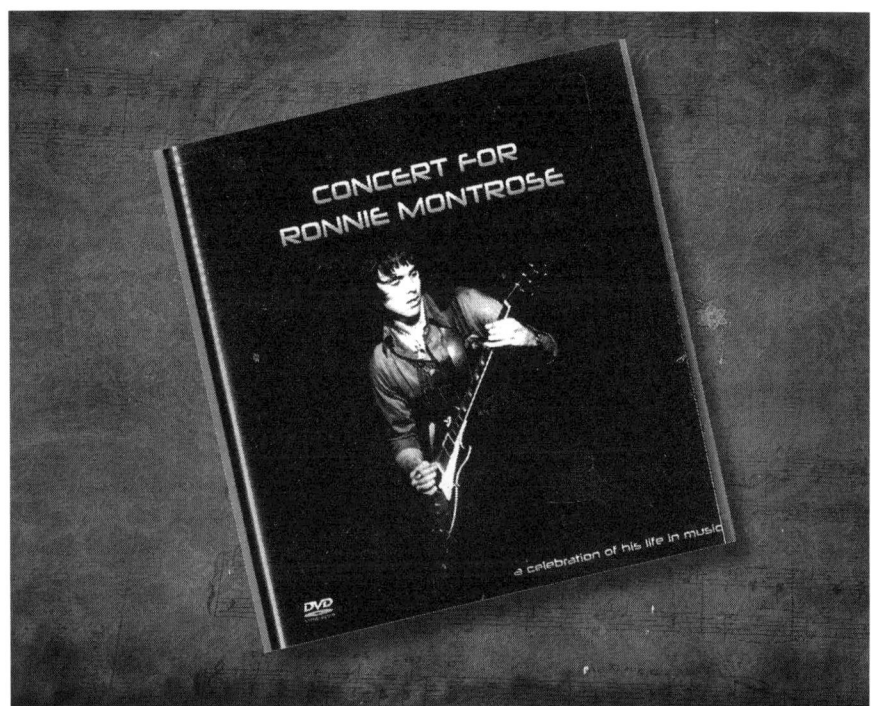

CHAPTER 12: Epilogue – Ronnie's Legacy: "Continually moving forward and wanting to be remembered for that"

On April 27, 2012, not two months after his death, Ronnie Montrose was celebrated in a tribute concert performed at the Regency ballroom in San Francisco. The star-studded set, issued in 2013 as *Concert for Ronnie Montrose: A Celebration of His Life in Music*, featured (exactly as printed on the DVD) Sammy Hagar, Neil Schon, Joe Satriani, Denny Carmassi, Bill Church, Davey Pattison, Glenn Letsch, Marc Bonilla, Tommy Suczek, Ricky Phillips, Steve Smith, Ed Roth, Eric Singer, Tommy Thayer, Jimmy Paxson, Eric Martin, Jeff Watson, CJ Hutchins, Tal Morris, Frank Hannon, Brian Wheat, Jeff Keith, Dave Rude, Troy Luccketta, Dave Meniketti, John Nyman, Brad Lang, Mike Vanderhule, Mario Cippolina, Chuck Terpo, Amber Morris, April Grisman, Michael Indelicatio, Steve Brown, Dan McNay and Randy Scoles. Ronnie's wife Leighsa, also credited as producer of the two-DVD package, was a comforting presence there as well.

Of note, Leighsa was also the driving force behind getting together *Live at the Uptown*, a DVD presenting Ronnie's band in action January 27, 2012.

"We actually played some Gamma songs, you know, towards the end," says Dan McNay. "It was basically like, he wanted to do both Gamma and Montrose material; he wanted to kind of sum it up. And we actually did that live video that I wouldn't say turned out the best. But I think it was his only thing he ever recorded like that, or that he let go, in his life. His wife, Leighsa, after he passed away, she kind of put it out too quick and didn't really take the care that it needed. Because let's face it, even the big boys like Zeppelin, everybody added shit on their stuff. And Ronnie was actually having... I wouldn't say it was one of his better nights."

Says Ricky Phillips of the brilliantly mixed-and-matched *Concert for Ronnie Montrose* show, "You know, there are a few things that surprised me about it. I loved what Mark Bonilla did with the Gamma set. And I thought his respect and care for Ronnie... I know that he was heavily influenced by Ronnie, but he had become such a virtuosic guitarist, that what he did with the Gamma set I thought was perfect. And it was just nice to hear the songs and it was nice to see everybody's interpretations, the guitar players who jumped in. I know that Neal Schon... it was no cakewalk for Neal. I mean, Neal can play just about anything, but we didn't really have any rehearsal. We were put in a room so we could discuss what we were gonna do. But we kind of had to do... just everybody flew in; I flew in from, I don't even remember where I was. But everybody was coming in from all over the place. A lot of people were actually from northern California, but they do have to get to San Francisco. And you think, 'Oh yeah, I know that song,' and then you get into actually running it down, and it's like, there's so much of Ronnie there. Ronnie's arrangement first of all, but Ronnie's hands, man, and the way he phrased and everything, makes the music that he created... and that's always the case, I guess, with the great guitarists. So for Neal to try to jump into those shoes, he realized that he had to contribute big pieces of himself to make it happen, to make it work, because there is no other Ronnie Montrose. But I noticed that with all the players. You can try, you can do your best, but it showed me how deep Ronnie was, seeing these great guitar players trying to interpret his work."

Asked who he was most excited to meet, Ricky says, "You know, I had never met Bill Church, so it was kind of cool for me to meet Bill, and we kind of palled around a bit when we were taking snapshots. But we didn't really get to hang too much that night, because there was just too much going on. Set changes, boom, boom, boom, boom. But it was great to meet Bill Church, great bass player. A lot of my unsung heroes throughout my musical influence past are guys like John Paul Jones. I mean, where would Led Zeppelin have been without him? John Entwistle, Chris Squire... I mean all these guys, everybody knows who the lead singer is and maybe the lead guitar player in all the rock bands that have come and gone, but Bill Church is one of those guys that did exactly the right thing for the Montrose material."

"That was an awesome trip," says Church, on the evening. "It was... well, all it was was me, Denny and Sammy. We had somebody play guitar, and since Sammy was doing his new band with Joe Satriani, you know, we had him along and it was a lot of fun. And of course, that night the music went on all night—all kinds of all-star players were there that night."

As Dan McNay explains, planning for the show revealed a side of Ronnie he hadn't really thought much about before-hand. "Yes, well, his legacy, I just sort of found this out through when he passed away. I had been playing with him, and I happened to have a pretty good relationship with his wife Leighsa at the time. It got weird after that, but she was helping me put together this concert with all these people, to honour Ronnie. I basically took the reins on that thing, and I said, 'Let me help any way I can.' She says, 'Well, I want you to try to figure out who Ronnie played with and contact them, and Ronnie's friends.'"

"And so I actually sat down and made a list. This is what I think Ronnie's legacy is. I'm taking a long-winded way to get to your question, but this is important actually. This is the one thing. When I think about him and I look at his pictures in my office... if you ask anybody... I mean, I had the dubious duty of calling all these people and saying, 'Hey man, do you wanna come down and play at Ronnie's thing?' These are all like rock stars. Nobody wants to get paid but everyone's got egos. And I mixed them all up, as far as playing together. We're just gonna play his music and whatever. Sammy Hagar and the boys would come up here. So yeah, Ronnie's legacy... all these guys were like, 'I don't want to play with so-and-so; I don't want to...'

And I would just shoot the shit on the phone with them, 'Well, why are you doing this whole thing? Why would you agree to do this for no money, and then...?' 'I'm doing it for Ronnie.' 'Well, that's right. That's what this whole thing is about.'"

"So anyway, when I wrote down all the names of everyone he's ever recorded with, and everyone he's ever toured with, the list was staggering. I mean, it was staggering. And I don't think anybody else you're gonna interview is going to tell you this, because they've probably never done this. But I did. And I wrote down all the people. I don't know if anyone's affected rock 'n' roll music behind the scenes, as far as recording, or taking on players that have affected rock music. Like, for instance, Eric Singer played with Ronnie first, right? Eric Singer plays in Kiss, right? You know, like Mario Cipollina, he played with Ronnie first and he went on to play in Huey Lewis, right? Mitchell Froom played with Ronnie first and now he's producing McCartney. It just goes on and on. Name after name. It shocked me. I think that is Ronnie's legacy. It's all these musicians that he… he had a way with people. All these musicians that he played with, that he gave the gift of music to. The music bug. I mean they obviously already had it, playing with him, but he gives you something extra, you know what I mean? Like after the fact. He gives you afterburners. Very inspiring to be around. But it'll blow your mind, if you make a list. If you look across rock and pop culture and you see how many guys he affected that way, that went on to do great things—that's his legacy."

When I asked Dan what Ronnie had to say about his time with Bob James, a wrinkle concerning this concert arose. "He liked Bob James. He thought Bob James was a little peculiar to deal with, but he said he was talented singer. And they tried to... I don't know about Bob James. He wouldn't even come to that tribute concert, because he wasn't sure it was the right form and he didn't want to take the stage unless it was the exact lineup of Montrose that he wanted. He wasn't having it. He wouldn't come sing. I said, 'You know, you oughta come sing anyway, dude. There's other people you can play with. There are some amazing players that will be there.' And I started going down the list, and I'm like, 'Everybody is qualified to rock with you, dude. Show up.'"

Recalls Mike Kelley, Bob's best buddy who also acts as his manager, and not exactly contradicting Ricky, "When Ronnie passed away, for the tribute in the Bay Area, they wanted to have Bob sing. But everything was being done through me. Bob said, 'Listen, I want to do it, I'm here. Just work it out. But I don't want to deal with any of it. You deal with all of it.' So I was a liaison. And everything was very diplomatic. And I said, 'Here is what Bob would like to do. He would like to do a song from *Warner Bros. Presents* and a song from *Jump on It*.' And I gave him some options. I said, 'Any of these songs would be great, he would love to do this, and he would like to do it with Denny. He would basically like to do it with the lineup that he was in the band with. With whatever guitar player you guys have, whoever you're going to use.'"

"And they said, 'Oh, well no, we already have…' They didn't want to do it for some reason. They were really kind of strange. They didn't really give any sensible reasons. But they said, 'No, no, we've got a section later where we're just going to have all these different configurations of people get up.' They wanted Bob to do one song, and they wanted him to do 'Twenty Flight Rock.' And Bob just said, first of all, I'm not even going to be playing with any of us who were in the band. They wanted to put him with an all non-Montrose lineup—no Denny, no Fitz, no Alcivar. It was just going to be whoever they picked, and him. He just said, 'Mike, you know, no.'"

"And believe me, we talked about it a lot and we really agonized over it. I said, 'Bob, I'm just your mouthpiece. Whatever you want to do.' He said, 'No, if, of course, I'm going to put in the time here, I'm going to put in whatever the time is necessary for this, and if I have to go up there and rehearse for a day or two I'm willing to do it. But how am I supposed to look at this as any kind of meaningful contribution for this guy when they're putting me with all people that were not even in the band, and they're going to have me do a cover song that wasn't even our song anyway?' It was weird. It seemed very strange. Believe me, I really lobbied them to say, hey, come on, at least Denny; at least you've got to have Denny. And who knows? Maybe Denny said, 'Fuck it, Bob James, no way, I don't want to work with him. I don't even want to be onstage with that guy.' I don't know. So I really don't know the politics behind it. But I know that it was on the table, and we just could not make it work. Very disappointing. Very disappointing especially for Bob. Because he really wanted to do it.

But the thing with Ronnie is, I knew there was bad blood between him and Bob. When Ronnie passed away, there was no love lost between the two of them. So I'm curious."

In addition to the action-packed concert, the DVD includes a pile of video interview segments where various of these players articulate Ronnie's legacy. And so we end our tale the same way, asking our story's characters what Ronnie should be remembered for, what his major accomplishments were, and, good or bad, what defines the story arc of this complicated man's roller-coaster of a career.

"If I were to be succinct, I would say Ronnie should be remembered as the father of American hard rock guitar," figures Tal Morris. "If you were to create a timeline of hard rock guitar and its heroes, you will find, I think, that his influence, specifically Montrose I, is the reason why everything that followed became what it is. Specifically, Van Halen I is a direct... the sound of that record, the way that they played as a band, and how they focused their energies sonically, is a direct result of *Montrose*, the sound and influence from that record. And even if you go into the way Ronnie wrote, Ronnie pioneered this technique where it is basically what I would call a static element in a moving element. So let's say a static bass mode, with moving chord shapes, and/or the opposite: a moving bass note with a static chord shape. 'Make It Last' and a few others are an example of this. And Van Halen basically took that... and there's documentation of it. When Ted Templeman said, 'How do you want your record to sound?' All they said was, 'Make it sound like this,' and they showed him Montrose I. So yes, to answer your question, Ronnie should be remembered as the father of American hard rock."

"I don't know why Eddie didn't mention the fact in interviews that Ronnie was a huge influence on them," continues Morris, "but the fact remains. They shared the same producer for the record, etc., and you can hear it. And I'm of the mind, specifically, that Eddie Van Halen isn't telling the truth when he talks about his tapping technique. I really feel that he knew Ronnie Montrose was the guitarist on 'Frankenstein,' and when he was young and heard that record, when he heard the synthesizer part, which is basically that tapping sound, he didn't know that it wasn't guitar, and he assumed it was Ronnie, and he tried to mimic it. And in doing so, came up with this technique. I really honestly feel that, but I can't prove it. He professed that he made it up based on things that he wanted to hear that he wasn't able to do with his left hand, so he came up with a way of doing it. But when you listen to 'Frankenstein' and that synthesizer solo, and you listen to 'Eruption,' the similarities are just astounding."

"So American hard rock was fathered by that record, period. End of story. I mean, the power of that record launched endless things. The influence is not calculable. It would be hard for me to believe that any of the powerful rock acts that followed... if they denied the influence of that record, I think they would be lying (laughs)."

Sums up Roger, "When Montrose first came out, they were the American Led Zeppelin. Ronnie was every bit as good a player as Jimmy Page, but never got the recognition that Jimmy did. That was a phenomenal record. Montrose - *Montrose* was heavy (laughs)."

"Oh yeah, the first Montrose was real groundbreaking for all my guitar and my band guys that I was hanging out with," reminisces Jeff Watson. "We got the album and listened to it in my sister's room—she had a stereo; I remember that (laughs). And we were just really impressed with Ronnie. I mean, he had come out of Edgar Winter's band, and we were real knocked-out with the songs, the production, Ted Templeman, the drum sound— Denny's kick drum on 'Rock Candy' was a real groundbreaking thing for us—obviously Sam's voice and how Ronnie played to the songs. His soloing was real song-oriented, and the riffs were real groundbreaking for the time. As for Ted, producing bands, especially really young bands, is like herding chickens, really. And I think he was good at gathering everybody together and making a signature sound. Like he did with the Doobie Brothers and that first Van Halen record. But everything about *Montrose* was new and fresh. Basically it was going to be the American Led Zeppelin; it really was. If that hadn't broken up, if Ron and Sam had not had that big fight on the airplane coming back from Europe, that band would've gone on to be amazingly huge."

"As a guitarist, to me, personally, none of them pose a challenge to perform," answers Jeff, asked about the technicality of Ronnie's playing. "But there's some real clever playing and all of it touched me in a great way. For parts—I look for parts. He was very clever in putting in very specific and intentional things that you wait for in songs, like that little slide part in 'Rock Candy,' which he showed me and I never mastered. He would put those here and there, but not over-use things. He was very smart about giving things space to breathe, and their moment. He wasn't into flash for flash's sake. That was something that was real important to him: just play to the song, whereas me, as a kid, I was going for the million-notes-a-minute thing."

"But that *Montrose* album was so important. I don't think you'll find anybody of our age and level of notoriety that wouldn't agree with that. From Eddie Van Halen to anybody who came out of that era, that was important listening for all of us. We all grew up listening to it. Everybody had their stuff that they chewed on to get themselves going, but that album was very important to us."

"And so as I said, the songwriting was very strong," continues the Night Ranger guitarist. "And Sammy's voice... to this day, I still think Sam has a great voice. It really was the first, I guess, heavy metal album of our time that came out of our country. And I know that Sam was a huge fan of Plant and Zeppelin. You can hear that influence in there. That's where it was going and that's what it was doing to all of us. And that continued, although the second album, *Paper Money*, had some nuance to it, where you could tell they were starting to struggle internally. There was a magic to the first lineup, with Sam and Denny and Bill and Ron, and then when they got Bob James, that's when it started falling apart. Not falling apart, but it was a different product."

It might be a bit much, giving Montrose so much credit for a new type of music or even so much credit for "influence," even if Tal's qualification is "American hard rock guitar." I mean, the point has been made by others throughout our story, and myself as well, but there's always cause to lift the foot off the pedal a bit because we are talking about a single album here, one record, *Montrose*, after which Ronnie and his band (and his next band etc.), just become part of a pack.

"Yeah, well, Ronnie unfortunately was one of the textbook examples of someone getting in their own way," concedes Morris, who explains how Ronnie would sabotage himself. "And Ronnie had issue with the fact that he was dependent on vocalists. And, you know, Montrose, in reality, was a band—it was a band. He couldn't have written all those songs without Sammy. And the sound that came out of that, he was responsible for in a large part, but as you know, magic recipes create their own effect. This has always been the problem within bands. Everybody wants to take credit for the alchemy of a group. I joined Credence Revisited, which was the CCR offshoot, of the rhythm section without John Fogerty. I toured with them for six years, and neither John Fogerty nor them had anywhere near the success that they had together. Look at when Mick Jagger and Keith left each other and tried to do their solo stuff. The alchemy is what it is, whatever it is. Ronnie is a victim of his own frustration of wanting to re-create the recipe, because he thought he was responsible for it, and it never happened. I guess you could make the argument that Ronnie needed an equal, an equally powerful partner, to re-create the effect that happened because of Montrose. Once Sammy was gone, he didn't have that. Because he didn't want to deal with that. And whatever dysfunction created problems, obviously, that same sort of chemistry created this magic."

So Tal recognizes this, the idea that as great as *Montrose* is, it was, to put it bluntly, your proverbial flash in the pan, somewhat of a happy accident.

"Sure, that was the biggest problem—they didn't see it through. If they had stuck together, it would've happened at the level that they all wanted. It would've happened. But they just didn't have the patience, and they didn't understand the work ethic, and they didn't understand—again, conjecture—that regardless of your personalities, you have an alchemy that can't be ignored. Which is what John Lennon and Paul McCartney recognized and what Keith Richards and Mick Jagger recognized. They were going to work. They weren't going there to be friends. They were going there to do a job, and the team worked. If you've got a company and it's doing very, very well, and #1 and #2 don't get along personally, but they're great at business? The stuff is working. Something is working. So put aside your differences and go to work. Pick your healthy boundaries and make it work. It doesn't have to be this magic thing where everybody gets along. You've got a powerful team and you've got stars and your craft is one thing and your personality is another. This is what ruins great actors too. All of a sudden they stop thinking about what they do as a craft and they start identifying with the effect they have as a persona and then they get lost."

Later in life, Ronnie had a way of recognizing it. "He would do this solidarity statement," says Tal. "He would say that Montrose is Sammy Hagar, Bill Church, Denny Carmassi, Ronnie. That's what Montrose is; Montrose isn't anything else. There's no such thing as a different incarnation of that. That's a statement that I heard him say. That was a magic arrangement and he realized that."

"But Ronnie was an intellect as well," notes Tal. "He was an inventor, he was highly artistic in terms of wanting to follow his passions. And focusing on an industry rather than being a pure artist is always a dilemma. And he always wanted to reinvent himself. I think there was a lot of pride in the fact that he was continually moving forward and wanting to be remembered for that, rather than acquiescing to whatever pressures his fan base would put on him to re-create what he had done before. Unfortunately, the fans are what's putting food on your table (laughs)."

And so the alchemy was gone, figures Morris, as early as the first singer switch, between *Paper Money* and *Warner Bros. Presents*. "I liked the Bob James albums; it was fun music. But there was an impact with *Montrose*, a feeling attached to it. And everyone, including me, when you first heard it, in my peer group, noticed this feeling. It's like, oh my God, I love that. And then you associate the people who are connected to it, and when it moves beyond that feeling and you're expected to remain loyal, that's tough."

And Ronnie really lost patience quick with people telling him how important that first album was. "Yes, he talked about it begrudgingly, in terms of even me as a fan saying, 'Please show me how to play "Rock Candy." I hear everyone is playing it wrong.' And he would show it to you like, 'All right, you've earned this kid,' kind of thing. But he would ignore fans' cries for these hits, because it was an instrumental tour, no vocals. And when you're battling with that, you want people to come to see him, and a lot of people expected those hits and still do. They were still wanting them before he died."

Dan McNay admired this quality in Ronnie. "You know what? If you're an artist and you happen to hold a guitar or a trumpet or a drumstick or a bass, and you record and you write, you just go where the heart wants to go, right? I mean, did Salvador Dali paint the same thing every time? You know what I'm saying? That just doesn't happen. If you're truly an artist, if you truly have things to express that are created inside of you, in your soul or your head... I mean, for all I know, Ronnie, had a regular tape in his head playing songs we've never heard 24/7. Because I know that I do. That's the thing. So why not that guy?"

And built into the cake, helping fuel Ronnie's propensity for change, is that he didn't come from a heavy metal place, particularly. "He was a Dick Dale fan," explains Watson, "and he was just a little bit too old enough, if that makes sense (laughs), to embrace that term. I don't think he respected that terminology. I think he hearkened more to his predecessors. Heavy metal started representing something he didn't want to be known as. That's my opinion, because I never specifically asked him that question. But no, when he came out with 'Town Without Pity' and he started showing his Jeff Beckness a bit, I think that showed that he wanted to be more than just a three-chord, loud, banging guy. He was an artist inside; he really was. He was a funny guy, Ronnie."

"Anyway, more of what I got from Ronnie was his assessment of gear," continues Tal. "The guy was an incredible technician when it came to amplifiers and tone. When I toured with him, he showed me so many things about room acoustics, how to compensate for that on stage, gain structures, gain staging, speaker choice, cabinet size, amplifier types. Just endless education that flowed from him. He was a very inventive person, but as an actual guitarist he had a lot of technical limitations. And he was a master at reinterpreting a similar technique over and over again, or something very simple and making it sound complicated when it wasn't. Like a lot of open string riffs. He was more about what type of effect could a musical idea or a guitar have, rather than the specific notes of it. You know what I'm saying? He was looking more for emotional response rather than to be known for an actual technical thing. He knew the power of timing. When to hit a note, the effect of a certain type of colour and sound, and what type of emotion or impression it would give. And so those are the kinds of tools that he worked with rather than chops. Because he knew he couldn't compete with Eddie Van Halen or Allan Holdsworth or Steve Morse or people that were out there. He knew that he didn't have that type of facility. But what he had was an incredibly powerful intellect and insight—he had the power of choice on his side."

"Like I said, he was very inventive with the tools he had, and he knew it. He was very aware of that, and that's why he would find new ways, permutations of his skill set, over and over again. What can I get and how can I get this, in a new way? And he would do it. And that's why he was so invested and captivated with gear and effects. Because he knew that it could give him new dimensions automatically, and so he developed the skill of treating his guitar tones in a way that would change him or advance things beyond his physical abilities. So sure, he was a great guitarist. When made him great was his ability to make great choices. You could say the same thing about Jeff Beck. Jeff Beck, as a legend, in the end, is going to be about inventiveness. And I could say the same thing about Ronnie. Ronnie was at this point—this strange point—where English rock was kind of ruling the universe, and he was obviously influenced by Jeff Beck and

Clapton and Zeppelin and everything else, just like everyone was, and he wanted to claim that real estate for American audiences. I really believe that. And that's what Montrose represents to me."

Jeff Watson wholeheartedly agrees with Tal on Ronnie as mad gearhead. "He was a tinkerer, and he was going into using these Lab Series amplifiers and trying different bits of gear, and he was really into Lexicon delays, digital stuff. He wanted to hear new sounds. He was really exploring things. And that's I think what took him to the album style he had with Gamma. And I'm sure he wanted to be on the radio, I think, as a guitarist... artist/guitarist, besides just being in a rock band."

As an example of Ronnie's mad scientist ethic beginning way back, Jeff says, "I knew Ronnie really well, and he was a very dear friend and he was my producer as well in the '70s. So he would spend a lot of time at my place, and we would talk constantly about the world and stuff. And he would pick up acoustic guitars and play some of those early Montrose things, and I was real knocked out by his dedication to replication of performance. He was a dedicated player. But we were working on some really funny things. Down at his house—he had a house down by the airport, below San Francisco, in the Belmont area—he was working on this thing. It was sort of like an ebow, but it was six little wheels made of, I don't know, fiberglass or plastic, which spun on little motors. So you would have a motor, and these levers would sit over the bridge of the guitar. You would have six little levers that would sit right above each string. And if you pushed down the lever, the motor would be running, and it would engage the little wheel and spin. It was like little, round violin bows. And we never got it working correctly. I think we did a bit, and he just gave me all the parts. It must be around here somewhere, in a box or something."

"But he was always tinkering, you know? Very inventive guy. He should be remembered for the fact that he was always curious, always exploring, wanting to better himself musically. That little device... what it was called? It was called the Gizmotron! And it must be a box in my studio somewhere, or down in storage. But that defines Ronnie to me. It's just him tinkering in his garage. I remember working on that thing endlessly, trying to get it working. And I'm sure it would've worked; today, you could do it with other products. But he was always curious. I would say Ronnie was the ultimate Gizmotron."

"And to be blunt, I think he was being personally indulgent," continues Morris, back on this idea of Ronnie not being concerned whether the music he was making was marketable or not. "That's how he operated—in his personal life and in his career. And so the results are not in the market, as it were. But with your own toolset, 'Look what I built with my own erector set.' 'What are you going to do with that?' 'I don't care. I did it for me' (laughs). And there are consequences to those decisions. Here's the funny thing. Like I've always said, success is relative. So we can be America and have clean water and food that won't kill us, and access to education relatively inexpensively if we wish it, because of technology and the college system or whatever. With persistence and drive you can basically do whatever you want in America. And you like to think that if you were to compare this to somebody in Senegal or a war-torn area in the Middle East, you would be thankful and somehow feel that advantage and feel thankful for it. Well, it's not really possible to tangibly feel that because it's not our culture. And so getting back to Ronnie, he's sustaining himself with music, and is a public figure and has opportunities to give interviews and be adored or whatever if that's important to him, and explore his interests, etc. Well, at what level? At what level does a person get satisfied when his peer group and also the entire genre of music that he basically fathered, is running away with millions of dollars that he doesn't get to participate in? I can't imagine what that felt like. He knew it was happening. And here he is, you know, trying to be possibly this historic figure, the island that is Ronnie Montrose, and he can't get there unless he plays ball."

Chuck Terpo makes the case that bands should play their hits, and that Ronnie's natural tendency to balk at this diminished his impact in the end.

"I'm 65 now and I've been playing since I was 16. And watching bands. When the Doobie Brothers were split up, I played with Tommy Johnson and Michael Hossack. Michael is passed now, but he was the original drummer. And Tommy Johnson, of course, is still the main lead singer and wrote all the early hits. And, you know, those guys are still doing great. They play great and they have a great band. But they're still doing 'Long Time Running' and 'China Grove' and 'Listen to the Music,' because people want to hear it. And Ronnie wouldn't want to do 'Bad Motor Scooter.' 'That was in the past.' So I think he hurt himself there, in that way. And then Sammy Hagar becomes more famous than Ronnie. You know, Ronnie played with Edgar Winter I was a big Edgar Winter fan way back, but I didn't know at the time that Ronnie played guitar for them. All I knew is, 'Hey, here's Edgar Winter.' And Van Morrison. And so I know that bothered him. A lot of people he worked with, that he contributed so much to their success... and still a lot of people didn't know who he was. Some people would ask me, 'Who are you playing with?' I would say, 'Ronnie Montrose.' 'Who?' Not everybody knows. And I'd say, 'Well, do you listen to rock 'n roll? Yeah? Then you've heard him.'"

"I'm happy I got to know him," continues Chuck. "And I definitely know we were friends—it was more than just music. I would definitely say Ronnie was a complicated person. Some people are not complicated; they're pretty straightforward and simple. Ronnie was complicated. And I don't know what else to say than I'm just really glad I met him. Plus I learned a lot from him musically; he would usually be quite patient with me, especially when we were learning some of the Montrose, when he asked me if I wanted to go out and play some of the Montrose shows with him. And I said, 'Obviously you must think I can do it or you wouldn't be calling me.' He says, 'Yeah, I think you can do it. I'll help you through some things. Because some of them have got a lot of chord structures and I changed some of them. I'll help you with it.'"

"Ronnie could have produced," continues Tal, which makes sense, given that his curiosity for the process obviously goes right back to the beginning. "I mean, how many people in these bands that completely adored him, if he says, 'Hey, let me produce a record for you.' Why wouldn't they say, of course, you know? He wanted to be an artist the whole time, and hanging up the spurs was not his way (laughs). And he could have possibly been an engineer—who knows? You know, these days, when you talk about someone like Jack White or these people that wear multiple hats... some people in the modern age basically have no qualms about wearing multiple hats and being proud of it, where Ronnie came from an age where if you became an engineer or producer, you've taken a step backwards. Or a role that you choose has to be singular, you know what I mean? It's kind of a different mindset to understand that, 'I'm a chef *and* I'm a race car driver.' It's okay."

Whether this was ego as well, Tal figures, "It's both. I mean, as anyone goes through their day, sometimes they are wonderful and sometimes they're not. I would say it's both. That's the honest answer. He knew that he had missed opportunities and misinterpreted situations based on his vantage point at that time; he readily admitted that. But at the same time, he's Ronnie Montrose. And whatever that means, he owned it. He had to, in order to sustain whatever it was that was going on. You can't reveal yourself to be indecisive or unconfident if you want to do business. He did both. But he wasn't like self-effacing, if that's your question. He was very much in command of the moment and he was the star of the show. He had to be. In order for the people who invested in him, the promoters, he had to fulfil that role, because that's what people expected."

"But to be perfectly honest, at the stage when I was with him, I was basically in awe. So it is very difficult to be objective at that point. I was in his learning mode, because he has so much to offer and so much experience and so much history. He could stop a conversation in seconds by telling you about the first time Boston opened up for them and what type of effect that had. It was just endless. But sure, Ronnie was more interested in pursuing his interests than trying to please an audience."

That's music, but in his personal interactions, says Tal, "Ronnie had a way of playing to the crowd, with regard to anyone he was with. So if you were in a room with people, and he knew you were into arranging flowers, he would talk about flowers and he would say something about flowers that was pretty poignant. If he was in a room full of whatever. So he would find out what you are into as a person, and then basically go down that road. So when we were touring, you know, we were doing instrumental music, and he was talking a lot about his associations with Holdsworth and what he did with Steve Smith and 'Town Without Pity.' He was focused on the job at hand. He wasn't reminiscing or talking about this or the future or what he regretted or anything. He was committed to the moment."

And as others have said, often in that moment, Ronnie could be a pretty funny and fun-loving guy. "Sure," says Tal. "In the van we'd play lots of English rock, lots of Led Zeppelin, Jeff Beck, that sort of stuff, and he was a fan of experimental synth music, textural stuff. But to be very truthful, we played The Jerky Boys probably more than anything (laughs). Jerky Boys in the van was the thing. We wore that to death. We would play the same first record over and over again. It was like a rerun television show. And then we would start memorizing portions of it and have dialogue from the tapes as we were doing sound check or at a restaurant or whatever. It was just running gag."

John Wardlaw adds additional colour to this idea that Ronnie will be remembered as an innovator, both through the music and through the tools to make it.

"He never liked repeating the same kind of music on any project, and he never liked using just the same old sound. He would get into a sound, he'd really love a certain guitar, a certain box and a certain amplifier, and then the next time he did an album he might use a similar guitar because he loved certain guitars, but suddenly it was, oh, I've discovered this box and this sound and this style of solo. Never wanted to be that guy who just played the same solo every record and sounded like the same record over and over. Which is why I think the lineups changed so much. So he was continuously trying to innovate. And sure, I'll agree with everyone else about the first album. Montrose were one of the first acts to play like heavy FM hard rock in the US. I don't really know when heavy metal in the US came out, but his stuff was getting close to early metal. The closest thing might have been Aerosmith and then obviously there was heavy influence on Eddie Van Halen. From the moment Eddie heard that record, he wanted that sound."

And then there was the independent streak, mixed up with ego, says Wardlaw. "Having spent some time with him, working with him and knowing a bit more about his life, he explains it himself about growing up in different bands but wanting you to do your own stuff. He played with Van Morrison, he played with Edgar Winter, but that wasn't enough—he wanted to expand. I know that his problem with Sammy... he thought Sammy is a genius vocalist with great writing talent, but some bands can't have two huge writing talents. The band was called Montrose, and I think he wanted to be the source of the music and a lot of other things. So I do think there was a bit of, if the vocalist really had a strong way they wanted to go, and it wasn't the way Ronnie wanted to go, given his name being on the band, that could create friction."

Jeff Watson recognizes all too well Ronnie's sense of ego, especially as it pertains to his relationship with Sammy. Speaking about the break-up between the two, Jeff says, "I hear it from both Sam and Ron, plus Fitz, who was there. What I infer is that Ronnie wanted Sam to not run around so much and steal the spotlight so much when Ronnie was doing his soloing and things like that. And Sammy was just the consummate entertainer, and still is. It was like the limelight was kind of overshadowing the decision making, I suppose. So I think he always had that thing up his butt about Sam, even though they got together at the end and Ronnie came up and played on a couple shows. But I don't think Ronnie ever got over it, what went down with that original band, because it had such potential. It was a huge thing in the making, and I think he realized that some of the downfall was his own doing."

"Plus don't forget, Sammy sees himself as a guitar player," adds Jeff. "Which I would give him grief about forever (laughs). He sees himself as a guitarist and a singer and he was relegated to the microphone. That happens to a lot of singers that play guitar. Joe Lynn Turner, my singer from my other band, Mother's Army, he's a good guitar player, but Blackmore... we all keep putting him on a mic stand. So Sammy wanted to play guitar and sing. And Ronnie wasn't going to have it. And that was another issue. And Sammy wanted... Sammy is the captain of his own ship—always. And when Bob James came in, he seemed like a sweet guy, to me, anyway. He was a real nice guy, and he had a real strong look and a strong vocal presence; I thought he sang really well. But Sammy is a consummate showman—he really is—and I don't know if Bob had those chops. Not to take anything away from him, but I thought Sammy was the perfect fit. Every now and again you get the right formula."

"But that band was so tight, and they could jam," explains Watson. "One thing I do know that was really important that Ronnie insisted on, was that—and I'm sure it was probably the same for Church and Denny—but Fitz told me they would go to the studio, S.I.R. in San Francisco, and they would just work with the rhythm section. Just bass and drums, working off the kick drum for the bass parts. And this was Ronnie really making sure he had a rock-solid rhythm section. Because in a three-piece band, that rhythm section has to be so strong and deep. I thought that was an interesting thing; I learned a lot from that. And they did a lot of jamming. There was a lot of time spent on instruments. That is one thing I did notice with those guys, more so than with a lot of other bands that had been around, that they really spent time on that."

As for his impressions of Davey and the whole Gamma era, Watson recalls, "I saw Gamma several times. Davey Pattison and I worked together, and the band worked with Davey a lot. We did a soundtrack for a movie having Davey sing with the Ranger lineup. We almost put Davey in the band; we wanted a singer. We weren't happy with our lead vocalist, except for Kelly, our drummer. But we worked with Davey, and we would go to shows; there was a lot of interaction between all of us. Davey is such a great singer. I remember Ronnie calling and going, 'Jeff, I found a singer in Scotland. You're not going to believe this guy.' And I went, really? 'This guy's got a voice like, you know, it's one of the best things ever.' And Ronnie also wanted to incorporate his vocoders, which is the thing that he plays where it sounds electronic and robot-like. He was really into experimenting with electronic sounds and different guitar approaches. He was always tampering with that. So that was his outlet for that; the Gamma thing was trying to be futuristic. He wanted to be a futuristic guy."

Continues Wardlaw, back to the idea of Ronnie and songwriting, "People talk about this idea of Ronnie being insecure and constantly having to feel he was achieving and improving himself... which obviously he did. But some people that are insecure about their own work might lash out at the people around them. If somebody else is getting more of the attention, even though they don't intend to be that way, there could be problems. I think I only offended Ronnie once. I won't go into the details. I accidentally insulted him. So I think he has a bit of that side. The insecurity came out that he felt I was saying, 'Oh, that wasn't good enough.' And I said, 'Hey, I didn't mean it that way' and we were good, right then and there; it was done and we were good. So I saw a little bit of that insecurity. But also when we recorded with him, he would do a solo, and he would look up at me and my friend Mark, and say, 'How was that?' We would go, 'Man, that's awesome, that's perfect.' And he'd say, 'Let's do it again.' He just had to keep going until *he* loved what he did. He was a bit of a perfectionist, and I think that may have caused some friction. I'd say certainly with some of his vocalists—because obviously he had a few."

Echoing a point made by Chuck Terpo, Ricky Phillips says that, "Ronnie Montrose is one of those kind of guys that maybe not everybody on the street knows, which I think is a shame, because every musician that's ever heard Ronnie... I mean, it's one of those industry things where everybody who's a musician knows maybe not all of the things that Ronnie has given to the industry, but he had some sort of magic. And he introduced sort of heavy-handed rock 'n' roll on the guitar to America, really, at a time when the players were, you know, Jimmy Page, Jeff Beck, Eric Clapton, bands like Humble Pie. Ronnie, with the band Montrose, sort of wrote the American version or take on hard rock 'n' roll. And it certainly wasn't heavy metal. Ronnie came from the Edgar Winter Group, which was a great place for him, because as he told me he learned a lot from Edgar and Dan Hartman, great writers and singers, about song structure and all that. By the time he got the Montrose band together, he was able to do all his cool heavy-handed riff rock compositions that Sammy Hagar sang so well. In fact, the whole band was great, with Bill Church and Denny Carmassi, who I had the pleasure of working with too."

"It's kind of hard to stop when it comes Ronnie, because people don't know Ronnie," muses Phillips. "Ronnie was kind of a special guy because he was a true friend. He knew a lot of people and had a lot of friends, and he was not a surface kind of guy. He got to know his friends. And when Ronnie called you on the phone, you'd better sit yourself down because you're gonna be there for a while. He didn't call to chitchat. He liked to check in with his friends. He was just a great dude, man, one of my favourite people and one of my favourite friends. And as a guitarist, if you watch him, for example, on some of those YouTube videos, he doesn't just play guitar with his hands, he plays with his whole body. His feet are stomping, he's marching around the stage, gesturing with the neck of the guitar, slamming it up and down—that was his voice. And that's the place where he, without a doubt, was not reserved. He did not have a shy bone in his body when he got to talking with his guitar. But Ronnie was also complex guy. He had deep thoughts and he felt life. He let it in. He cared for the common guy in the street. If you saw a homeless person, he'd say that's somebody's baby. He was a very, very personal kind of guy."

When I asked Ricky about hearing the *Montrose* record for the first time—he would have been about 20 when it came out—he says, "Well, first of all, you start adding as many of those songs to your set list as you can, as you're playing the bars or whatever. Yeah, it's kind of like wow, okay, finally—and it's American. It was a proud sort of feeling. It was a far cry from... oh, I don't want to pick on any bands. But it was a far cry from what we had been getting. And then it sort of started the ball rolling. All of a sudden, bands started cropping up, all the way up into Van Halen. *Montrose* was sort of the template for what they wanted to do, so much so that they not only recorded with Ted Templeman, but I think they recorded in the same studio as well. And Sammy Hagar himself had his stint with the band."

"I even got a lot of influence from Ronnie from his time with Edgar Winter. How you can have such a great song-oriented band with those tough guitars, and it adds to it rather than detracts? I mean, it added so much. Things like 'Frankenstein,' which Ronnie said to me, 'After we recorded it, it was a mishmash of stapled together pieces of music and bits that just kept growing and growing out of jams and sound checks and this and that, and that's why they called it "Frankenstein."'" It was all stapled together, but he said even after they recorded it, they still were changing and adding things, and Dan Hartman was changing and adding bass lines, which I discovered from watching YouTube. Even after Rick Derringer was in the band, they were still changing it."

But we keep forgetting that the *Montrose* album wasn't exactly a sales success. Says Ricky, "Now that you put it that way, I guess my view of it is limited to Northern California, but I thought it was huge. I thought it was universal. I thought that Montrose had really hit its stride. But everywhere I go, even the musicians I work with, I'm sure one of the reasons Jimmy Page and David Coverdale got Denny Carmassi and I to work on that record that they did... I know that my connection was basically, I had been on the road when I was in Bad English opening up for Whitesnake, and that's how Dave saw me. But I would imagine that it was Montrose, not Heart, that was the reason they went after Denny."

Esteemed Creem writer Jaan Uhelski was there when the *Montrose* record hit the industry, and she's had an interest in Ronnie ever since.

"I loved that album, I loved Ronnie, and actually I loved that *They Only Come Out at Night* album anyway. I thought he was just a star. The minute I saw him and those popping green eyes, you know he just was fierce. He just had... whatever it is, he had it, so I wasn't surprised. When I interviewed Sammy Hagar, he thought this was going to be the band that would take him to the top like it was Led Zeppelin. He even had an astrology chart drawn up about from the moment of the inception of the band. It was a phenomenal album, and they were just big songs. I think the problem with Montrose was that the songs were getting less big over time. When you talk to the people in the band, it seems like if Ronnie didn't do it... I mean, it's all one-sided but he seemed to resent Sammy Hagar getting to be a more accomplished songwriter. So instead of pooling their energies and making this thing bigger, he took it down. It's sad because, God, talk about thwarted potential. Again, a man with great vision and great drive but why can't he sustain it? I think there's something that goes off in his head, like some time element. Like he can do something for maybe three, four years and then..."

But perhaps also causing this implicit impatience is the simple idea that Ronnie didn't like heavy metal. In a way, maybe he stumbled into it somehow, aided and abetted by meeting the 1000-watt force of nature that was Sammy Hagar, and even Denny, hard-whacker of the drums, and Bill "Electric" Church, wild man of the bass.

"I know! You kind of wonder, is it the semantics? Like, what doesn't he like? There are those few videos on YouTube and you see him, and he's so in the moment and so enlivened by it, like he's shot from a cannon, I still can't believe that he doesn't like it, no matter what he says. I think he's a contrarian. I think back in the day; he had that thing when he was on stage and even with the Edgar Winter Band, that thing he did with his leg and he'd bend back. I thought he really had a big stage persona back then. You can't really say that in later years because you'd see him and he was like a pale imitation of himself. But when he did that one show with all the metal guitarists, maybe ten years ago, I thought he really held his own. I don't think he's proficient. He's not Eric Clapton, he's not even Slash, but there's some kind of demon energy that he has. It's like he has tapped into something. Like the way you said it, he 'stumbled;' I think you actually nailed it because that's him."

Last word goes to the mighty man himself, Ronnie Montrose, from my last conversation with him, in fact, fittingly, from the *end* of that conversation. This was a chat we had as a dry run—what we called a pre-interview—for having him appear on *Metal Evolution*, an 11-episode series on the history of heavy metal I worked on with Banger Films. Try as we might, offering to pay for flight and hotel to LA for both Leighsa and himself, we couldn't get Ronnie on board, later, over time, after it was obvious at first that he was looking forward to it and all good to go. As a result, the story point around the importance of *Montrose*, in an episode on "early US heavy metal," was supported mostly by Sammy. All told, we feel proud having emphasized Ronnie's and that record's legacy in a high-quality VH1 Classic TV series that has been seen all around the world and is in steady if not constant rotation still years later.

And so this was just our sign-off, but it's just good to hear his voice again, to hear him make plans, to hear him want to talk and impart what he knows. Along with all the other points we've just heard on the facets of Ronnie's personality, from the inspiring to the problematic, perhaps this is the best way to remember him—as engaged with the world, not in the least bit intent on "dying of nothing."

Closing with a few final musings upon the record that made his reputation, Ronnie says, "Well it was ten years later—I think ten years later—that it went gold. I mean the band had already been disbanded. I think I was actually doing Gamma at the time it went gold or platinum. It was just one of those slow, steady builders."

Due to what?

"Due to the fact… the one thing I know that I'm comfortable with, was it was like we just spoke about. It was an album that the four of us did—that first record—that we were all maxed-out and we gave it everything we had and we were doing everything that we knew at the time as hard as we could. And that stuff stands the test of time."

After Ronnie drops another nugget as we sign off, namely that he "was scheduled to produce one of Van Halen's records one time," he tells me, "It's been good talking with you and keep in touch. I apologize for being long-winded—that's me. It's been fun talking to you, and as you can tell I'm a non-stop talker. Don't worry about time. I booked my afternoon off for you. I went from my nice mountain hike this morning up in the hills behind my house, to our call—it's your dime, so go ahead, my brother."

Not wishing to overstay the welcome, I do venture a few more questions before voluntarily begging off. In light of what was to happen, I wished I'd kept him talking all Goddamn day. "This could be phase one," chuckled Ronnie. "We could have this whole conversation on another level tomorrow."

Attempting to nail down plans to interview him with a camera crew, Ronnie says, "Well, let me know because I certainly don't have a problem if you want to fly me down to LA for the day. But it's just tight at Thanksgiving. I mean it's family and it's Thanksgiving, and this is my wife's and my busy month. She's in the flower industry and she does weddings and is a really successful floral and event designer. And then we've also got many, many—which is really good—we have good friends and events we're going over and cooking for. I just cook—I love to cook. So I'm the designated cooker."

"If it's something that had to be done..." continues Ronnie, "I'm just feeling so good now coming back from this whole wicked battle with cancer, and I just want to… I mean I wake up and I'm doing this entire acoustic guitar thing, I'm really diving into it full-scale. But I think I'm planning on going out and doing quite a few Montrose shows with this singer that I have now. His name is Keith St. John and he's just… he's like a young Sammy; I mean he's got it. I love playing and I wake up every morning feeling good. You don't know what it's like to be pain-free until you're pain-free. I've regained my joie de vive."

DISCOGRAPHY

Given that the focus of this book is the Montrose and the Gamma catalogues, I've provided detailed discographical information for those records only. Compilations, as well as Ronnie's solo albums (and not Sammy's or Davey's or anyone else's), are also listed, but not with extended credits. As with all my books, vinyl-era albums get a Side 1/Side 2 designation. Timings and writing credits are taken from original vinyl copies, but CD in the case of Gamma 4. Personnel (including order of naming) and what they do is similarly cited directly and exactly from the original album releases, save for punctuation variants. Guest cameos are not included. The rule of double quotes around songs was set aside for neatness' sake. US issue is used for catalogue numbers. I've decided not to do singles, as both Montrose and Gamma were album bands, with, alas, no hits!

Montrose

Montrose

(Warner Bros. '73; BS 2740)

Produced by Montrose and Ted Templeman

Personnel: Denny Carmassi – drums; Bill Church – bass; Ronnie Montrose – guitar; Sam Hagar – vocals

Side 1: 1. Rock the Nation (Montrose) 2:57; 2. Bad Motor Scooter (Hagar) 3:43; 3. Space Station #5 (Montrose, Hagar) 5:17; 4. I Don't Want It (Montrose, Hagar) 3:02

Side 2: 1. Good Rockin' Tonight (Brown) 2:57; 2. Rock Candy (Carmassi, Church, Hagar, Montrose) 5:17; 3. One Thing on My Mind (Hagar, Montrose, Sanchez) 3:40; 4. Make It Last (Hagar) 5:29

Paper Money

(Warner Bros. '74; BS 2823)

Produced by Ted Templeman and Ronnie Montrose

Personnel: Ronnie Montrose – guitar, vocals; Sammy Hagar – vocals; Denny Carmassi – drums, vocals; Alan Fitzgerald – bass, synthesizer

Side 1: 1. Underground (Rappaport) 3:33; 2. Connection (Jagger, Richard) 5:42; 3. The Dreamer (Hagar, Montrose) 4:05; 4. Starliner (Montrose) 3:36

Side 2: 1. I Got the Fire (Montrose) 3:06; 2. Spaceage Sacrifice (Hagar, Montrose) 4:55; 3. We're Going Home (Montrose) 4:52; 4. Paper Money (Hagar, Montrose) 5:01

Warner Bros. Presents

(Warner Bros. '75; BS 2892)

Produced by Ronnie Montrose

Personnel: Jim Alcivar – keyboards; Denny Carmassi – drums; Alan Fitzgerald – bass; Bob James – vocals; Ronnie Montrose – guitar and vocals

Side 1: 1. Matriarch (Alcivar, Carmassi, Fitzgerald, James, Montrose) 4:33; 2. All I Need (Alcivar, Carmassi, Fitzgerald, James, Montrose) 4:18; 3. Twenty Flight Rock (Fairchild) 2:42; 4. Whaler (Alcivar, Carmassi, Fitzgerald, James, Montrose) 6:54

Side 2: 1. Dancin' Feet (Montrose, James) 4:03; 2. O Lucky Man (Price) 3:14; 3. One and a Half (Montrose) 1:39; 4. Clown Woman (Montrose) 4:20 5. Black Train (Kardt, Richards, Fried) 4:36

Jump on It

(Warner Bros. '76; BS 2963)

Produced by Jack Douglas

Personnel: Ronnie Montrose – guitar; Bob James – vocals; Denny Carmassi – drums; Jim Alcivar – keyboards

Side 1: 1. Let's Go (Alcivar, Carmassi, James, Montrose) 4:16; 2. What Are You Waitin' for? (Hartman) 3:50; 3. Tuft-Sedge (Montrose) 2:48 4. Music Man (Montrose) 4:17

Side 2: 1. Jump on It (Alcivar, Carmassi, James, Montrose) 3:32; 2. Rich Man (Hartman) 4:24; 3. Crazy for You (Montrose, Rappaport) 3:25; 4. Merry-Go-Round (Montrose) 5:37

Mean

(Enigma '87; ST-73264)

Produced by Ronnie Montrose

Personnel: Ronnie Montrose – the guitar; Glenn Letsch – the bass; James Kottak – the drums; Johnny Edwards – the voice

Side 1: 1. Don't Damage the Rock (Montrose) 5:06; 2. Game of Love (Ballard Jr.) 2:57; 3. Pass It On (Montrose, Edwards, Kottak) 3:37; 4. Hard Headed Woman (Montrose) 3:50; 5. M for Machine (Montrose) 3:59

Side 2: 1. Ready Willing and Able (Montrose) 4:19; 2. Man of the Hour (Montrose) 4:23; 3. Flesh and Blood (Montrose, Edwards, Kottak) 4:36; 4. Stand (Montrose) 4:46

Gamma

1

(Elektra '79; 6E-219)

Produced by Ken Scott

Personnel: Ronnie Montrose – guitars; Jim Alcivar – synthesizers; Davey Pattison – vocals; Alan Fitzgerald – bass guitar; Skip Gillette – percussion

Side 1: 1. Thunder and Lightning (Montrose, Pattison) 4:34; 2. I'm Alive (Ballard Jr.) 3:13; 3. Razor King (Montrose, Pattison) 5:53 4. No Tears (Pattison) 4:53

Side 2: 1. Solar Heat (Montrose) 3:08; 2. Ready for Action (Montrose) 3:39; 3. Wish I Was (Newbury) 5:13; 4. Fight to the Finish (Montrose, Alcivar) 6:21

2

(Elektra '80; 6E-288)

Produced by Gary Lyons and Ronnie Montrose

Personnel: Ronnie Montrose – guitars; Jim Alcivar – synthesizers; Davey Pattison – vocals; Glenn Letsch – bass guitar; Denny Carmassi – drums

Side 1: 1. Meanstreak (Montrose, Pattison, Alcivar) 4:45; 2. Four Horsemen (Montrose, Pattison) 4:40 3. Dirty City (Montrose, Pattison) 4. Voyager (Montrose, Pattison) 5:36

Side 2: 1. Something in the Air (Keene) 3:16; 2. Cat on a Leash (Montrose/Stahl) 4:04; 3. Skin and Bone (Montrose/Stahl) 4:51; 4. Mayday (Montrose, Alcivar) 5:39

3

(Elektra '82; E1-60034)

Produced by Ronnie Montrose

Personnel: Ronnie Montrose – guitars; Mitchell Froom – keyboards; Davey Pattison – vocals; Denny Carmassi – drums; Glenn Letsch – bass

Side 1: 1. What's Gone is Gone (Montrose, Froom, Stahl) 5:29; 2. Right the First Time (Montrose, Froom, Stahl) 4:00; 3. Moving Violation ((Montrose, Froom, Stahl, Carmassi) 3:37; 4. Mobile Devotion (Montrose, Froom, Stahl) 6:37

Side 2: 1. Stranger (Froom, Stahl) 3:00; 2. Condition Yellow (Montrose, Froom, Carmassi) 4:07; 3. Modern Girl (Montrose, Froom, Stahl) 3:33; 4. No

Way Out (Montrose, Froom, Stahl) 4:05; 5. Third Degree (Montrose, Froom, Stahl) 4:49

4

(RoMoCo '00; 0-2004)

Produced by Ronnie Montrose

Personnel: Ronnie Montrose – guitars; Davey Pattison – vocals; Denny Carmassi – drums; Glenn Letsch – bass; Edward Roth – keyboards

1. Darkness to Light (Montrose, Pattison) 5:35; 2. Love Will Find You (Montrose, Hutchins) 4:18; 3. Resurrection Shuffle (Ashton) 4:36 4. Oh No You Don't (Montrose) 4:30 5. Bad Reputation (Montrose, Pattison) 4:05; 6. Last Man on Earth (Montrose) 7:54; 7. The Only One (Montrose, Pattison) 3:52 8. Out of These Hands (Montrose, Hutchins) 5:24; 9. Prayers (Montrose/Pattison) 3:36 10. Low Road Home (Montrose Pattison) 6:33

Ronnie Montrose

Open Fire (Warner Bros. '78)

Territory (Passport '86)

The Speed of Sound (Enigma '88)

The Diva Station (Enigma '90)

Mutatis Mutandis (I.R.S. '91)

Music from Here (Fearless Urge '94)

Mr. Bones (SegaSoft '96)

Roll Over and Play Live (RoMoCo '99)

Bearings (RoMoCo '99)

Miscellaneous

Gamma - The Best of Gamma (GNP/Crescendo '92)

Montrose - The Very Best of Montrose (Warner Bros. '00)

Montrose – Original Album Series (Warner Bros. '11)

CREDITS

Interviews with the Author

Alcivar, Jim. June 19, 2016.
Carmassi, Denny. June 21, 2016.
Church, Bill. July 22, 2016.
Church, Bill. July 26, 2016.
Douglas, Jack. 2010.
Earl, Roger. June 8, 2016.
Eckerman, Ron. April 27, 2012.
Edwards, Johnny. June 17, 2016.
Gillette, Skip. August 22, 2016.
Hagar, Sammy. May 30, 1997.
Hagar, Sammy. March 3, 1999.
Hagar, Sammy. October 27, 2000.
Hagar, Sammy. May 29, 2003.
Hagar, Sammy. August 7, 2006.
Hagar, Sammy. June 14, 2007.
Hagar, Sammy. May 21, 2008.
Hagar, Sammy. October 15, 2008.
Haggerty, Mick. 2010.
Hammett, Kirk. June 10, 2016.
Hammett, Kirk. July 12, 2016.
Haze, Leonard. December 19, 2014.
James, Bob. June 4, 2016.
James, Bob. June 17, 2016.
Kelley, Michael. June 3, 2016.
Kelley, Michael. June 4, 2016.
Letsch, Glenn. August 28, 2007.
Letsch, Glenn. June 21, 2016.
McNay, Dan. July 7, 2016.
Montrose, Ronnie. June 1, 2000.
Montrose, Ronnie. 2001.
Montrose, Ronnie. 2009.
Morris, Tal. June 16, 2016.
Pattison, Davey. August 1, 2005.

Phillips, Ricky. December 16, 2013.
Powell, Aubrey. July 14, 2016.
Ranno, Richie. 2010.
Terpo, Chuck. July 7, 2016.
Trower, Robin. August 1, 2007.
Wardlaw, John. July 7, 2016.
Watson, Jeff. June 16, 2016.
Wiersema, Roger. July 20, 2016.

Additional Sources

Allmusic. Gamma 3 record review by Whitney Z. Gomes.
Anti-M.com/Montrose. Interviews with Denny Carmassi, Ronnie Montrose and Davey Pattison by John Wardlaw. 1997, 2000.
Billboard. *Paper Money* record review. November 2, 1974.
Billboard. Magnet – *Worldwide Attraction* record review. March 17, 1979.
Billboard. Gamma 1 record review by Mike Hyland. January 19, 1980.
Circus. Montrose—The Band to Take Over the World by William Pratt. Vol. 8, #5. February 1974.
Circus. *Montrose* record review by Ed Naha. March 1974.
Circus Raves. *Montrose* record review by Jon Tiven. March 1974.
Circus Raves. *Montrose* record review by Gordon Fletcher. March 1974.
Circus. Coney Island Sensurround: Montrose & Douglas Make Sonic Cinerama by Kathi Stein. 1975.
Classic Rock Revisited. Gamma 3 record review by Jeb Wright.
Creem. *Warner Bros. Presents* record review by Joe Fernbacher. January 1976.
Dunn, Sam. Interview with Sammy Hagar. 2009.
Elektra/Asylum Records. Gamma bio. 1979.
Guitar Player. Ronnie Montrose by Steve Rosen. October 1976.
Hit Parader. Guitar Workshop with Gamma's Ronnie Montrose by Andy Secher. 1980.
Kansas City Star, The. 'Heavy Metal' Rock Wins Applause by Donna Palatas. April 2, 1978.
Melody Maker. Montrose Country. January 11, 1975.
Music Express. What Makes Sammy Run? by Lenny Stoute. Issue #55. March/April 1982.
National Post. Sammy Hagar got his start in guitarist's band by New York

Times staff. March 9, 2012.

Raw Power. Swan by Quick Draw. Vol. 4. Oct.-Nov. 1977.

Rolling Stone. *Montrose* record review by Gordon Fletcher. #158. April 11, 1974.

Rolling Stone. *Warner Bros. Presents* record review by Andy McKaie. #202. December 18, 1975.

Rolling Stone. Is Montrose Lost in a Power Play? by John Grissim. #208. March 11, 1976.

Rolling Stone. *Jump on It* record review by Charles M. Young. #228. December 16, 1976.

Warner Bros. Records. *Paper Money* bio. 1974.

Warner Bros. Records. *The Very Best of Montrose* liner notes by Ronnie Montrose and Martin Popoff. 2000.

Photo Credits

Rudy Childs – Johnny on the spot capturing Gamma in their prime.
Richard Galbraith – my Oklahoma buddy who shot everybody of note in the late '70s. That's him standing with Ronnie back in the *Jump on It* chapter, although specifically the two clinked a drink during a stop on the *Open Fire* tour.
Ted Roarke – killer vintage Gamma shots making Ronnie looking fine indeed. Nice.
Jim Summaria – consummate pro, who provided the front cover shot and one of the back shots, plus a few more throughout.
Paul Vincze – capably capturing history by shooting the little-documented Gamma lineup of 1992, Michele Graybeal included.

Special Thanks

Not only did prolific and wunnerful underground musician and film-maker John "Wedge" Warlaw open for biz the very first official Ronnie Montrose website, but he also collaborated with the man, provided some shots for this book, and performed top-shelf scanning duties on other shots used throughout, particularly those by Paul Vincze.

In addition, thanks to Rob Warren for getting the ball rolling, with a few contacts, but also just, "Why the hell don't you do a book on Montrose?" Dude just basically talked me into it over the course of a few emails, so cheers, Rob!

I also wish to mention my buddy Steve Olson, who applied his meticulous proof-reading skills, as the only other set of eyes on this thing before we decided to go to press.

Design Credit

The graphic design and layout of this book is by Eduardo Rodriguez, who can be reached at eduardobwbk@gmail.com. Pleasure working with the guy—he's done about a dozen for me now.

About the Author

At approximately 7900 (with over 7000 appearing in his books), Martin has unofficially written more record reviews than anybody in the history of music writing across all genres. Additionally, Martin has penned approximately 80 books on hard rock, heavy metal, classic rock and record collecting. He was Editor In Chief of the now retired *Brave Words & Bloody Knuckles*, Canada's foremost metal publication for 14 years, and has also contributed to *Revolver, Guitar World, Goldmine, Record Collector, bravewords. com, lollipop.com* and *hardradio.com*, with many record label band bios and liner notes to his credit as well. Additionally, Martin has been a regular contractor to Banger Films, having worked for two years as researcher on the award-wining documentary *Rush: Beyond the Lighted Stage*, on the writing and research team for the 11-episode *Metal Evolution* and on the 10-episode *Rock Icons*, both for VH1 Classic. Additionally, Martin is the writer of the original metal genre chart used in *Metal: A Headbanger's Journey* and throughout the *Metal Evolution* episodes. Martin currently resides in Toronto and can be reached through martinp@inforamp.net or www.martinpopoff.com.

Martin Popoff – A Complete Bibliography

Rock the Nation: Montrose, Gamma and Ronnie Redefined (2016)
Metal Heart: Aiming High with Accept (2016)
Ramones at 40 (2016)
Time and a Word: The Yes Story (2016)
Kickstart My Heart: A Mötley Crüe Day-by-Day (2015)
This Means War: The Sunset Years of the NWOBHM (2015)
Wheels of Steel: The Explosive Early Years of the NWOBHM (2015)
Swords And Tequila: Riot's Classic First Decade (2015)
Who Invented Heavy Metal? (2015)
Sail Away: Whitesnake's Fantastic Voyage (2015)
Live Magnetic Air: The Unlikely Saga of the Superlative Max Webster (2014)
Steal Away the Night: An Ozzy Osbourne Day-by-Day (2014)
The Big Book of Hair Metal (2014)
Sweating Bullets: The Deth and Rebirth of Megadeth (2014)
Smokin' Valves: A Headbanger's Guide to 900 NWOBHM Records (2014)
The Art of Metal (co-edit with Malcolm Dome; 2013)
2 Minutes to Midnight: An Iron Maiden Day-By-Day (2013)
Metallica: The Complete Illustrated History (2013); update and reissue (2016)
Rush: The Illustrated History (2013); update and reissue (2016)
Ye Olde Metal: 1979 (2013)
Scorpions: Top of the Bill (2013); updated and reissued as Wind of Change: The Scorpions Story (2016)
Epic Ted Nugent (2012)
Fade To Black: Hard Rock Cover Art of the Vinyl Age (2012)
It's Getting Dangerous: Thin Lizzy 81-12 (2012)
We Will Be Strong: Thin Lizzy 76-81 (2012)
Fighting My Way Back: Thin Lizzy 69-76 (2011)
The Deep Purple Royal Family: Chain of Events '80 – '11 (2011)
The Deep Purple Royal Family: Chain of Events Through '79 (2011); reissued as The Deep Purple Family Year by Year (to 1979) (2016)
Black Sabbath FAQ (2011)
The Collector's Guide to Heavy Metal: Volume 4: The '00s (2011; co-authored with David Perri)
Goldmine Standard Catalog of American Records 1948 – 1991, 7th Edition (2010)
Goldmine Record Album Price Guide, 6th Edition (2009)

Goldmine 45 RPM Price Guide, 7th Edition (2009)
A Castle Full of Rascals: Deep Purple '83 – '09 (2009)
Worlds Away: Voivod and the Art of Michel Langevin (2009)
Ye Olde Metal: 1978 (2009)
Gettin' Tighter: Deep Purple '68 – '76 (2008)
All Access: The Art of the Backstage Pass (2008)
Ye Olde Metal: 1977 (2008)
Ye Olde Metal: 1976 (2008)
Judas Priest: Heavy Metal Painkillers (2007)
Ye Olde Metal: 1973 to 1975 (2007)
The Collector's Guide to Heavy Metal: Volume 3: The Nineties (2007)
Ye Olde Metal: 1968 to 1972 (2007)
Run For Cover: The Art of Derek Riggs (2006)
Black Sabbath: Doom Let Loose (2006)
Dio: Light Beyond the Black (2006)
The Collector's Guide to Heavy Metal: Volume 2: The Eighties (2005)
Rainbow: English Castle Magic (2005)
UFO: Shoot Out the Lights (2005)
The New Wave of British Heavy Metal Singles (2005)
Blue Öyster Cult: Secrets Revealed! (2004); update and reissue (2009); updated and reissued as Agents of Fortune: The Blue Oyster Cult Story (2016)
Contents Under Pressure: 30 Years of Rush at Home & Away (2004)
The Top 500 Heavy Metal Albums of All Time (2004)
The Collector's Guide to Heavy Metal: Volume 1: The Seventies (2003)
The Top 500 Heavy Metal Songs of All Time (2003)
Southern Rock Review (2001)
Heavy Metal: 20th Century Rock and Roll (2000)
The Goldmine Price Guide to Heavy Metal Records (2000)
The Collector's Guide to Heavy Metal (1997)
Riff Kills Man! 25 Years of Recorded Hard Rock & Heavy Metal (1993)

See **martinpopoff.com** for complete details and ordering information.